Material Conflicts

Parades and Visual Displays in Northern Ireland

Neil Jarman

BERG

Oxford • *New York*

First published in 1997 by
Berg
Editorial offices:
150 Cowley Road, Oxford, OX4 1JJ, UK
70 Washington Square South, New York, NY 10012, USA

Berg is an imprint of Oxford International Publishers Ltd.

Library of Congress Cataloging-in-Publication Data

A catalogue record for this book is available from the Library of
Congress.

British Library Cataloguing-in-Publication Data

A catalogue record for this book is available from the British Library.

ISBN 1 85973 124 4 (Cloth)
     1 85973 129 5 (Paper)

Typeset by JS Typesetting, Wellingborough, Northants.

Printed and bound in Great Britain by WBC, Bridgend, Mid Glam.

For Alison and Hal

Contents

Acknowledgements

My research into parades and visual displays in Northern Ireland began in the summer of 1990 for an undergraduate dissertation at the Department of Anthropology at University College London; it has steadily continued through my Ph.D. work, on which this book is based, into more policy-orientated research into parades as a political problem, on which I am working at present. My funding has come from a number of sources. I began with a local authority undergraduate grant from the London Borough of Newham (without which I would never have gone to university as a mature student). Postgraduate work at UCL was initially supported with a grant from the Central Research Fund of the University of London and then with a three-year research grant from the Economic and Social Research Council. Post-doctoral work has been supported by a Fellowship from the Cultural Traditions Group held at the Department of Social Anthropology at Queen's University, Belfast and by research work at the Centre for the Study of Conflict at the University of Ulster at Coleraine. I am extremely grateful to all of these bodies and organisations and the many people within them who have assisted my work.

There are always too many people to thank for their support and encouragement, and I hope there will be no offence taken by those whom I do not mention. I just want to acknowledge a few people to whom I owe a special thanks. In London, Danny Miller and Barbara Bender, among the staff at UCL, have given me many years of help and encouragement, as well as supportive and critical readings of my work. In Belfast I have worked extensively with Dominic Bryan, since he first gave me a lift to a Hibernian parade in Draperstown in March 1993. Although we have largely pursued our separate research agendas, he has been of immense assistance in helping me to maintain, and to extend, my interest in the subject.

Finally, I want to thank Maggie, Kyle and Ruari, for putting up with my seemingly endless visits to parades in odd locations, and without whom none of this would have happened.

Remembering I, Apprentice Boys, Londonderry, August 1992.

Remembering II, Workers Party, Milltown, Easter 1993.

Remembering III, Sinn Féin, Milltown, Easter 1994.

Remembering IV, Brian King Parade, Shankill, August 1995.

Chapter 1

The Performance of Memory

Some societies need no re-enactment to reactivate history; the process seems to be ingrained, habitual. Unassuaged injuries and injustices often lead men to conflate remote with recent times and even with the present. Many Irish continue to experience the Danish invasions, the devastations of Laud, the Famine of 1847, as almost contemporaneous events. Irish memory has been likened to historical paintings in which Virgil and Dante converse side by side. But the Irish do not 'live in the past; rather, Ireland's history "lives in the present". All previous traitors and all previous heroes remain alive in it', as in the 'bottomless memory' of an O'Faolin character in which 'one might see, though entangled beyond all hope of unravelling', the entire saga of Ireland's decay

(Lowenthal 1986:250).

The above embodies a widely held view of the Irish use of history, in which the concept of 'folk' or 'race' memory is used to explain persistent or recurrent social beliefs and practices that are transmitted apparently almost without trace (MacDonagh 1983a; Rose 1971; Smyth 1992; Stewart 1989). Although the past retains an unusual prominence in Irish social and political life, can we talk of a bottomless memory in which nothing and no one is forgotten? Are such memories really sustained habitually with no re-enactment? How is it even possible to talk of a singular 'Irish memory' in an island that has been subject to centuries of colonial domination, an island that now has two distinct, ideologically opposed ethnic communities? And what impact will the fact that the island has sustained a military conflict for the past generation in which one of the most prominent features has been the conflicting interpretations of Irish history, have on a sense of collective belonging? While one may criticise Lowenthal's sweeping generalisation of the understanding and use that many Irish people have and make of their past, it is a perspective that can be accommodated within many popular interpretations of the 'Irish

1

problem.' Ireland is all too readily regarded as a society trapped in the past: the contemporary conflict has been likened to medieval religious wars, or alternatively described as an unresolvable conflict between two mutually hostile tribes. Both of these approaches consign the Irish (or perhaps only those Irish who live in the northern part of the island) to a primitive or backward state that in turn perhaps makes their irrational, bottomless memory more understandable.

However, no matter how critical or dismissive one might be of the 'religious war' or 'tribal conflict' approaches (Jenkins, Donnan and MacFarlane 1986), it is impossible to ignore the prominent role that historical events and characters continue to play in the political and social life of Northern Ireland. One might ask why battles of the seventeenth century are still remembered as important events 300 years later? Why does a seventeenth-century British king who is all but unknown in England feature as an icon of British identity in Northern Ireland? What do historical and mythological figures, such as King William III and St Patrick, mean to people living in the north of Ireland? How have the complex identities subsumed within the populist rhetoric of 'Protestant' and 'Catholic' been created, developed and maintained since the arrival of colonists from England and Scotland in the seventeenth century? And why are they the most prominent anchors for collective identities? This study considers these questions by analysing some of the ways and the means by which past events are remembered in contemporary Northern Ireland. It focuses in particular on the numerous commemorative parades that are held each year to explore just what is being commemorated and remembered at those times. In Britain the practice of holding annual parades, which flourished in the nineteenth century, has now largely died out; but in the north of Ireland the practice continues stronger than ever. In tracing the history of this custom, I aim to show how parades have been used in the past and how they have changed, and to indicate why these popular commemorations and festivities have not only survived but are thriving in Ireland, when similar events have failed to survive the transition to urbanism and industrialisation in other Western European and North American countries (Burke 1978; Cressy 1989; Davis 1986; Malcolmson 1973; Storch 1982).

I will also consider the relationship between these acts of remembrance and celebration and the violence of the Troubles.

While republican and loyalist paramilitary violence has been subjected to extensive analysis, less interest has been spent on understanding how political violence (as a general practice rather than any specific acts) retains some legitimacy within the population at large. From the beginning of the Troubles in the late 1960s until the ceasefires of August and October 1994, paramilitary groupings have caused a considerable amount of death, destruction and injury while still retaining substantial support within otherwise law-abiding and church-going communities. They did this while appealing to abstract ideals of nationality and to the precedent of history. To the question 'How is the past remembered in Northern Ireland?' one must add 'How is political violence legitimised through the acts of commemoration?'

Finally, I am concerned with the use of visual displays as a part of this process. The two principal forms of imagery in which I am interested are painted silk banners carried on the parades and mural paintings that adorn the gable walls of the working-class areas of Belfast and Derry. The banner displays are a conservative body, and many of the images and symbols have been carried since last century. In contrast, although murals have been painted in Belfast since the early part of this century, the body of work considered here is largely a product of the past twenty years. Nevertheless, many of the images and themes of the murals are linked to the images displayed on parades. To understand this contemporary use of images I discuss how and why these two bodies of images have been established, what they mean and how that meaning is changed and used within broader ideological debates. I analyse the connections and differences between images used within each community, but also explore the connections and differences between the Protestant/Unionist/Loyalist images and the Catholic/Nationalist/Republican images. This also involves looking at the media of presentation, the space, the form and temporality of display and how these factors relate to the images: where murals are painted and where they are not, where parades go and where not. Collectively the parades, banners and murals present a comprehensive display of history, symbols and icons that underpin the distinctive and opposing identities of the two dominant groups. The anniversaries and the images are an opportunity to give public expression to the collective memory of the Ulster Protestant and Irish Catholic communities.

Social Memory

Social memory is similar to, but remains distinct from, a more formal sense of history. History follows a form of logic, of structure, of pattern, of narrative and of progress that is absent from the more chaotic and disjointed content of memory. Halbwachs (1980, 1992) contrasts history, that which is concerned with documenting change, with the collective memory, which is rooted in a sense of permanence and continuity. The writing of history is concerned with imposing some sense of narrative and direction on the past, while a collective memory is more concerned with emphasising the sense of repetition, of situating the event or experience within a pre-existing category. In a similar fashion Pierre Nora regards memory as the traditional medium for understanding the past, but one that has been supplanted by reconstructed history in our 'hopelessly forgetful modern societies, propelled by change' (1989:8). But, as Redfield (1994) argues, this opposition and separation between history and memory is never so complete and fixed: history will always be balanced, and sometimes opposed, by a multiplicity of social or collective memories. And, just as the past recalled by memory may question that authorised by historians, so the memories of one group may contrast with those of another. This sense in which collective memories conflict with one another and with written history is one of the themes explored in this study. I am not concerned here with understanding how memory works *per se*, but how a collective or social memory, or rather a plurality of social memories, is generated and maintained. Here it is useful to be aware of the difference between auto-biographical memory and historical memory: between events that are remembered from personal experience and are specific to the individual, and memories of past events that 'can only be stimulated in indirect ways through reading or listening or in commemoration and festive occasions when people gather together to remember in common the deeds and accomplishments of long-departed members of the group' (Coser 1992:24).

This idea of a memory of unexperienced events insists that memory is not simply a repository for sensory data that are merely stored away, only to be retrieved unchanged and as new when required. Instead, remembering must be an active process, in which memories have to be worked on and used in order to be maintained. Memories, as a medium for understanding the past, are a part of the wider cultural practices that are continually being adapted and rephrased to meet the needs of the present. Social memories 'are not "recollections of times past" but part of the present understandings of the past', people use 'images of the past [as] a justification for the present relationship' and not 'images from the past' (Morphy and Morphy 1984:462). It is the desires and aspirations of the present that shape our views of the past, while at the same time those present aspirations are partly formed by our understanding of our past. We use the past by remembering selectively those events that help to explain or justify what is happening in the present, a present that can therefore be portrayed as the inevitable and only outcome of those same events. The changing needs and circumstances of the present mean that memories are monitored and re-evaluated, and our understanding of the past is adapted to changing circumstances. Some memories will be readily abandoned and forgotten, and some long-ignored events may in turn be recalled, as history is subject to reappraisal. Usually this is a subtle process 'of persistence and change, of continuity and newness' (Coser 1992:26); but in periods of dramatic social change and upheaval, attempts may be made to make wholesale changes to the collective remembrance of the past. Such attempts to refocus history were made after the French Revolution (Ozouf 1988), and again more recently in Nazi Germany (Connerton 1989; Mosse 1975) and during the Stalinist period of the Soviet Union (Lane 1981). The fact that the social memories that were imposed at those times have largely been forgotten illustrates the problem of trying to create new memories of the past that conflict with an emergent understanding; of trying to rewrite history to conform to a larger 'objective' truth. The current restructuring of national, ethnic and political identities across much of Eastern Europe has in turn produced another refocusing of collective memories. Much of the recent past is being swept away in an attempt to recall a better and more appropriate past from which to launch new state formations. Just as the idea of Stalingrad was swept away by a previous generation, so one now is encouraged to imagine a return to the imperial glories of St Petersburg, as Lenin's position as Soviet icon is whittled away and his preserved body removed from view. The importance that a sense of the past has in people's daily lives, in providing continuity in the face of change, makes it almost impossible to wipe the slate clean and begin again.

Social memory is the understanding of past events that are remembered by individuals, but within a framework structured by the larger group. The group may range in scale from a single family, or residents of a particular town or village, right up to a national or state-based identity, which always relies on a particular form of social memory (Anderson 1983). As well as kinship and geographical groupings, individuals may share memories based on ethnic, class and political affiliations or structured by age and gender. Each individual is therefore enmeshed within many different pasts at any one time. Although not all will be equally important, each set of memories offers the possibility of a different future if a different sense of the past is given weight.

For this study the most important form of group affiliation is that of ethnicity. While the labels Protestant and Catholic have been widely interpreted through a religious idiom, the two communities function as discrete ethnic groups in so far as they remain largely endogamous, culturally distinct and symbolically bounded, and most importantly, see themselves as distinct (Smith 1986). The two communities emphasise this difference by claiming allegiance to opposing political nations, the British and the Irish, while living in a territory that remains contested by both states. While an ethnic or national identity is often seen as an essential and unchangeable feature of one's being, it is in practice a much more fluid and unpredictable formation (Anderson 1983; Banks 1996; Eriksen 1993). In Ireland the formations of the distinct Ulster-British Protestant and Irish Catholic ethnicities were largely a product of the nineteenth century; but they are none the less real for all that. While the Irish Catholic identity has formed within the generalised rhetoric of nationalism, the Protestant identity sits at an uneasy intersection of Irish and British culture and history that has come to be called Ulster.

As a social construction, ethnic identity is given form and substance by being situated in time and in space. The group must have a memory of itself that recounts a sense of origin and distinctiveness (Smith 1986). A social memory becomes a central facet of the ideological armoury of the group, helping to legitimise and rationalise difference by rooting it in the far-distant past and thus placing weight on the primordial or essential nature of the antagonisms or otherness. Different media and forms of remembering may be more or less appropriate, depending on the number and range of people involved in creating a shared memory. It is difficult to produce and sustain a consensual memory of the past for a large and diverse group of people, even if they accept the common rubric of ethnicity, except when dealing with very general understanding or with the far-distant past. Even within the ethnic group, sub-groups may hold radically differing memories of what is a common past. As Papadakis (1993) discusses with reference to the recent political history of Cyprus, these differences may be a result of memories that are based on personal involvement rather than simply learnt history, but they may also be complicated by political, age and gender differences. We must therefore consider what are the most suitable means to maintain and transmit memories, both for individuals and for the group, to come to an understanding of the form and the expression in which past events are communicated.

At the level of the ethnic or national group, the historic event and symbolic icons are likely to be some way removed from individual experience. To be established as a social memory they need be conceptualised or encoded into an 'internal context', that is, isolated or freed from their specific history or external context and 'transformed into images (or) arranged into stories' (Fentress and Wickham 1992:68–73). This encoding involves a process of simplification: removing or ignoring extraneous details that blur the certitudes and so reduce the event or figure to little more than a schematic outline, the event or hero becomes mythified and decontextualised from any concrete past. The schematic structure can then be built upon and elaborated to fit different situations. Reducing the past to a formalised and generalised ideal allows for a multiple layering of memory whereby events and people over widely differing periods of time can be equated with one another. It also allows the specific individuals or actions that are remembered to be replaced by, or conflated with, others. Memory becomes less a means of conserving a distinct lineal history than a generator of meaning. The smooth temporal flow of history becomes a jumble of distinct and separate events lacking any obvious ordered narrative form, yet in which similar events seem to recur. Removed from their generating context, social memories function as signifiers without signifieds, as themes or metaphors in which the meaning is generated and added in the process of remembering. As the external context of the remembering changes, so the meaning may change, and social memory becomes an 'active search for meaning' in which the events of the past have a didactic as well as an explanatory function. Duplication or overlap merely serves to reinforce this feature (Harwood 1976:795).

Ritual and Memory

In reviewing Maurice Halbwachs' work, Lewis Coser suggests that social memories are stimulated indirectly, through 'reading or listening or in commemoration and festive occasions' (1992:24). This formulation groups together widely differing processes of confronting the past: the quiet reflective intimacy of reading or being told a story (perhaps these days of watching a documentary on television), or of visiting a memorial, is quite different from participating in a public commemoration or festival (which in turn incorporates a broad range of events). The one focuses more on the details and meaning of the past, the other engages more with the emotive and bodily processes. Paul Connerton (1989) suggests that these are distinct and separate processes, and he argues that it is the active participation in ritual events that is the significant means of encoding social memory into the individual body. He therefore emphasises the importance of the ritual form over its content in the remembering process. However, I want to give more equal weight to both bodily and cognitive processes, and I will begin by considering the importance of the performative aspects of 'festive occasions' before returning to the role of extracting meaning from ritual events, in this case through the interpretation of symbols and images. Form and meaning are therefore complementary parts in the creation and maintenance of the social memory, rather than alternative approaches. Expressed through a multiplicity of media, memory moves from an intensive experience to an extensive penetration of social life, from the liminal to the habitual.

Most, if not all, states utilise ritual commemorations to celebrate their past glories and future aspirations and to help sustain the imagined community (see for example da Matta 1977; Gregory 1994; Handelman 1990; Kapferer 1988; Lane 1981; Mach 1992; Vogt and Abel 1977). These ritual events are formalised, stylised and repetitive symbolic activities that are constrained within a tightly structured format and restricted to specific times or places that are outside the normal flow of routine daily life. Although an idea of marginality or liminality is often central to an analysis of ritual

(Turner 1969, 1974), the power and efficacy of rituals are not restricted to the ritual occasion itself. Rituals are 'porous' activities: the meanings and values spill over into normal time, their effect begins before the event itself has begun, and continues after it has ended (Connerton 1989:44). The focus of interest at ritual events may be a rarefied or an abstracted facet of communal life, and the proceedings may be structured so as to distance the event from routine activities; but it none the less remains central to the social world. Rituals require preparation and organisation, they are subject to debate and argument, to reflective discussion and comparison, and, increasingly, to numerous modes of recording, from amateur photographs and videos to TV and documentary productions. As the scale of the event expands, so does the overall importance of the ritual outside the formal ritual time. In this way the ritual creation of memory begins to collide with other media, such as oral narratives or the routine contact with memorials. In some cases the ritual process seems to be in danger of becoming a total way of life, rather than constrained by liminality.

But not endlessly so. To remain effective rituals need to be restricted activities, but ones that must also be repeated. Rituals are often repetitive, both in their internal structure and within the calendrical cycle; which further enhances the feeling that they never change. The rhythmic patterning helps confirm their natural state as an integral part of society. It is the formality and repetitiousness that give much of the power to ritual and generate a sense of belonging, a sense of order and a sense of continuity between the individual and the group, and between the group, the larger world and its past. This repetition might be the weekly visit to church, or it might be the annual attendance at the local war memorial; but the apparent invariance in ritual routine, its resistance to change, its archaic or formal language or dress, all imply and assume a legitimacy derived from the past, based on continuity and tradition. Participation integrates the individual into the larger social body, while exclusion helps define the parameters of that body. But many rituals do more than just imply a vague continuity with past events: they explicitly link the present with the past, explaining the present in terms of the past or re-enacting a narrative of past events. Judaism, Christianity and Islam all structure their ritual calendars around recalling and re-performing founding or formative events (Connerton 1989). This is equally true of political rituals that commemorate key dates in the formation of a state or social order. The apparent historical continuity of ritual is an important feature of its power, the unchanging form is itself a major attraction, to join in and carry on a tradition, to follow in one's father's footsteps, or to wear 'the sash my father wore'. This continuity of form inevitably hides changes in meaning. If a ritual remains central to social life of a community it is because of this paradox: that it is at once unchanging and yet ever changeable.

Ritual events are essentially performative: they demand the active involvement of the participants. This does not mean that everyone must participate to the same extent, since the ritual process can and may be central to the differentiation of roles; but it is difficult to remain on the sidelines at such events, to be present physically but not emotionally. The rhythmic repetition of sounds, whether liturgy, singing, chanting or music helps to create a sense of a collective identity where before there was only a collection of individuals. As the sound expands, attention becomes focused, levels of expectation are raised and the body is drawn into the performance. Once engaged, the formalism of the ritual is extended to bodily posture, forcing the participants to extremes of physical control or exertion, either through extended or repetitive activity or the opposite, enforced non-activity. The participants become the subject of the performance, which, for Connerton, is nothing less than a re-enactment: through physical involvement each of the participants shares in the primal suffering or the privations of the communal ancestors. When a ritual is moved out of the closed quarters of a building, a formal separation between active performers and passive audience seems more apparent. As people are allocated distinct spaces and places, some are more central to the event, while others appear sidelined, reduced to spectators; but in public events the barrier between central and marginal performers, the active and the passive, may be more apparent than real. This is because 'it can be just as important for the spectators to be seen by the "actors" or by other spectators as it is for the viewers to watch' (Marin 1987:227).

The totality of the ritual performance extends to include the audience, who play a role as much as those more demonstrably on display. In this environment of watched watchers, participation, and by extension, membership of the commemorating community, is confirmed by a range of physical activity, by a bodily expression of the encoded and habituated ritual routines. Active bodily involvement is therefore fundamental to commemorative rituals. Rather than simple recognition or acknowledgement of the importance of the past, participation in the ritual event generates a collective re-enactment of the past. By such a re-enactment, the past, now mythified and decontextualised, is transformed into an 'unchanging and unchangeable substance' and becomes an indispensable part of the present (Connerton 1989:43).

However, one must be cautious of developing this into an argument in which collective participation is the same as having a single understanding of the importance or meaning of the ritual, as an example of the Durkheimian collective consciousness. This is one problem with Connerton's over-reliance on the form of the ritual rather than the content. Although ritual events appear as singular celebrations, they often incorporate many diverse interpretations within the apparently unified mass. But the efficacy of ritual stems in part from its very ambiguity and its openness to multiple interpretations. The ambiguity and openness allows people to participate for different and sometimes radically diverging reasons, and as the scale of the ritual event expands, so may its meaning (Cohen 1993). Rituals can and will be used by different sections of society at different times. They may mean different things to different groups at the same time, or different things to the same class or group over time (Bloch 1986; Boissevain 1965, 1984; Cressy 1989; Goody 1993b). Rituals may be contested and fought over, praised and condemned and ultimately completely transformed in meaning, while retaining an apparently constant form. This is an important process to investigate, because of the importance that is given to 'tradition' when disputes arise over the ritual process in Ireland. Rather than being a rigid and constraining facet of society, ritual can be extremely flexible and adaptable. While in itself this suggests something of the vitality of the ritual process, and thereby explain why rituals have flourished when it is predicted that they might disappear (Boissevain 1992a,b), it also creates problems for Connerton's argument in favour of form over content. Even when the form remains stable it does not imply that the meaning is static: in fact discontinuity between form and meaning may contribute to the persistence of a ritual by increasing the multivocality of the event and thereby its ambiguity, and in turn, its vitality. The ambiguity of the ritual process is an important factor in its accessibility to a large number of people. This ambiguity stems from the different roles individuals have in the ritual or from their varied interests, but is also linked to the central role that symbols play in ritual communication. Symbols always have a certain vagueness about them: since they can always embody a diversity of ideas within a single form they can rarely be reduced to a single precise meaning. They can be used both to stress different things at different times and to different people, and to elaborate variations of a central ideal. It is the wider context of presentation of icons and symbols that is a key feature in anchoring them to any one particular understanding or meaning.

The Visibility of Memory

The close links between the visual senses and memory were recognised in some of the earliest existing writings on mnemonics (Yates 1966). Cicero, writing in the first century BC, argued that in order to develop a good memory the individual must construct a mental geography of places or buildings; facts or ideas that must be remembered can then be converted into images and stored within this mental architecture. Ideally a memorised map or space should be based on a real place, well known to the individual; but the stored images need not be literal representations of the things to be remembered – they can simply be arbitrary and personal signifiers. As well as asserting that images were the most reliable medium for retaining memories, Cicero also regarded sight as the keenest of all senses, and he argued that things that have actually been seen are more 'easily retained in the mind' than 'perceptions received by the ears or by reflection' (quoted in Harwood 1976: 793).

However, recent research suggests that visual memories of familiar objects are readily distorted or fragmentary if the details have not been closely observed or noted. Although we retain some prominent features, we easily forget or misremember the background or incidental details (Richardson 1993). How do we reconcile this apparent contradiction, that on the one hand the visual senses are the most sensitive for purposes of remembering, yet that on the other visual images are only poorly recalled? One suggestion is that the problem of accurately remembering visual images is due to the fact that they often include too much information. They include too many focal points and too many possible interpretations, a feature that on the one hand makes images difficult to control, or restrict in meaning, while on the other it also makes them difficult to recall. Gombrich (1980), for example, argues that if images are to be memorable and easily remembered they must be simplified, and broken down into smaller images or schematic outlines, 'visual concepts' in Gombrich's terminology. The key features must be enlarged or centred, while the colours are made brighter, the backgrounds simplified and unnecessary details removed. We are left not with a work of art, but with an image of childlike simplicity as the base on which an elaborate memory can be built.

In spite of the memorability of images, pictorial representations have not been widely regarded as an appropriate medium for conveying memories. Instead, verbal transmission is more usually presented as the most appropriate or dominant means by which memories are shared. However, the practices of story-telling offer some useful indications of what may be important in conveying memories visually. Here repetitive and formulaic conventions are used as an *aide-mémoire* for both the narrator and the audience. These formulae both enable the story to be told correctly and provide cues for the audience when introducing dramatic episodes. Repetition permits the key episodes to be stressed and to be told from different perspectives and from the viewpoint of different characters. The process of telling is therefore less a verbatim recitation of a known text than an extended improvisation within a more or less bounded structure. It is more or less bounded because the audience will have a good knowledge of the story which is being told and therefore will expect it to be told in a certain manner. The audience as much as the narrator will know what is appropriate as part of the story and what is out of place. They are largely being told something they already know. Social memory works at the level of recalling shared meanings and not through creating surprises. It confirms rather than challenges.

But this does not mean that memory is inflexible or rigid: the process of improvisation allows the narrative to be adapted to changing circumstances and to incorporate new characters or events where it is appropriate. Because of this shared knowledge and relative flexibility the story can be broken down into a number of distinct episodes or 'tableaux', a form known as 'paratactic narrative'. In a paratactic narrative the episodes are recounted in only a rough sequential order, with no strong narrative thrust between one segment and the next: each episode is relatively complete in itself. This form permits longer and shorter versions of the narrative to be told by omitting some episodes and including others at different times (Fentress and Wickham 1992, Chapter 2). It also allows new events, which conform to the structured expectations, to be readily incorporated into the social memory without disrupting the existing remembered temporal flow.

Images were used in this manner in medieval times in a range of media, in stained glass windows, on tapestries and as marginal illustrations in books. Broken down into simple segments, they could be viewed in a number of ways: as a series of single striking images, as a continuous narrative or as a group of structured moral oppositions. The aim was not just decorative: they were also allegorical, educational aids, constructed as signposts guiding people to higher truths (Carruthers 1990; Kemp 1991).

More recent studies, by Jewsiewicki (1986) of popular painting in Zaire and by Evans (1992) of political stamps in Poland, have shown how a variety of simple visual images can be used as a political weapon to challenge the dominant views of history. The two dominant communities in Northern Ireland have long utilised visual displays to convey their distinct and specific understandings of a shared history. The emphasis on a visual expression permits a certain openness of meaning that on the one hand allows for varying interpretations, but on the other prevents the containment of meaning within a centralised discourse. The clarity and simplicity of an image, which makes it readily recognisable, at the same time makes it harder to define.

Interpreting Visual Images

The most widely used theoretical model for analysing visual images is derived from semiotics, and in particular the work of Roland Barthes (1973, 1977). Barthes explores the ways that images are used as a system of communication, both to express meaning in a readily understood manner, through denotation, and also within a coded, symbolic system, through connotation. The connotative level requires a greater degree of cultural knowledge to read: the meaning is more allusive and uncertain, and may be interpreted differently by different people, or even denied altogether. The connotative sign is less controllable and more readily connected to other signifiers, so that its meaning is potentially endless. Connotative meanings have the potential to be expanded both vertically and horizontally, paradigmatically through metaphor and syntagmatically through metonym. Metaphorical connections are made via recognition of equivalences, that something is or functions in a similar manner to the sign in question rather than being exactly equal to it; while metonymic expansion is a function of some form of logical connection to the sign. While this opens up a wide range of possible symbolic meanings for any sign, these are nevertheless culturally specific, relevant to a particular time and place; and just as signs may take on new specific symbolic values, they can also lose them. Analysis of systems of symbols must necessarily consider the particular social and political culture in which they are used and be sensitive to changes of use and meaning through time.

While denotation and connotation expose the image to multiple interpretations, the intended meaning is often directed or focused through the use of words. A text often acts as an agent of those cultural and historical brakes that are already placed on the chain of signification and further constrains or directs the reading or understanding of an image. Texts are an attempt by the producer of the image to exert control and reduce possible ambiguity. Unlike written texts, visual representations are an extremely poor medium with which to be precise in saying things. Although images may be successful in conveying generalities, moods, atmosphere and impressions and in condensing numerous ideas within a small space or amount of work, an image is always relatively unfocused and out of control (Gombrich 1980). A caption or the like can direct the reader to one particular reading or open one particular door in a syntagmatic chain of meaning. For Barthes (1977:39), this linking of words or captions with images serves primarily as a form of 'anchorage', to focus attention on one aspect of the image rather than any other, and therefore to constrain the range of interpretations; but it can also serve to move the image along by a process of 'relay'. Although Barthes discusses relay in relation to moving images, such as film, it can be an important aid to the narrative process, by alluding to non-depicted but related events or as a bridging medium in paratactic narratives. While the creator of the image may seek to constrain these potential readings by such means as verbal anchors, framing devices and restrictions on access, the image is always relatively distanced from its producer and relatively autonomous, and therefore open to new and unexpected interpretations (Ricoeur 1981).

We can consider how these theoretical concepts apply to an understanding of some of the images under consideration in this study. The most common image among the loyalist community is the depiction of a man on a white horse. One can recognise that this image functions first and most simply at what Panofsky (1970) calls the level of pre-iconographical literal description, where all that is required is a basic cultural knowledge to recognise it as an image of man on horseback. The majority of the population of Ireland will recognise that this image denotes King William III, what Peirce (1940) calls an 'icon', something that conveys meaning or signifies because of its similarity to an object (Panofsky's second level of iconographical analysis). The source of this image is an eighteenth-century oil painting that ultimately serves as the referent object.

But few Irish people have seen this original work of art; recognition of the iconic King Billy who appears in Northern Ireland depends not on the similarity to an original painting, nor to a resemblance to the historical figure himself, but to the inclusion of certain components, certain sub-iconic features, from which the icon itself is constructed. The most important features of any iconic representation of King Billy are his historical dress (often coloured red, white and blue as a further symbolic device), his hand holding a sword aloft, and his white horse, depicted walking through water. The single most important signifier of his 'King Billyness' can be reduced to the white horse. It is these features alone, rather than any notion of style, quality or likeness, that denote the identity of the figure. As I shall explore in detail below it is those essential features that denote the subject that in turn connote his symbolic meaning.

Similarly, the portrayal of St Patrick commonly found on the banners of the Ancient Order of Hibernians is denoted not by any resemblance to the fifth-century historical figure but by the portrayal of the snakes that he is casting out of Ireland. His appearance in the dress of a Catholic Archbishop and the modern-looking church in the background denote him as a modern-ish figure. This in turn creates an opening to stress his symbolic importance as both ancestor and contemporary. Both iconic figures are already highly conventionalised, although they are still functioning at a non-coded denotative level. This stylisation acts in a similar manner to text, to anchor and focus our understanding of the symbolic importance of the figures and direct it into specific metaphoric and metonymic systems. Words are also used to anchor the range of interpretations by linking the group bearing the image and the image itself, so that the group comes to be a living embodiment of the ideal, be this the dead hero/ancestor or the moral virtue. Other mottoes or slogans also function to direct the reading: often they add a philosophical or moral epitaph to a historical person or event, and aim to complete the process of closure, so that the intended meaning is clarified and ambiguity restricted.

While both the image and the text are contained and constrained by their interconnectedness, by the overall framing of the image and by its distinctiveness from other images, it is impossible to understand the images in isolation, separate from each other and self-contained. This is a problem with many studies, which tend to treat the images in isolation, as self-contained objects, and the frame of the image as the limit of analytical consideration. Meaning or meanings emerge from within rather than from clashes on the margins, although, as Berger (1977:152) points out, in practice images exist in a wider social world of unlikely conjunctions and juxtapositions that impinge upon them. The images on the banners and on walls are not displayed in isolation: the process of relay or connectedness between images is very important. At each parade a wide range of images are displayed – images that all relate to a common theme, but which are jumbled together in no particular order. Individual banners proclaim their own rhetorical message, but this is always only a part of a larger whole; while the individual frame of an image marks some sort of limitation on the range of meanings, individual images also begin to dissolve into the whole. Metaphoric and metonymic connotations become entwined. Historical events mixed with Biblical events, real people with mythic, kings with commoners and saints with warriors. Parades take on the aspect of a slow-moving chaotic cartoon, with no obvious logical beginning or end to its story, but with constant variations on themes of individual and collective faith, betrayal, sacrifice, resistance and victory, endlessly repeated and connected together. Which is how some parties like to portray Ireland's history: a cyclical and unresolvable, timeless conflict.

For mural paintings, a single image is far more common, and consequently less elaborate concepts and ideas are communicated. However, a single image often includes a wide selection of symbols that have little meaning except as metaphoric equivalences, in which traditional or normative readings of a sign are moved on or refocused. Fixed in space but extended in time, their presence becomes part of the routine environment, and the message is the more readily accepted because of its very mundanity, as part of the unchallenged *habitus* (Bourdieu 1977). Anchoring an image to a particular place may be a key feature in its effectiveness: both its rhetorical force and resonance are increased (Schudson 1989). I have already noted the classical mnemonic practice of conjoining objects and ideas to be remembered with particular spaces or places, a practice that can be extended to include many con- temporary societies for whom memories of the recent or the mythical past are maintained by their anchorage in specific house sites, gardens, tracks or features of the natural landscape (Feld 1982; Küchler 1987, 1989; Morphy and Morphy 1984; Rosaldo 1980). Murals are therefore also a medium in which memories and ideology, the past and the future, can be brought together, and provide anchors for the identity of a particular community.

The Structure of Presentation

This study explores the role of parades and visual displays in structuring and maintaining sectarian divisions within contemporary life in the north of Ireland. My fieldwork began in 1990, and although it is still continuing, over time the point of interest has changed and expanded (see Jarman and Bryan 1996). My initial work was confined to loyalist parades and displays, but this soon extended to the nationalist community, my intention being to offer a comparison of the use of the differing media both within the two communities and between them. There is an immense amount of material available that I could have used, and, while I try to provide an overview, some branches have been crudely trimmed and some obvious avenues have been ignored. The intention is not to offer a detailed analysis of parades or the Orange Order or any other of the subjects touched on, but to show how they contribute to a local sense of identity and understanding of the past.

The book is divided into four distinct sections. The first part looks at the history of parades and parading and the use of visual displays in the north of Ireland from the seventeenth century to the present. It explores the changes and developments in the practice and the background to the 'inevitability' of the sectarian divide. The second section deals with the ethnography of parading, its importance in social and political life, showing how sectarian geography is mapped out and sustained by the parades, how parades are used to commemorate specific events by re-enacting battles of the past, and how in turn the parades help sustain the conflict in the present. The third section documents and analyses the contemporary use of banner displays on the parades to discover what parts of history are actually being remembered during the marching season. The final section, on mural painting, explains how the commemorations of the marching season are extended into the rest of the year and into areas less central to the parades. It shows how this medium is used by differing groups, sometimes of necessity, sometimes of choice; how the paintings sometimes form part of an internal critique and at others act as an expression of a more extreme voice that would need to be more guarded in other, more formal settings. In each case I focus first on the practice within the loyalist community and then go on to the nationalist practice. This is because in each case the loyalist tradition is either more developed and extensive or more widely documented. Protestants have paraded more often over more areas in the past; they likewise parade more in the present day, and they parade with a larger and wider range of banners. They also established the mural painting tradition. The reasons for these differentials will be explored fully within the body of the text.

Photographs

Although I have just stated that the text is divided into four parts, there is in fact a fifth part to the book, which is presented photographically. I have used photographs extensively in my fieldwork: initially this was to record and document the banners, murals and other displays for later analysis – as a form of fieldnote; but I soon extended my use of the camera to explore other, less obvious, aspects of the culture of parading. Over the years that I have been working in Northern Ireland I have amassed several thousand images, a small proportion of which are included in this volume.

Visual anthropology does not have a very high profile within the discipline, and photography is a poor relation to film and video within the sub-discipline. Much of the analysis of photographs has focused on the ways that they have been used in the past, in an attempt to construct an 'objective' or 'scientific' record, and has recalled debates about the subjectivity of images, or more simply the value of them within verbal texts (Crawford and Turton 1992; Edwards 1992; Taylor 1994). But interest in the importance of photography and its role in ethnographic practice does appear to be growing. The 1995 exhibition *The Impossible Science of Being* and the Anthropology and Photography conference at the 1996 RAI Film Festival have marked a further raising of its profile.

However, in spite of the improvements in technology and the relative ease with which images can be incorporated within texts, anthropologists rarely use many photographs, and rarely use them to provide more than an apt illustration (although see Chaplin 1994; Harper 1987; Tilley 1994), while some of the best visual anthropology has been produced by non-anthropologists John Berger and Jean Mohr (1975; 1989). It would have been easy to use my photographs just as apt illustration, as an adjunct to the verbal descriptions of often complex images; and many of them can be used in that way. But I have also tried to go further and use the inherent polysemic quality of images to address some of the less easily expressed facets of the culture of parading, some of the areas that I have not addressed verbally: the physical, the expressive, the extensive nature of the events, and the involvement of the less prominent and marginal roles that these events demand. The photographs are presented in small groups, each with a common theme (although some images are included just because I like them as photographs), and they run through the length of the book according to their own structure, which runs in parallel to the verbal text, although sometimes these intersect more closely than at others. I cannot say that I found this particularly easy to do; but I do feel that the images add something that more words simply could never do.

Finally, to deal with some absences. In attempting to cover an extensive range of material some corners have been cut. There is already an extensive body of literature on Northern Ireland dealing with the historical, geographical, demographic and political background to the society and to the conflict. I acknowledge this where appropriate, but do not intend to duplicate it. This is not a work of history, but rather a study of how the past is selectively used in the present or perhaps in numerous presents; it is not a study of social geography, although it is concerned with the construction of place; it is not about Politics with a large P, but instead it is about the structures and beliefs that underpin a particular aspect of politics – how history, geography and identity are interwoven to create and sustain a sense of difference.

Orangeman, Belfast, Twelfth 1992.

Part I

The Tradition of Parading

On the way home, Sandy Row, Belfast, the Twelfth, 1994.

Tradition is one of the most over-used words in contemporary Northern Ireland. It is used when referring to habitual, customary practices that are, or appear to be or are claimed to be, rooted in the past. The term has a particular resonance when invoked in connection with the right to parade. Loyalist groups in particular readily claim their 'traditional' rights to march along 'traditional' routes throughout the 'traditional' marching season. To outsiders and to nationalists this 'tradition' often seems to invoke the right to march where they will, when they will. Changing circumstances of geography or demography are rarely regarded as acceptable reasons for giving up one's 'traditional' rights. Time passes but traditions remain. They are regarded as unchanging and unchangeable, connecting the present to the past and affirming the meaning of that past for those in the present. Identity is built on a sense of the continuity of tradition and traditional rights. But maintaining one's identity does not involve invoking tradition but actively maintaining it, year in, year out. Maintaining a tradition means being seen to maintain it. To have meaning, traditions must be made visible in the public life of Northern Ireland and made visible on a regular basis. Any challenge to a tradition is therefore also a visible, public event, and, as such, is a threat to one's status, one's identity and one's history. To have a tradition revoked, whether it be the playing of the national anthem at the Queen's University graduation ceremony or the right to parade along Belfast's Ormeau Road or the Garvaghy Road in Portadown (two major disputes during 1995 and 1996), is seen as a potentially devastating threat to communal identity. Revoking a tradition is the slippery slope to change. For unionists all challenges to tradition are seen as a capitulation to the IRA. They are a threat to the Union, to one's identity as British and as a Protestant. It is the beginning of the road to Rome-rule, to Dublin-rule, and to integration into a United Ireland. Any change to tradition is resisted to the utmost with an attitude expressed by the slogans 'Not an Inch' and 'No Surrender', or more brutally with a simple 'NO'.

Nationalists are less prone to invoke these same rights, largely because they have 'traditionally' been excluded from equal participation in the public sphere of Northern Ireland. Their commemorations have been marginalised. They have been less keen to invoke traditional rights, and instead have demanded civil or equal rights, or in the current terminology, 'parity of esteem'. Nevertheless, they are ready to acknowledge the power of the language of tradition when appropriate. In August 1985 Sinn Féin claimed that a parade through Downpatrick was 'traditional' because it had been held since 1982, and in 1986 Gerry Adams insisted the annual Internment Commemoration Rally on the Falls Road would go ahead, in spite of police opposition, because it was 'traditional' (Irish News 9.8.82, 10.8.86). This all suggests that tradition is a dynamic aspect of socio-political life in the north of Ireland. Traditions can be increased as much as they can be reduced, they can be expanded and extended. Traditions are an active part of the creation of identity and of the maintenance of difference. And as active facets of cultural life we should expect the traditions themselves to undergo change. We should expect the practices that are reified as 'tradition' to be invoked in different ways in different times. They may be used by different interest groups and given different meanings; but none the less, as local practice becomes sedimented as tradition, it will be built on by later generations.

In this first part of the book I want to trace the development of the 'tradition' of parading in Ireland from the late seventeenth century onwards, with particular focus on the celebrations to mark the Williamite wars of 1688–91. The history and customs of parading have been largely ignored by academics (although see Hill 1984; Kelly 1994; Simms 1974; Wright 1996), and to do the subject justice would require a major study. This is not an attempt to provide that study; instead, I trace some of the historical threads of this custom to provide a wider perspective and a deeper context to my ethnographic data. Williamite commemorations are unique in so far as they can be traced in some detail over a period of 300 years. Over these centuries the anniversaries have been used by a number of different groups and sections of society to support diverse political opinions. This development provides the context of my history: to consider the emerging sectarian character of politics in Ulster, the nationalist base for local identity and the role of parades in these processes.

It has been suggested that the events of the Williamite era only came to be considered of real importance within the political environment of the late nineteenth century, and that the 'evidence about lack of interest in these events during the 18th and much of the 19th century ... is conveniently forgotten' (Walker 1992:61, 1996). Walker points out that the centenary of the Battle of the Boyne was largely ignored by Protestants, while the campaigns of the 1690s 'were not major events to be commemorated every year' because they had 'largely faded from memory' (p. 58) and were only rediscovered in the later nineteenth century as part of an emerging unionist political consciousness. He regards these anniversaries as little more than an 'invented tradition', one among many similar traditions that were constructed across Europe in the period 1870–1914, and through which a more or less spurious history was invoked to give cohesion to radically changing social formations (Hobsbawm and Ranger 1983). While fundamental and wide-ranging changes did occur in the nature of the Williamite commemorations in the nineteenth century, the events of the late seventeenth century were far from ignored until this time. Until the later nineteenth century these celebrations were more in the nature of a custom: a routine activity that was established and maintained by practice, but one that varied in response to local circumstances and context, and was re-enacted in a largely unreflexive manner (Hobsbawm 1983:2–3). From the 1870s a more formalised, unified and invariable tradition was constructed from the practices of the predominately rural, lower classes, as their (often disruptive and unruly) festivities were gradually controlled, refined and elaborated in the process of being co-opted to the explicit interests of the Protestant bourgeoisie.

But rather than consider the Williamite celebrations as a simple case of 'before and after', or as a contrast between custom and tradition, I want to break the history down into three distinct periods. Until the formation of the Orange Order in 1795, William was used symbolically by a number of different interest groups throughout Ireland. The parades began as displays of authority and privilege by the *ancien régime*, but they were soon emulated by the emerging Protestant middle class in Dublin. Parading was consolidated as a cultural practice in the late eighteenth century because of its possibilities as an overt political instrument to challenge the existing order. But having successfully achieved their political demands, the middle classes abandoned the use of such displays for almost a century. From 1795 to 1868 parading was largely restricted to the rural lower classes in Ulster. Their parades always verged on the edge of legality, and often crossed the boundary into uncontrolled violence. As a result the interest of the state and the respectable members of society was directed at controlling and constraining these events. But the parades were only one of a number of 'uncivilised' practices that were subject to the censorious eye of the ruling classes in Victorian Ireland. Modernity and industrialisation could not accommodate the localism and disorder of Irish social life, and a diverse range of popular customs and practices were seen as being at odds with the 'civilising process' (Elias 1982). Constraints were imposed on a diverse range of activities: rural sports, such as cock-fighting, were banned; the revelry of fairs and popular religious holidays, including the barely restrained licence of the Belfast Easter holidays on Cave Hill and the festivities at Donnybrook, were restricted or closed down; excessive drinking and distilling of whiskey were countered by laws and temperance crusades; 'immoral' sexuality and courting practices were subject to renewed challenge from the religious authorities; 'unchristianlike' funeral celebrations at wakes were banned by the Catholic Church; and forms of recreational violence, from duelling to faction fighting (including the northern parading practices), were all confronted by a restructured police force and a reformed judiciary. All these activities and more were targeted and tamed in the years between 1840 and 1880 (Connolly 1982; Donnelly 1981; Gray 1983; Malcolm 1986; Rafferty 1994).

However, it proved impossible to eradicate parading: it was too deeply embedded as a popular expression of identity. Instead, parades were legalised from 1872, and, now incorporated into the broader body politic, they became an increasingly prominent part of the political process. The parades were supported and utilised by the political leadership of the two communities in the north, and major anniversaries became occasions for mass mobilisations of support: parades ended in major political rallies dominated by large numbers of speeches and, more importantly for this study, were the occasion for ever more elaborate and extensive visual displays. In tracing this history through 300 years I will explore how people have expressed their understanding of the past through ritual performance and an associated material culture, discuss how the form and meaning have changed, and thereby indicate how the 'folk memory' of the Boyne and other annivers-aries has been maintained and transmitted.

Creating Identity I: King Billy; Belfast, Twelfth 1994.

Creating Identity II: Maid of Erin; Ballyholland, August 1995.

Chapter 2

A Custom Established, 1690–1790

England established a presence in Ireland in the twelfth century when Norman adventurers arrived seeking new lands; but these were few in number, and it was only in the second half of the sixteenth century that Elizabeth I sought to establish firmer control over the island. Until this time Ulster had remained largely independent of England's colonising and military presence. Geographically, Ulster was isolated, defended by a wild border country of hills, woods, rivers and marshes; but persistent military campaigns from the 1560s onwards led to the defeat of the native forces, under Hugh O'Neill, Earl of Tyrone, at Kinsale in 1601. In 1607 Tyrone and Tyrconnell abandoned Ireland (the Flight of the Earls) and their lands in the west of the kingdom were confiscated by the English Crown and made available for plantation. From 1609 the Government began the systematic plantation of Counties Armagh, Cavan, Derry, Donegal, Fermanagh and Tyrone with settlers from England and Scotland. The Merchants Companies of the City of London were encouraged to develop the plantation and establish towns (their legacy remains in the renamed city and county of Londonderry, and smaller settlements and townlands such as Draperstown and Taylorstown); but the major colonisation of Ulster was via an influx of Scots, who crossed the North Channel into the eastern counties of Antrim and Down. The most significant feature of this settlement was that the colonisers were Protestants, a mixture of Anglicans and Presbyterians, while the native Irish remained Catholic.

The government envisioned a substantial replacement of the native population by the colonisers, but the result was a much more diverse settlement pattern, since it proved hard to attract the number of planters necessary to complete the government plans. Many Irish remained in their native areas, although they were often reduced to living on the poorer upland soils rather than in the fertile valleys. Ulster became a varied and fragmented region as settler and native, coloniser and colonised, Protestant and Catholic lived side by side. Although intermarriage, religious conversion and acculturation undoubtedly did occur, the two communities remained largely distinct and separate. Old resentments remained, and when the time seemed right these were acted on: in 1641 the Irish rebelled under Rory O'More, and in many places revenge was taken and settlers were put to the sword. But retribution followed, as Oliver Cromwell arrived in Ireland in 1649 and in his turn slaughtered, confiscated lands and banished the Irish landowners to the barren western area of Connacht. Cromwell's campaign confirmed the British presence.

> [A]lmost all Catholic landowners disappeared in Ulster . . . Land was granted to soldiers and 'adventurers' . . . A fresh set of landowners and jobbers arrived in Ulster, but this time there was no real attempt to remove the native cultivators. The Gaelic aristocracy, already shattered by the Ulster plantation, was all but wiped out and the foundations of the Protestant Ascendancy had been firmly laid (Bardon 1992:141–2).

Upon accession to the throne of England in 1685, James II assumed executive power and began to restore Roman Catholics to public positions. Fearing the restoration of a Catholic ascendancy, a number of leading Protestants approached a Dutchman, William, Prince of Orange, and, assuring him of popular support, they asked him to lead a military force against the King. William landed at Torbay in November 1688 and, as he advanced towards London, James fled. William was married to James's eldest daughter Mary, and they were crowned joint monarchs in February 1689. James rallied his supporters in Ireland, and it was here that the military campaign for the kingdom was fought. There had been no initial panic over James's accession, nor was there any overwhelming support for William among Irish Protestants; but as law and order began to break down in the rural areas the balance of opinion shifted (Gillespie 1992). The Protestants of Londonderry resisted the arrival of the Jacobite army, and the city was besieged from December 1688 until relief arrived in August 1689. The following year William landed at Carrickfergus to lead his army. The two forces met at the River Boyne on 1 July 1690 (Old Style). Militarily the battle was inconclusive, and the campaign continued; it was not until 12 July (Old Style) the

following year that the decisive victory was won at the Battle of
Aughrim, that consolidated the Glorious Revolution and cemented
the position of the Protestant faith in the two kingdoms. However,
the symbolic importance of the two monarchs leading their armies
into battle, and James's defeat and subsequent flight from Ireland
meant that the Battle of the Boyne would be remembered as the
key event.

Parading Power, Parading Loyalty

The first formal Williamite celebration in Ireland was held only
months after the battle of the Boyne, when on the King's birthday,
4 November 1690, a military procession was held through Dublin.
Throughout the city bonfires were lit and church bells rung, and
in the evening there was a firework display for the public, while
the Lords Justices hosted a dinner for the nobility and leading
citizens (Simms 1974; Hill 1984). Only a few days earlier the defeat
of the 1641 Irish rebellion had been commemorated with 'great
solemnity' in a similar manner. Throughout the following century
William's anniversary was marked each year by an elaborate
procession, and a diverse range of loyal and royal anniversaries
were marked in a similar way (Kelly 1994). These Dublin processions were in turn a local expression of a Europe-wide custom
by which public authorities celebrated royal anniversaries,
religious festivals, military victories and civic commemorations
(Bergeron 1971; Cressy 1989; Darnton 1984; Muir 1981; Rubin
1991). Such celebrations were occasions for the display of wealth,
grandeur and status of both individuals and institutions of state.
The great and the good physically reaffirmed their collective
control of the streets, of society, and with military accompaniment
they visibly demonstrated the extent of their power.

Habermas argues that within the world of the *ancien régime*
authority, power, status and virtue had to be formally publicised,
that is given public representation 'not for but "before" the people'
(1992:7–10). The hierarchy of power and authority, normally
remote or concealed in the city, was thereby confirmed at the most
immediate and democratic level, that of the street. In their pomp
and finery the processions portrayed an idealised representation
of the civic and political order to the watching populace. The

parades were often structured to mirror the formal hierarchies of
rank and power, and the whole aimed to demonstrate to spectators
a unity of purpose and unchallengeable authority. The contrast
between the elegance and finery of those processing and the dress
of the spectators emphasised the unbridgeable social gulf between
authority and the people, and further distanced the agents of the
state from the mundanity of daily routine. In general such
demonstrations 'served not so much the pleasure of the participants as the demonstration of grandeur . . . the common people,
content to look on, had the most fun' (Habermas 1992:10).
Excluded from formal participation, the role of the lower classes
was to observe and bear witness to the dignity of their betters.
Away from the procession, and after the nobles had retired indoors
to enjoy their banquet in a more relaxed and private realm, the
public celebrations continued in a carnivalesque, and sometimes
riotous, manner as people gathered around the numerous bonfires,
eating and drinking, watching the fireworks and firing guns long
into the night.

The Dublin authorities used the processions on 4 November to
imply that the ideals of 'civil and religious liberty' were as much
a feature of Irish social and political life as they were in England.
William's accession was seen to signify a victory for freedom of
speech, tolerance and parliamentary democracy over arbitrary and
autocratic government, and William was promoted as a symbol
of constitutional government rather than as the military conqueror
of Catholic Ireland. In this spirit it was appropriate to celebrate
the King's birthday rather than to commemorate the military
victories over the Irish. But while there was a sense in which
William could be promoted as a non-sectarian national figure, his
public meaning was constrained by other events of the ritual
calendar. November 4th was bracketed by two other major
commemorations in Ireland: 23 October marked the defeat of the
1641 rebellion, and 5 November marked the anniversary of the
discovery of the Gunpowder Plot (Barnard 1991). Both anniversaries were the cause for widespread public celebrations, and
on both dates sermons, giving thanks for Protestant deliverance
and warning of the continued threat of Catholicism, were delivered
from the pulpit. Many of these sermons were then published,
giving them a wide circulation. The two-week period from the
end of October to early November was therefore one of concentrated public commemoration and rejoicing that focused on

the repeated Protestant deliverance from Catholic treachery. Sir John Temple's *The Irish Rebellion*, which recounted the events of 1641 and likened the Irish Protestants to God's Chosen People, went through several editions in the eighteenth century, thus further consolidating this reading of history (Bartlett 1992). The continuity of the Williamite celebrations must be understood within this wider framework, which meant that from the beginning they were open to alternative interpretations of his memory.

State processions continued through Dublin into the early nineteenth century, but it proved ever more difficult to control the exuberance of the popular celebrations and the meaning of the memory of the victor of the Boyne. November 4th became the focus for competing claims on William's memory: on the one side by the representatives of the Crown, and on the other by the Volunteers, who demanded political reform of Parliament (see below). The Government steadily reduced its public involvement and concentrated on attempting to control the excesses that the day inspired. This gradual abandonment of Williamite anniversaries acknowledged the fact that it was impossible to neutralise William's memory. Dublin Castle turned to the figure of St Patrick as a symbol of national unity, and promoted 17 March as a day for popular celebration (Hill 1984). By 1822, although flags were flown from Dublin Castle and church bells rung for the day, state processions were no longer held; furthermore, armed guards were mounted around King William's statue in College Green to prevent it being decorated (*Belfast News Letter* 12.11.1822).

While the state struggled to control the formal commemorations of the late King, popular celebrations to mark the anniversary of the battles themselves had long been established as parallel events (Kelly 1994). In 1740 the Boyne Society, one of many such loyal clubs, broke with the custom of celebrating the anniversary with a private dinner, and instead initiated a new era when they decided to mark the Golden Jubilee of the battle by marching to St Catherine's church for a sermon and then afterwards parading through Dublin, accompanied by music and the discharging of guns and pistols. Within a few years their annual celebrations were being described as a 'warlike parade' (*Dublin Courant* 30.6–4.7.1747). The Aughrim Society also adopted the custom of parading, but they avoided the same military emphasis and 'made a very decent appearance' with 'Orange cockades and green Boughs in their hats' when they paraded through the city 'with proper Effigies, Musick, Drums etc.' (*Dublin Courant* 14–17.7.1744). This became a regular practice in Dublin, and similar public celebrations were also held in Cork, Drogheda and Londonderry. However, in general the wealthier classes in Ulster still preferred to mark the day in a more private manner: a visit to the theatre, a charity ball or a dinner were all popular forms of celebration, but while the lower classes celebrated around bonfires there are no indications that they held parades to mark the day.

Public processions were not restricted to the Williamite commemorations: many anniversaries were marked in a similar manner. Guild processions on Corpus Christi had been recorded in Dublin since 1498 (Webb 1929), and the guilds still processed the Liberties and Franchises to mark the boundaries of the Mayoral jurisdiction, carrying their colours and flags, in Dublin and other towns into the eighteenth century (*Faulkner's Dublin Journal* 3–7.8.1731; Barrington 1803; Loftus 1978). The Freemasons also held occasional parades. They marked St John's day (24 June) 1725 by a procession of 100 brethren, wearing 'their Aprons, White Gloves and other parts of the Distinguishing Dress of that Worshipful Order', and the same day the Journeyman Taylors, for whom St John was also patron, marched to St John's church for a sermon and 'afterwards to the Walshes Head where they had a splendid entertainment' (*Dublin Weekly Journal* 26.6.1725). Masonic parades were recorded in Coleraine and Cork in following years, while various journeymen associations paraded on patron's day and to express their loyalty in Belfast, Cork and Lurgan (Crawford 1972). In spite of numerous laws banning both combinations and public assemblies, they continued through much of the eighteenth century; as Boyle notes, 'processions had long been dear to tradesmen who assumed much of the pageantry of the guilds' (1988:41). Unfortunately, these events remain poorly documented, and their historical significance has yet to be addressed.

Williamite commemorations were part of this urban custom of parading, which was developed and maintained by a range of fraternal bodies. All of the features that were to become a regular aspect of the Boyne celebrations previously appeared as a part of either patron's day parades or state-sponsored festivals. Eating and drinking was a common attraction of all public festivities, whether aimed at the nobility or the general public; but parading the streets in group formation, wearing some form of distinguishing dress and carrying flags or effigies, was a central part of the day. The popular parades drew heavily on the example and visual rhetoric of the state ceremonials and of the guilds. They were an opportunity to display the corporate dignity of the respective bodies and announce the public presence of otherwise private associations. From the early eighteenth century it became common for groups to emulate the state practice and take their celebrations out of the dining rooms and on to the streets. The parades drew attention to, or, more explicitly, publicised, the emerging presence of an organised middle and artisanal rank of society, who, while not breaking with the traditional norms and proprieties, were beginning to establish their own agenda. This corporate image still displayed itself in the language of the theatre, in the type of costumed performance that Sennett (1993) sees as a residue from the regimented social placings of the previous century. Within the context of the *ancien régime* such displays were still apolitical, in so far as there was no formal oppositional political intention behind the early parades, although by mimicry of the state events they offered an oblique challenge and threat to the existing order.[1] However in the changing social, economic and political climate of the eighteenth century, parades were soon to become the medium that gave visible form to the demands of the emerging Protestant middle classes in Ireland as they sought to translate their increasing wealth into political capital.

Parades and Protest in the North

Beyond the urban centres there is less evidence of the popular ceremonial or political world of the peasantry. There are few indications that the lower classes participated in formal cele- brations except as an audience, or that they were able to mobilise themselves as a political force. One exception was the Oakboy movement of 1763, a mass protest of Protestant artisans, farmers and shopkeepers against local tax increases. This erupted in north Armagh at the end of June and spread rapidly through adjacent counties before being subdued by the military in early August

1. Supporters of the Jacobite cause displayed their presence with processions in Dublin and elsewhere on the Pretender's birthday on a number of occasions during the 1720s. These assemblies caused concern to the authorities, who went as far as banning the wearing of white roses and 'other marks of Distinction' in 1729 (*Freeman's Dublin Journal* 11.6.1726; 7–10.6.1729; Connolly 1992:239).

(Donnelly 1981). The Oakboys often paraded in large numbers in broad daylight: up to 20,000 took to the roads in Armagh in mid-July; 10,000 assembled at Errigal on the Tyrone–Monaghan border on 14 July; and 10,000 met at Monaghan on 20 July; on another occasion, near Markethill 'they fill'd at least two miles of the road and were formed into companies, with each [having] a standard, or colours, displayed; of which [companies] he says he counted thirty with drums, horns, fidlers and bagpipes' (letter in the *Cork Evening Post* 11.7.1763, quoted by Donnelly).

These disturbances flourished in an 'atmosphere of carnival', but this disguised the true purpose of the Oakboy parades, which was to warn and intimidate the local gentry. While there is no suggestion that the Oakboys acknowledged any Williamite anniversaries, their protests were most visible at a time when popular demonstrations might be expected. Only a few years later and in the same area there was a conjunction of customary celebration and political discontent when on 12 July 1775 a 'very respectable group of the Protestant Gentlemen of the town' from Tandragee, County Armagh, spent the day eating and drinking before they marched through the town 'preceded by a band of music; with flags etc.'. The marchers decorated themselves with orange cockades and ribbons, while an orange and blue flag bearing the motto 'Protestant Interest' was flown from the Market House. The report concludes that 'the afternoon was spent in mirth, sociality and joy; with bonfires, firing of guns etc. The town was elegantly illuminated and had grand fire-works. The number of people assembled on the occasion was prodigious' (*Belfast News Letter* 18–21.7.1775).

These examples offer fragmentary evidence of a rural custom of parading in a disciplined and quasi-military manner with flags and music among the Protestant community in the north, and indicate that they were willing to mobilise in support of their interests. In fact the 1770s witnessed the beginnings of a more widespread and systematic use of public parades and displays as the Protestant gentry of the north of Ireland took to the streets in support of their political demands. The 1770s and 1780s marked a rupture with the old tradition of social displays that emulated the state, and instigated a period in which the parade became established as an instrument of political action. The Irish Parliament in Dublin, dominated by landed interests, was subservient to the wishes of England and unable to legislate for itself. The head of state, the Lord Lieutenant, a member of the British Cabinet appointed by London, was often absent from Ireland. Furthermore, Ireland's exports and foreign trade, and therefore her financial autonomy, were heavily constricted by London. This situation was increasingly unacceptable to an ever-larger portion of Irish Protestant society, who, represented in Parliament by the Patriots, attempted to restore Ireland's political autonomy. The issue had been rumbling away since the 1720s (Swift's *Drapier's Letters* were an early expression of this dissatisfaction); and by the 1770s discontent was coming to a head. It was also widely felt that the internal Roman Catholic threat had finally been laid to rest, and many of the Penal Laws, introduced after the Williamite victories, were being ignored or repealed. Some members of Parliament like Henry Grattan were beginning to talk of a common interest of all Irishmen, Protestant and Catholic (Boyce 1991). It was in this environment that the Volunteer movement was founded.

In the Spring of 1778, while the British army was confronting rebel colonists in America, privateers began raiding in Irish coastal waters and, with a lack of soldiers in Ireland, there was concern that the French might take the opportunity to invade. As the British government had no funds to pay for a militia, the Protestant gentry and middle classes took it upon themselves to set up a paramilitary defence force of Volunteer companies. However, the Volunteers outlived the immediate concerns of security, and developed into an extra-parliamentary force in the cause of Ireland, adding their support to the rhetoric of the Patriots. Between 1779 and 1782 the combined forces of the Patriots in Parliament and the Volunteers on the streets brought about many political and economic changes: Ireland was to have the same trading rights as England, legislative independence was restored to the Irish Houses of Parliament, and the Irish House of Lords was given final legal jurisdiction. The constitution of 1782 and 'Grattan's Parliament' established some degree of autonomy for Ireland and achieved many of the Patriot Party's demands (Bardon 1992; Smyth 1992).

Some of the Volunteer companies continued to press for further reform of Parliament, repeal of the Penal Laws and the reintro- duction of Catholics to the public life of Ireland. These demands proved too radical for such a broad alliance, many of whose more conservative members were content with the already secured reforms; and, as the alliance disintegrated, the power and influence of the Volunteers declined (Stewart 1989). While the Volunteers represented 'the first successful example of the bringing of the gun into Irish politics' (Smyth 1979:136), they also confirmed the importance of parading, and extended the use of visual displays as an integral part of the political process. The Volunteer period witnessed a new development in the culture of parading, in which ceremonial, commemoration and political demands become inseparably entwined.

The first Volunteer Company was formed in Belfast on 17 March 1778. By the middle of 1780 an estimated 60,000 men had enrolled, and by 1782 more than 300 companies had been raised in Ulster alone (Rogers 1934; Smyth 1974). Parading immediately became a prominent feature of their activities, and was taken up with great enthusiasm across Ulster. Most parades involved some form of military display; and many reports emphasised the colour of the spectacle, the smartness of the men on parade and the large numbers of spectators that were attracted to the parades. In 1778, the Belfast Volunteers paraded to church on 28 May, on 4 June to mark the King's birthday, again on 21 June, on 1 July to mark the Boyne, on 1 August to mark the Hanoverian succession and on 4 November (*Belfast News Letter* 26–30.5, 2–5.6, 22–26.6, 30.6–3.7, 31.7–4.8, 3–6.11.1778). The following year both the anniversary of the Boyne and William's birthday were marked by parades in Dublin and throughout Ulster (*BNL* 5–9.11.1779). These parades and the larger-scale reviews, held in Ulster from 1780, kept the Volunteers constantly in the public eye. In the late 1780s, after the split between the radical and conservative wings, the Volunteers abandoned their commemorations of the Williamite anniversaries: 'it was unanimously resolved, in future not to commemorate as formerly, any day that directly tends to keep up the remembrance of the Civil Wars of Ireland. It is nearly a century since they ceased and full time to forget them' (*BNL* 3–7.8.1787), but they continued to parade in support of their radical causes until they were disbanded (and others soon took up the Williamite memory). Parades were used as a recurrent public display of strength of the middle ranks of society, and were an expression of the weight of public opinion (as well as a fashionable activity and an entertainment; see Jarman 1997). And, in so far as they helped to extend connections between the ranks of Protestant society and further the dissemination and debate of ideas, they were also a key part of the democracy of the movement.

The Volunteers were not simply prepared to parade in support of their ideals; they also developed and extended the use of visual displays in the form of slogans, symbols and emblems to convey their ideas. Displays of some kind, flags, banners, effigies or smaller devices had probably always been used on parades. The guilds had long carried flags and banners decorated with their patron saint and the coat of arms of the town, and the journeymen associations and probably the Freemasons adopted similar practices, although the descriptions are all rather vague (Loftus 1978; Webb 1929). The Volunteers drew on these customs, as well as the practices of the formal military units, and linked them with more immediate political demands. The Dublin Volunteers paraded to William's statue each year on the morning of 4 November and left it decorated with political slogans and demands. In 1779 they demanded 'Short Money Bills, a Free Trade or Else!' and 'Relief to Ireland', but also supported 'The Glorious Revolution' (*BNL* 5–9.11.1779); in 1783 they called for 'An equal representation of the people' (*BNL* 7–10.11.1783) and in 1785 the banners stated 'The volunteers of Ireland will support the Trade and Constitution or perish in the ruins' and 'Reject the English Propositions or Else' (*BNL* 24 8–11.11.1785). Besides these agit-prop slogans, the Volunteers publicised themselves through a range of more conventional symbols. Some of these appeared for the first time at these parades, but have subsequently become central to the diversity of Irish political culture. The material culture of the Volunteers expresses something of the range of ideas and opinions within this heterogeneous organisation. They were able to display a variety of images and symbols within a single framework that in later years would come to be seen as essentially polarised and contrasted as either explicitly unionist or nationalist. At this time it was still possible to be loyal to the ideals of the 'Glorious Revolution' and to consider oneself an Irishman. It was within this ideological framework that William III remained an important figure for the Volunteers.

Some companies used a simple coat of arms: the Dublin Volunteers carried both a blue flag with the Dublin arms in a shamrock wreath and a crimson flag with the Irish harp of the Leinster arms; the Merchants' Regiment used an orange flag with the arms of Ireland and a figure of Liberty; and the Goldsmiths' Regiment carried a cream flag with the 'Irish arms imperially crowned' (*Belfast News Letter* 5–9.11.1779). Other companies had more elaborate designs: the Loyal Ballyshannon Volunteers, the Caledon Volunteers, County Carlow Legion and Castleray Fencibles all bore representations of Hibernia resting on an Irish harp on their colours; the flag of the 1st Armagh Volunteers depicts a sunburst through clouds and a harp surmounted by a crown and wreathed in shamrocks; that of the Ballymena Volunteers has a harp and the cipher of King William; and the flag of the Killeavy Volunteers has a portrait of William and the mottoes 'Our King and Country' and 'William's Great Cause' (Hayes-McCoy 1979).

Some of these, the harp, the shamrock and references to King William, were specifically Irish symbols, but other features of the iconography were drawn from a range of sources. The feminised representation of Ireland was common in Gaelic traditions, while Ireland had been represented as Hibernia, crowned with laurel and oak leaves and bearing a Phrygian cap from William's time, and was used as a counterpoint to Britannia. Hibernia was also similar to representations of Liberty that appeared in revolutionary France (Agulhon 1981; O'Cuiv 1978; Warner 1985), while the sunburst was a Freemason's symbol, representing knowledge and enlightenment and, as such, was widely known in western Europe in the eighteenth century.

The Volunteer movement can therefore be seen as the Irish expression of a more widespread challenge to the established social order – one that drew on both internationalist ideals (parliamentary democracy, liberty) and local customs (parades) as its means of converting and sustaining public opinion. In 1791 and 1792, at what were to prove to be the last displays of the radical rump of the Volunteer movement, this international solidarity was prominently displayed in Belfast on Bastille Day. In 1791 portraits of Benjamin Franklin and Mirabeau were carried beside slogans denouncing the slave trade (Stewart 1993). The following year they carried the flags of 'the five free nations', Ireland, America, France, Poland and Great Britain, and displayed

> the Great Standard, elevated on a triumphal car, drawn by four horses with two volunteers as supporters, containing on one side of the canvas a representation of 'the Releasement of the Prisoners from the Bastille', motto 'Sacred to Liberty'. The reverse contained a figure of Hibernia, one hand and foot in shackles, a volunteer presenting to her a figure of Liberty, motto 'For a people to be FREE, it is sufficient that they WILL IT'.

This final parade, to the Falls review grounds and back, involved over 800 Volunteers, and another 180 people followed them marching behind a green flag (Joy and Bruce 1792–3).

By 1793, when the Volunteers were disbanded, public parades with music and decorative flags and banners had been transformed into an established feature of political life of the north of Ireland. Although the Volunteers had maintained the memory of King William, it was his role in the 'Glorious Revolution' rather than his military conquests that remained important. Attention was focused on the aspiration for a unified, national identity rather than evoking the memories of difference and exclusion that were to dominate the public stage in the next few years. Although many of the constituent features of parading politics had appeared by the end of the eighteenth century, they remained largely within the patterns and aspirations of bourgeois life. The transformation of social practice, which established parades and public display as a regular feature of popular culture and politics, only occurred in the early decades of the nineteenth century. Although the Volunteers were formally brought to an end in 1793, their legacy was immense. They had always been a diverse body of opinion; and, as the movement fragmented, this varied membership was important in continuing the radical tradition, through the United Irishmen, and also in consolidating the conservative forces of society, through the Orange Order. It was the Orange Order that were to have the most impact in extending the custom of parading.

Creating Identity III: Crown and Bible; Ormeau Road, Belfast,
July 1994.

Creating Identity IV: St Patrick; Toome, St Patrick's Day, March 1995.

Chapter 3

Riotous Assemblies, 1796–1850

While the Volunteers were celebrating the success of the French Revolution, in rural Armagh Protestant and Catholic peasant bands, known as Peep o'Day Boys and Defenders, had been fighting and raiding each other regularly since 1784. These clashes culminated in the Battle of the Diamond, near Loughgall, in September 1795 (Miller 1983, 1990). In part these were a continuation of the agrarian protests that had erupted across Ireland since the Whiteboys had first appeared in 1761 (Beames 1983). But they also introduced a new sectarian dimension that, initially, was specific to the proto-industrial social and economic conditions of County Armagh. This sectarianism was compounded by the heightened political tensions that were produced by the raised profile of the Catholic and national questions in the wider political arena since the 1780s (Gibbon 1975; Smyth 1992; Whelan 1996). The 'battle' would probably not have been of lasting significance had not some of the Protestant victors met afterwards to create a more structured organisation to counter the Defenders. This society was to become the Orange Institution. The Orange Order, as it is commonly known, received support from sections of the rural gentry and middle classes and spread rapidly across southern Ulster, although local groups remained largely independent of centralised control until the second half of the century.

The new organisation adopted parading as the appropriate means of displaying their loyalty and their strength. At the first Orange Boyne parade in 1796 some 2,000 men walked from Portadown, Loughgall and Richhill to Lord Gosford's demesne at Markethill. They arrived, he reported to Lord Camden, the Lord Lieutenant, at

> about five o'clock in the evening marching in regular files by two with orange cockades, unarmed, and by companies which were distinguished by numbers upon their flags. The party had one drum

and each company had a fife and two or three men in front with painted wands in their hands who acted as commander . . . The devices on the flags were chiefly portraits of King William with mottoes alluding to his establishment of the Protestant religion, and on the reverse side of some of them I perceived a portrait of his present Majesty with the crown placed before him, motto God save the King . . . They were perfectly quiet and sober . . . each company . . . saluted me by lowering their flags (published in Crawford and Trainor (eds) 1969).

This first parade clearly owed much to the practices of the Volunteer companies. The lodges adopted a pseudo-military format: the men marched in formation and carried expensive flags decorated with the image of King William, and whenever possible they liked to be reviewed by members of the local aristocracy or military figures. But they also drew on the more ephemeral tradition of the agrarian bands who had similarly marched to music in a military manner, appointed officers and identified themselves with cockades and floral displays. Lord Gosford, who had otherwise been antagonistic to the Orangemen, suggests that the day was peaceful and orderly; however, the *Belfast News Letter* notes that, in the afternoon, following 'words' between a Mr M'Murdie and a member of the Queen's County Militia, M'Murdie 'received a stab of which he died' (*BNL* 15.7.1796). The following year large Orange parades in Lurgan and Belfast passed off peacefully, but an 'affray' between Orangemen and members of County Kerry Militia in Stewartstown, County Tyrone, left 14 people dead and many more wounded (*BNL* 14.7, 17.7.1797). These early encounters set the tone for Orange commemorations for the next few decades. The parades were tolerated, if not overtly encouraged, by the gentry, and vilified by liberals and by the Whig press, but were able to be defended as a rural custom until a flashpoint produced an eruption of violence. In the heightened tensions of this period surrounding the United Irishmen rising of 1798 and the Act of Union of 1800, violent incidents were common; and whenever the issue of Catholic rights was raised on the political agenda in years to come, parades became a persistent flashpoint. While they were used as emblems of identity across the north of Ireland, they remained a thorn in the side of the authorities.

Orangeism remained strongest in the rural areas, and membership in Belfast remained small until the 1860s. The Twelfth was soon widely celebrated, especially in Counties Armagh, Down and Tyrone; most parades were small affairs, but sometimes they drew much larger crowds: 7,000 people were reported at Lurgan in 1815 and 20,000 were claimed at Waringstown the following year. Most reports of these early events are perfunctory, especially if there was no violence, but occasionally we are given a fuller picture of the growing local importance of the day from the scale of the decorations and preparations. In 1812 Dr John Gamble described Tandragee as 'a perfect orange grove' and noted the 'lofty arch, which was thrown across the entire street', in which 'orange was gracefully blended with oak leaves, laurels and roses' and bits of 'gilded paper' were interwoven with the flowers; doors and windows were also decorated with 'garlands of the orange lily'. He also remarks on the number of banners, which were all decorated with King William 'grim as a saracen on a sign post' and which he describes as 'more remarkable for loyalty than taste or variety' (McClelland 1980). Dr Thomas Reid describes a similar scene at Caledon, County Tyrone in 1822: 'The way was strewn with Orange lilies, and at particular places was thrown over it triumphal arches, decorated with orange festoons, and garlands innumerable. The scene was quite delightful, and reminded me of the fabled stories of fairyland I had read at school' (Reid 1823:189).

The banners continued to be dominated by representations of King William until much later in the century, but a range of street decorations flourished in this early period, and arches became a major element in local displays. The idea of a triumphal arch had originated in ancient Rome, as a device to honour victorious military leaders. Persons passing under the arch supposedly shared in the virtues and qualities which decorated it (Saxl and Wittkower 1948). In the sixteenth and seventeenth century arches were used extensively in royal pageantry in England; elaborate designs incorporating floral decorations were erected across principal streets to mark royal visits and coronations; and they remained a popular form of welcome into the nineteenth century: one was erected in Bristol in 1816 to mark the visit of the Duke of Wellington, and they were often erected by friendly societies and similar bodies (Bergeron 1971; Gosden 1961).

The earliest reference to a triumphal arch in Ireland dates from 1790, when the Bishopgate in the Londonderry city walls was rebuilt in honour of King William. In 1795 Ferryquay Gate and in

1810 Butcher's Gate were remodelled in a similar style (Miller 1989). These stone-built, permanent arches contrasted with the ephemeral floral displays; but this is presumably the inspiration for the triumphal arch at Orange celebrations. Most arches were little more than bunches of orange lilies, purple rocket and evergreen suspended from a cord spanning a principal road; but even these were potent symbolic displays. Some were more elaborate: two arches were erected in Enniskillen for the anniversary of the Battle of Newtownbutler in August 1828: one was decorated with 'God save the King' and references to William III, George IV and the defence of Enniskillen, and the other bore the slogan 'Wellington, Peel and the Present Administration' (*BNL* 19.8.1828).

This is an early example of more explicit political displays on an arch, a use that would became more common as the century progressed. Where once such displays were contained within a moving body of men, they were now an extension of the public architecture; these developments mark the beginnings of the visible sectarianisation of space, for although the earliest descriptions suggested scenes of arcadian pleasure to the visitor, of villages and towns gaily decorated with flowers, the idea of the 'triumphal' arch points to the darker background of conflict and to a vanquished population as well as to the victors. These developments in visual displays occurred at a time of increasing sectarian tensions over O'Connell's campaigns for Catholic rights; arches were used to declare the identity of a village, and demanded recognition of this. In Dromore for example, the 'Grand Arch' was affixed to the house of a publican and spanned the 'road leading to Dublin; under which every coach (and) cart . . . was obliged to pass' (*Northern Whig* 20.7.1826).

However, if arches were expressions of Orange triumphalism, their location often provoked resentment and reaction. In 1829 two arches in Newry, decorated with orange ribbons and 'surmounted with a likeness of King William on horseback' were taken down by the police, while at Maghera riots broke out as Catholics attempted to remove an arch (*BNL* 17.7.1829). Despite the protests, objections and attacks, arches were firmly established as part of the Orange celebrations, and they appeared in large numbers every year. In contrast, green arches were rare: some were erected for O'Connell's monster Repeal meetings in the 1840s, but they were not tolerated in Ulster. It was not so easy to stop Catholics from taking to the streets in commemorative parades, however, and the 1820s and 1830s witnessed a general escalation of the culture of parading; this in turn led to an increase in sectarian clashes and violence which proved difficult to constrain.

Ribbonmen and Freemasons

The legacy of the Volunteers, the Freemasons, the United Irishmen, the Defenders, and of popular involvement with political activity and debate, left a deep mark in Ulster. This was especially true in the linen triangle, which stretched from east Tyrone, through Armagh and Down, to south Antrim. This was the area where fraternal organisations had long been, and remained, strongest. It was an area with numerous book clubs and reading clubs, and it had the highest literacy rates in Ireland (Adams 1987; Hewitt 1951). Daniel O'Connell's campaign for Catholic emancipation coincided with an increase in displays of political identity within the Roman Catholic community in the years after 1820, and it was around this time that the name 'Ribbonmen' began to appear regularly in news reports. The Ribbonmen inherited the role of defenders of rural Catholics (Garvin 1981, 1987). They organised across the north to counter the Orange threat, and espoused a vague nationalist political rhetoric, which was largely concealed by the secretive, undocumented structure of their organisation.

Ribbonmen came from a wide range of social backgrounds with the farming, trading and artisanal ranks of Catholic society prominent in leadership positions: this helped to unite the otherwise local defence groups into a more coherent political movement. The Ribbonmen were also prominent in establishing a custom of parading among the Catholic community, one which reflected the growing importance of religion as a marker of collective identity (Wright 1996). It was at this time that St Patrick's day was confirmed as a popular and specifically Catholic event; funeral processions were also utilised as a suitable opportunity for public displays of solidarity. It is not clear when St Patrick's day parades began, but in 1822 *The Irishman* reported that 'there has been an immemorial practice of walking in procession on the anniversary of St Patrick',and claimed that 20,000 people had paraded in Downpatrick the previous year (22.3.1822). St Patrick's parades were regularly held in Castledawson, Downpatrick,

Newry, Toome and in the Glens of Antrim, all areas with a large Catholic population, while smaller celebrations were recorded in Belfast. Ribbon parades adopted all the customary trappings: the men appeared in 'regular marching order, with a drum and fife' wearing white and green colours and 'sashes corresponding with their head dresses', and they paraded 'with colours flying and music playing' (*BNL* 19.3.1824, 21.3.1826). However, it is not until 1847 that a report from Seaforde, Co. Down, gives more inform-ation: 'flags, inscribed with mottoes and devices . . . several having the portrait of St Patrick' (*NW* 20.3.1847). Therefore St Patrick seems to have been co-opted and sectarianised as a Catholic Irish saint, in the same way and at broadly the same time as King William was redefined as a Protestant hero. He was adopted as the patron of one section of the lower classes of a society that was increasingly divided in its loyalties and aspirations. This seems to have been accepted by many historians as an almost inevitable outcome of the violence of 1798; however, there are indications that this was not the only option.

Although the divisions between Orange and Green were becoming more apparent at this time, there was still a vibrant, popular non-sectarian tradition in the north, which was expressed through Freemasonry. The widespread occurrence of oath-bound secret societies in rural areas from the 1760s onwards is probably due to masonic inspiration. Ulster experienced a rapid growth in masonic lodges in the 1770s and 1780s and again in the early nineteenth century. Although a Grand Lodge had been established in Dublin in 1725, it struggled to exert central control over local bodies until late in the nineteenth century, and in the rural areas of Ulster unofficial lodges or 'hedge-masonry' remained strong (Beatty 1933; Stevenson 1990). Freemasonry was a varied and heterogeneous organisation that brought together a socially diverse range of individuals, in an environment that often stimulated debate and radical ideas and encouraged self-help in education and literacy. Membership of lodges varied according to the local situation, but in rural Ulster a single lodge might include gentle-men, farmers, weavers and artisans (Beatty 1933; Crossle 1909; Johnston 1977; Leighton 1938). This was a similar social back-ground to the other fraternities, although without a formalised sectarian separation, for in spite of Papal edicts in 1738, 1751, 1821 and 1825 that forbade Roman Catholics from becoming Free-masons, they constituted a large proportion of the membership

(Smyth 1993). It is not clear how many individual lodges were of mixed faith, but a number in Ulster had both Catholic and Protestant members who paraded to church together each St John's day (Grange 1980). However, in the early-nineteenth-century political climate of Ulster it was difficult to avoid being identified as either Protestant or Catholic, individually and collectively, and this may help to explain why we find reports of Masons clashing with Orangemen, with Defenders, and later with Ribbonmen (Smyth 1993; de Vere White 1973). But, rather than disappearing with the growth of sectarian politics, Masonic lodges had their most dramatic expansion in the early nineteenth century, and the area that witnessed the most growth was the region of Ulster that also sustained the Orangemen and the Ribbonmen (Crossle 1973).

Many of the founder members of the Orange Order were Freemasons, and it has been widely acknowledged that both Orangeism and Ribbonism owed much of their symbolism, structure and organisational practices to Freemasonry (Dewar, Brown and Long 1969). We should add to this list the masonic custom of holding commemorative and funeral parades, which, in Ulster, had been established in parallel with the Volunteer practice. St John's day parades were held regularly in Belfast and throughout Counties Antrim, Armagh and Down from the 1780s onwards. In the early nineteenth century they were at least as widespread as, if not more numerous than, Orange parades, although Freemasons attracted little of the notoriety or opposition that the Orangemen incurred. Funerals were also important events for masonic lodges in the nineteenth century, with some lodges averaging more than one funeral parade every year (Simpson 1926).

In 1824, and again in 1836, as violence at parades increased, the Grand Lodge of Ireland banned all masonic parades. However, as the official historian of the order notes: 'The processions on St John's day were immensely popular with the Craft, particularly in the North of Ireland and the Grand Lodge encountered a good deal of opposition when it had to prohibit them' (Parkinson 1957:57). In fact, any attempt to ban parades was usually ignored, and although many lodges suffered repeated suspensions, the St John's day parades remained a regular feature of rural Ulster life until the 1870s (Beatty 1933; Grange 1980; Simpson 1924, 1926). While most attention has been focused on the polarisation of the sectarian divide after the defeat of the 1798 rising, the strength of

Freemasonry suggests that many in the north were still prepared to reject both camps and follow a non-sectarian path.

Riotous Assemblies

The campaign for Catholic emancipation had the effect of raising tension, fear and uncertainty in the north. But there had been a steady increase in violence at parades from 1818 onwards. This attracted the attention of the social élite and louder calls for action. The *Northern Whig* announced that Orangeism was the 'well-head from which these evils spring', and it proclaimed

> we cannot but lament how fallen is the colour, how degraded is the cause, when these 'canaille' who shout loyalty, and show their rags, annually, are permitted to prostitute both, by their drunken squabbles, and attacks on the peace of society. King William would have been the last man . . . who would have countenanced the proceedings of such a body, as the Orangemen. He fought to secure toleration not to establish persecution (*NW* 8.7.1824).

In 1824 the Grand Orange Lodge of Ireland responded to public pressure and tried to cancel all parades; but this was ignored by the membership. The following year the introduction of the Unlawful Societies Act outlawed both Daniel O'Connell's Catholic Association and the Orange Order; but it had no effect on restraining popular support for parades. The magistrates and local law-enforcement agencies were equally unsuccessful in controlling parades, even when they resorted to confiscating banners and removing arches. In 1827, the *Northern Whig* (19.7) noted that 'scarcely a town or village in the North of Ireland can boast of . . . obedience to common sense, and the laws of the land'. A year later the Twelfth demonstrations in Belfast were cancelled, in deference to the wishes of the local authorities, but parades went ahead elsewhere: in Dungannon 170 lodges turned out, among them 'several Protestant Gentlemen of Rank'; in Armagh 30,000 people took to the streets; at Lurgan, the crowds were estimated to reach 50,000–60,000, at Monaghan 6,000 and at Ballibay 11,000 (BNL 15.7.1828, 18.7.1828).

It was during this period, when parading was particularly contentious and significant as a marker of local dominance, that the Orangemen began to parade on a wider range of anniversaries. Commemorations of the battle of Newtownbutler and the raising of the siege of Derry were held each August at a number of locations, and parades were held on St Peter's eve, on 4 November and in August to honour the King's birthday (*BNL* 4.7.1823, 24.8.1824, 19.8.1828, 22.8.1828, 10.11.1829). Violent clashes followed many parades throughout this period: Orangemen attacked Ribbon parades and vice versa, and both attacked masonic processions at various times. In 1829, amidst a growing fear of more violence, the Grand Master of the Orange Order once again cancelled all parades; again this was ignored, and Orangemen paraded in over 30 locations. Rioting followed in Armagh, Bellaghy, Comber, Greyabbey, Maghera and Portadown. At Strabane three people were wounded, at Stewartstown a person died, at Clones seven were killed and at Enniskillen eight were left dead or seriously wounded. The following year the Lord Lieutenant banned all processions, and though many went ahead they were largely peaceful. An editorial in the *News Letter* supported the ban, claiming that parades 'have now in great measure lost their utility' (9.7.1830). In 1832 the Party Processions Act, prohibiting all parades, was passed, and a Select Committee of the House of Commons was set up 'to inquire into The Nature, Character, Extent and Tendency of Orange Lodges, Associations or Societies In Ireland'. Its report of 1835 shows, from police reports, that although many parades were still held, they were much smaller than a few years earlier and they were largely peaceful. As a result, when the Act expired in 1845, it was not renewed. The following year the *News Letter* exclaimed optimistically: 'In these days of education and enlightenment, Protestantism and Loyalty have discovered better modes of asserting themselves, than by wearing sashes and walking to the music of fifes and drums.'

However, the newly restored legality of parading encouraged an even wider range of organisations on to the streets, and a profusion of display. Freemasons, Ribbonmen, 'Thrashers or Repealers', the Belfast Teetotal Societies, the Independent Tent of Rechabites, Dr Spratt's Teetotalers and Father Mathew's Benevolent Society all took to the streets with their bands and elaborate flags and banners. But as usual it was the Orangemen who held the most parades and mounted the most elaborate displays. Arches were prominent in Coleraine, Comber, Seaforde and Ballymena (where 'several beautiful arches were erected'); in Dungannon the Orangemen carried 'many new flags'; in Tandragee over 150 flags were paraded; and in Belfast, Sandy Row Lodge No. 247 attracted special attention with their 'very handsome flag', composed of needlework on purple velvet, with a crown and sceptre on one side and King William crossing the Boyne on the reverse (*BNL* 14.7.1846). The violence of the previous decade was quickly forgotten as the *News Letter* waxed lyrical: 'the banners were of the most costly fabric and the most elegant design and as they floated in the morning breeze they presented a spectacle of great beauty and splendour' (13.7.1848).

The following year the paper wrote 'we cannot avoid arriving at the conclusion that the [Orange] Institution is now becoming more than ever part and parcel of the very genius of the Ulster character' (*BNL* 13.7.1849). However, this optimism was expressed too soon: in spite of the apparent festival atmosphere at many parades, violence was never far below the surface. Trouble followed Orange parades in Armagh and Newry in 1846; in March 1848 the St Patrick's day parade at Downpatrick ended in a riot when Catholics were attacked; trouble also occurred at Ballynahinch and Hilltown; while parades at Coleraine and Derry were cancelled after warnings from Orangemen (*BNL* 21.3.1848). The following year a Ribbon parade at Castlewellan was attacked, and the 1,500-strong parade at Crossgar ('there were twelve flags – pitiful, paltry rags; a large drum and two or three fifes') was also attacked by Orangemen. In the riot that followed a policeman and a young woman were killed (*NW* 20.3.1849). Then on 12 July 1849 an Orange parade returning from Rathfriland was attacked by a party of Ribbonmen at Dolly's Brae, near Castlewellan. The Orangemen retaliated, and 8 men were killed.

In 1850 the Party Processions Act was renewed. Some parades continued to be held, but these were small affairs and they received little publicity. A crowd of 10,000 that celebrated the Twelfth outside Lisburn in 1858 were dismissed as 'chiefly farmers son's and girls' (*BNL* 13.7.1858). Arches and decorations were still erected, but not on the scale of the late 1840s, and lodges returned to meeting in their rooms to celebrate the day with food and drink. St Patrick's day received a similar response, and parades were abandoned in favour of 'drowning the shamrock'. Some masonic lodges in Antrim and Down persisted in parading on St John's day, and several had their warrants regularly suspended through the 1850s as a result (Simpson 1924, 1926; Leighton 1938). In general the Party Processions Act was successful in controlling the parades and the consequent violence; when they eventually resumed as a legal practice it was within a different political environment.

Custom and Politics

From the isolated Twelfth of July parades organised by the nascent Orange Order in the late 1790s, an extensive range of annual commemorations were established across Ulster which were used to define and to mark ideologically distinct and opposing identities. Parading rapidly became sedimented as the popular expression of cultural identity and difference. In a period of relative prosperity, but of political uncertainty, parades were a means of marking territory, of showing local party strength and solidarity with neighbours, and a way of displaying cultural identity and allegiances. At a time of simmering tensions – the rebellions of 1798 and 1803, the union with Britain in 1801, the recurrent moves for Catholic emancipation – parades were one of a number of occasions when local antagonisms could be vented. Parading practices followed a recurrent cyclical pattern. Peaceful displays increased in scale until they provoked an aggressive response from the 'other party'. There then followed a period of escalating violence before the authorities banned or attempted to ban all parades; but these bans were only obeyed where absolutely necessary. When the ban was allowed to lapse, the cycle began again.

These cycles of rising violence coincide loosely with the larger themes of early-nineteenth-century political life in Ireland, and they soon developed a momentum of their own: the major escalation of violence began well before O'Connell launched the campaign for Catholic emancipation in 1823. After this there was a reduction in random violence and a greater emphasis on formal parades. During this period of agitation there was an expansion of Orange parades and displays across the north, as Orangemen reacted to O'Connell's campaign by marching more often, in more places and with more people. A parade could only ever be a temporary and localised display of strength, and with a background of political uncertainty one response was to take to the roads to mark more anniversaries. The parades were local expressions of power and dominance, assertions which needed constant reaffirmation, and the threat of violence remained as a constant undercurrent, even if it was not always realised (Wright 1987).

But this growing culture of parading also served both to build more connections between people and places of similar faith, and at the same time to intensify the social distance from those of the other faith. Commemorative parades thereby helped to consolidate the sense of difference and distinctiveness between Protestants and Catholics. For a time the Freemasons appeared to bridge the divide; but ultimately the march to polarisation was too strong. The state was largely unable to contain the parades, although the 1832 legislation and the subsequent reform of the police service were successful in constraining outbreaks of violence. Commemorative displays of identity were still insistently marked, and, when parades were legalised after seventeen years, the established anniversaries were celebrated more energetically than ever. This in turn almost immediately provoked a descent into more intense riotous behaviour.

During this period, Ulster was of marginal importance on the wider political stage; it was relegated to the wings as the major tactical plays were made between Dublin and London. The changing nature of the displays and parades can therefore only partly be explained in conjunction with major political and economic events of the time: the participants responded to these changes, but were not determined or bound by them. Orangemen, Ribbonmen and Freemasons fought out their battles on the smaller arena of local disputes, and of rights to walk and dominate a local public arena. The popular commemorations remained largely outside the influence of the respectable members of society. Local authority and the law were largely unable either to control or to direct the energies of the lower classes to their agendas. The events documented above appear largely unpoliticised in relation to outside events and to matters of state; but parades, and the attendant displays, gradually became one of the major expressions of lower-class socio-political aspirations as sectarianism emerged as a major factor in Ulster life.

In the 1780s and 1790s this had been mapped out by sporadic violence and nocturnal raiding, and was acted out on the margins of society. By the 1840s the sectarian division had become openly celebrated, structured and clarified by the ritual ceremony of commemorative parades. In the 1780s King William and Hibernia, the crowned harp and the shamrock could still be displayed as diverse facets of a single movement, and St Patrick could be considered as a possible national unifying symbol. Fifty years later this was no longer possible: these symbols now signified opposing political desires. But the sectarian division of Ulster society was by no means a foregone conclusion: the evidence of the Freemasons suggests alternative possibilities, that a third path was still open even after the violence of 1798. When the parades were once more legalised in 1872 it was in large part as a result of populist politicians' recognising the potential of Orange lodges and Ribbon societies as popular mass movements in support of the national debates. The third path had disappeared.

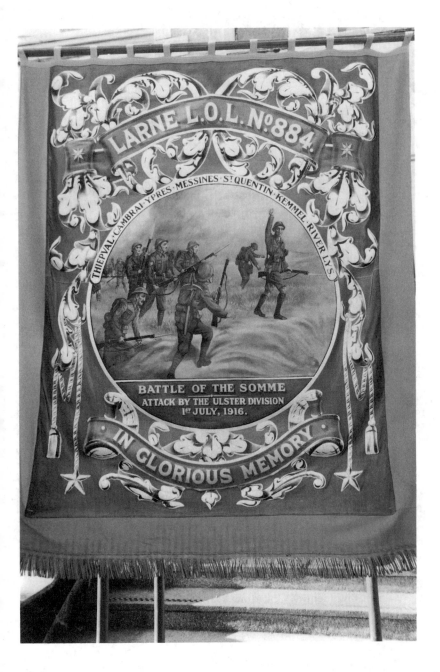

Creating Identity V: Battle of the Somme; Larne, May 1995.

Creating Identity VI: Padraic Pearse; Ballyholland, August 1995.

Chapter 4

Parading Identity, 1870–1968

Opposition to the Party Processions Act was mobilised by the radical populist Orangeman William Johnston, who was elected MP for Belfast in 1868, with a commitment to secure the repeal of the act. This was achieved in 1872 (McClelland 1990). Thereafter parading resumed as a popular activity, but now with increasing support of the respectable middle classes. Parades were held against a background of polarised political demands. The campaign for Home Rule and for land reforms grew through the 1870s and 1880s, and the Catholic population mobilised behind these demands. Land reforms were realised by Acts of Parliament between 1870 and 1909; but the demand for Home Rule was less widely acceptable. The rapid growth of the linen and shipbuilding industries in the Belfast area during the nineteenth century meant that the north-east of Ireland had become closely interlinked with the British economy. The Protestant population viewed moves towards Home Rule as a threat to both their religion and their economic standing. From the 1880s Ulster Unionists represented the only concentrated opposition to Home Rule, and the 33 Parliamentary seats in Ulster were divided equally between the two positions. Unionists were mistrustful of British intentions and felt threatened by the rise of Irish Nationalism. Home Rule bills were defeated in Parliament in 1886 and 1893, but the continuing land reforms, the rise of cultural nationalism in the form of the Gaelic Athletic Association, the Gaelic League and the literary Celtic revival movement, plus anti-British support for South Africa during the Boer War, all contributed to their increased insecurity, and intensified the search to define and refine their own position. Home Rule legislation was finally passed in 1913, only to be stifled by the onset of war.

After the legalisation of parades in 1872 both the Twelfth and St Patrick's day became closely drawn into the wider political process. The extension to the franchise under the 1884 Reform Act meant that the working classes had a greater impact on the formal political process, and politicians, both unionist and nationalist, began to use public commemorations as an opportunity for direct access to a wide constituency of potential support and to link the celebrations of the past to the contemporary political process. Although Orangemen had occasionally used the Twelfth assemblies to deliver political eulogies alongside the usual sermons, the practice of using the Field as a platform for political rallies, with speeches delivered by politicians rather than by churchmen, largely dates from this period. At the same time as the Orange Order was becoming more respectable, the Ancient Order of Hibernians emerged as the representatives of rural, conservative Catholic Ulster, and St Patrick's day and Our Lady's day (15 August) were adopted as nationalist parading days. Civilising the parades was never completely successful, they were still popular events among the rougher elements but by the 1890s faction fighting, sectarian rioting and general disturbances were no longer such a recurrent or widespread feature of the summer parades. When violence did occur it was more closely linked to a general rise in political tension or at election times, rather than a response to commemorative displays per se, and it no longer had the cyclical momentum of earlier years (Boyd 1987; Foy 1976; Wright 1996).

'Erin go Bragh'

From the 1870s nationalist parades were prominently linked to the wider political agenda. Parades were regularly held in towns with a substantial Catholic population, such as Derry, Downpatrick and Lurgan, and more irregularly in Belfast and many smaller centres. These parades were supported by a wide range of politicians and groups, such as the Hibernians, the Irish National Foresters and the United Irish League. This more assertive Catholic presence was barely tolerated by unionists, especially with the growth of more overt political displays. Violence had never been slow to erupt when the northern Catholics sought to celebrate their traditions, and on many occasions the threat of Orange violence was enough to stop planned parades. Parades and meetings to mark Our Lady's day at Cookstown and Gilford were cancelled in August 1872 after Orange counter-demonstrations were announced, and violence occasionally broke out on St Patrick's day in Belfast through the late 1870s, in Derry through the 1880s, and at many parades in Lurgan (Boyd 1987; Doak 1978). Home Rule parades in particular were widely confronted, in 1883 the Grand Orange Lodge mobilised against the threat of 'Nationalist Invaders' when it was announced that Charles Stewart Parnell was to address a meeting in Tyrone, and he had to be replaced by less controversial speakers (Boyce 1990). Later in the century attempts to commemorate the centenary of the 1798 Rising in Belfast were also met with violent attacks (O'Keefe 1992). However, the repetitious violence of earlier years was not allowed to become re-established as a feature of the marching season. Disturbances at parades were, wherever possible, treated as minor scuffles and resolved at a local level, although this statement should be qualified by the admission that violence and rioting became more regular features of the Belfast marching season.

As Catholic anniversaries became more openly political, so too did the visual displays. In August 1872 the banners carried to Hannahstown, outside Belfast, were restricted to tried and trusted mottoes: 'Remember Limerick', 'God Save Ireland', 'Erin go Bragh' ('Ireland for ever') alongside the crownless Irish harp, while in Derry they portrayed St Patrick, Pope Pius IX and Daniel O'Connell (*BNL* 16.8.1872). But two years later, at Downpatrick, banners appeared bearing the motto 'Home Rule' and portraits of William Orr and Robert Emmett, political heroes from the United Irishmen era, and at Lurgan the banners, which 'showed considerable taste and skill', portrayed Emmett, Wolfe Tone and the Manchester Martyrs, three members of the Fenian Movement whose public execution following the killing of a policemen in Manchester in November 1867 generated angry protests across Ireland (*BNL* 18.3, 17.8.1874; Newsinger 1994). In Monaghan in 1884, banners depicted leading political figures Michael Davitt, founder of the Land League, T. J. Heally and C. S. Parnell, along with the slogans 'Land for the People' and 'Ireland for the Irish' (*BNL* 16.8.1884).

However, alongside these current heroes were numerous references to earlier historical and religious figures: Patrick Sarsfield, leader of James II's armies in 1691; Rory O'More and Hugh O'Neill, two of the last great Gaelic chiefs; St Patrick, St Columbcille, and the Pope. There was also a wide range of symbols and slogans: the crownless harp; the wolfhound; the roundtower and 'Erin go Bragh', 'Faith of our Fathers' and 'God Save Ireland'. While openly politicised, the banners were used to link the contemporary campaigns with Irish history. Although Home Rule was a peaceful movement, the banners acknowledged the violent traditions of previous bids for political independence, with the unspoken suggestion that the violence of the risings of 1798, 1803 and 1867 might be needed once more. They also linked the future aims for the Irish nation with both a Gaelic and Catholic past. The implications were that the heroes and martyrs of the past had gone to their deaths fighting for a distinctly Catholic Ireland, and that this ideal was still worth dying for.

Some arches had been erected at the time of O'Connell's mass rallies in the 1840s, but they had never been a prominent feature of nationalist celebrations. But in the resurgent political atmosphere of the 1870s and 1880s 'green arches' were regularly erected in many towns as a further means of displaying political heroes. In Belfast in 1875: 'In Pinkerton's Row a green arch was erected with a green flag in the centre, bearing likenesses of the Pope and Dan O'Connell' (*BNL* 17.8.1875). In March 1878 arches were erected in Derry bearing portraits of Emmett, Fitzgerald and the Manchester Martyrs, topped with the green Irish flag and the French tricolour (Doak 1978:159), while at Monaghan in 1884 'three or four green arches with crownless harps and portraits of Robert Emmett and Daniel O'Connell . . . were erected' (*BNL* 16.8.1884). Descriptions such as these are rare, but make one wonder how elaborate and widespread nationalist displays may have been. The attitudes of the press meant they rarely showed any interest unless the displays caused controversy; but, given the opposition they seem to have attracted, nationalist arches may never have been established as an accepted feature of their commemorations. The arches in Derry, described above, were soon pulled down by the police, and the following year a crowd of angry Protestants gathered in Downpatrick to prevent a green arch from being erected in the position traditionally occupied by an Orange arch each July (*BNL* 19.3.1878, 16.8.1879). The most controversial nationalist arch was erected in Winetavern Street, Belfast in August 1900, and carried the mottoes 'Remember Spion Kop' and 'Bravo De Wet' alongside portraits of the Boer general and the slogan 'Let England not forget there's a day of Reckoning yet'. Nationalists took the Boer side in the war, seeing parallels between their fight for autonomy from the British Empire and the Irish campaign. The *News Letter* described this display as 'exceptionally objectionable', and police were called in when a group of Protestant youths tried to destroy the structure (*BNL* 16.7.1900; *NW* 19.8.1900).

Although Catholics in Ulster took to the streets more readily than they had before 1870, and paraded more widely than elsewhere in Ireland, this was still only possible in those areas where they were numerically strong. If the forces of law and order were more ready to allow nationalist parades and decorations on the streets, unionists consistently opposed them, even if now this was more often rhetorically rather than physically. St Patrick's day parades were often relocated or cancelled in the face of an Orange threat. The unionist attitude to nationalist commemorations was to yield 'Not an Inch'. The constitutional nationalists who dominated the public sphere at this time were often willing to accede to unionist threats rather than to antagonise them further, expecting that in the end the Ulster Unionists would accept their place in an independent Ireland. However after the centenary commemorations of 1798 were attacked and memorials destroyed across the province (O'Keefe 1992), is it any wonder that the activities of the Boers were taken up as an inspiration alongside the Irish rebels of past generations?

Orange Renaissance

The Orange Order returned to the streets *en masse* even before the Party Processions Act was repealed: in 1870 an estimated 100,000 people paraded from Belfast to Derriaghy carrying over 140 flags and passing under numerous arches, and in 1874 the Twelfth was celebrated at over 80 locations across the north of Ireland (*BNL* 13.7.1870, 16.7–17.7.1874). Street decorations were once more prominent, and ever more elaborate: in Coleraine, at least 15 arches were erected, incorporating representations of William III, the Relief of Derry, the Boyne Obelisk and 'other emblems of the Revolution', while in Lurgan the public weighbridge was decorated with flags and flowers, surmounted by an emblem of a Bible, although the Crown was 'conspicuously absent', a protest at the disestablishment of the Church of Ireland in 1869 (*BNL* 13.7.1870,

15.7.1871). By 1882 the *News Letter* felt able to report that the time of 'stringing flowers on a cord and calling this, when stretched out like a clothes line, "an arch" has gone. Beautiful pictures and appropriate symbols and mottoes met the eye [a]ll through the town' (*BNL* 13.7.1882).

Through the 1880s and 1890s the scale and extent of arch building steadily increased, particularly in Belfast. Many spanned the main thoroughfares, and, as more and more streets erected their own displays, competition developed between neighbouring streets, which encouraged still greater elaboration. In York Street, Belfast in 1884 the arch was

> formed of iron rods, over which is carefully stretched wire netting and its form is an embattled bridge with six arches between, separated by five Martello towers each being surmounted by a handsome flag. The design . . . is surmounted by the Bible and Crown . . . [and] a large well executed oil painting of King William . . . each of the towers bears a heraldic shield on each side . . . [it] is surmounted by a line of bannerets, the Royal Standard and the Irish ensign being most prominent . . . [it] has never been paralleled in Belfast (*BNL* 12.7.1884).

Alongside these Williamite representations other heroes were beginning to be portrayed on the streets: in 1877 an arch on the Shankill Road carried a painting of Henry Cooke, a firebrand preacher from the earlier years of the century. Cooke also appeared on an arch in Antrim in 1879, along with Thomas Drew, a similar figure from the recent past (*BNL* 12.7.1877, 14.7.1879). Political figures began to form a larger part of the display: in 1894 Queen Victoria, the Prime Minister Lord Salisbury, A. J. Balfour, Joseph Chamberlain and Lord Randolph Churchill, who had coined the phrase 'Ulster will fight, and Ulster will be right' during a visit in 1886, all joined King William on arches in Ballymena and Belfast (*BNL* 13.7.1894). The main developments were in the sheer scale and profusion of the street decorations. Erecting the arch was an important communal activity in Belfast; from the 1890s they became larger and more elaborate and also more numerous, as streets strove to outdo each other in scale and technical sophistication. In 1900, after tramline installations had prevented any arch from being erected for a number of years, seven arches were built on the Shankill Road and another twenty-three in side streets running off it. Arch designers came up with technical improvements as well: many arches were still suspended affairs, though made more complex by creating double or triple arches to incorporate a wider range of images and slogans; but the suspended string arches were increasingly replaced by solid pole or frame structures, and by 1898 at least one arch, at Bridge End, was being illuminated by electricity.

The resumption of parades and the continued expansion of arch displays gives the impression that little had changed in the popular commemorations. But the Twelfth was now an occasion for a much wider expression of Protestant unity. Celebrating King Billy's victories became a respectable part of the broader political calendar. Orange parades and displays were no longer an embarrassment to the Ulster Protestant middle classes: they were now seen as a key to maintaining their power base. At a time when Unionism was emerging as a distinct political response to nationalism, it needed to define itself clearly, to create and refine its myths and symbols, and state what made 'Ulster' distinct from 'Ireland'.

Ernest Gellner has argued that newly emerging nation states had two options, they 'could either grow around pre-existing states and/or High cultures, or they could as it were roll their own culture out of existing folk traditions . . . In the latter case, a consciousness and memory had to be created, and ethnographic exploration (in effect: codification and invention) were mandatory' (Gellner 1994:192). Irish nationalists and Ulster unionists were both in the process of redefining themselves and their traditions in relation to the British state. Nationalists drew on Catholic and Gaelic folk traditions that were welded to the history of political rebellion and resistance to define a new Irish nationalism, distinct and separate from an inclusive British identity. But for Unionists it was more complicated: they had to convince the British government that they were an inalienable and legitimate part of the British state, and not just Irish. Unionists had to define themselves as British and also to redefine Ulster as within the British, rather than Irish, sphere of culture. They had to blend High Culture and folk tradition rather than choose an either–or solution. Once the folk culture of parading was civilised and tamed, it was then refocused as a vehicle to define and display the nature of Unionism. The energy that had been consumed in the violent creation of sectarian difference was redirected to the expression of an Ulster Protestant identity.

Many of the symbols and historical personalities represented at the July celebrations provided continuity with the earlier part of the century, but a much wider range of individuals were now displayed. Initially this change was confined to arches, but the new images soon began to appear on banners as well. King Billy on his white horse, the monarch and the 'Crown and Bible' were the only designs recorded on Orange banners prior to the 1870s; but almost as soon as parades were legalised a number of banners depicting 'Brother Johnston of Ballykilbeg' appeared (*BNL* 14.7.1876). In 1888, the banners in Belfast 'bore the portraits of the friends of Protestantism and the leaders of the Conservative Party', including Henry Cooke, Thomas Drew, William Johnston and Lords Salisbury and Churchill. Local contemporary figures such as Edward Saunderson, MP for North Armagh (one of the first people to suggest publicly that it might be necessary to resort to physical force to resist Home Rule) were also portrayed (*BNL* 13.7.1888). Over the next twenty years, through the heat of the Home Rule debate, banner-making became increasingly professionalised and industrialised (Gorman 1986). With this commercial development came a standardisation of size, shape and design and, most importantly, an expansion of the subject-matter and range of images. At the turn of the century the local press also began to take an interest in these new, professionally produced, banners that were appearing at parades:

> Several of the banners bore excellent portraits of King Edward VII ... six banners had portraits of the late Queen ... while 4 or 5 [portrayed] ... the late Dr Cooke ... those which did not depict scenes of 1690 or bear an emblem of the Bible and Crown, were devoted to portraiture [including] ... the Late Lord Farnham, Sir James Haslett MP, Sir James Henderson DL [and] ... Col Wallace (who is at present out in South Africa with his regiment) [this list continues with the names and titles of a number of lesser personalities who were depicted on the banners] (*BNL* 13.7.1901).

The local press recorded 77 new banners as they were ceremoniously unfurled and 49 on their first appearance at the Belfast parades between 1904 and 1914, most of which were designed by the prominent Belfast banner-maker, William Bridgett. These give a useful cross-section of the new images that were appearing at this critical time for Unionists and help to illustrate some of the changes that were taking place.

Subject	Unfurling	Parade
King William	55	39
Williamite Events	22	14
Politicians	13	9
Local Dignitaries	20	7
Biblical Stories	9	4
Monarchs	8	2
Protestant History	6	5
Crown + Bible, etc.	9	8
Local Places	2	11

Although King William still dominated the corpus, and images of the Crown and Bible and the monarch were still in demand, a greater range of historical events were beginning to be depicted, and large numbers of banners portrayed local places, politicians and personalities. The banners were no longer restricted to abstract historical, religious and imperial ideals, but increasingly focused on a localised identity. King William was not only portrayed in his role as the Protestant victor over the Catholic King James, but in terms of the fact that the campaign took place in Ireland and that William himself journeyed through the north of Ireland. His status was enhanced by his physical presence in Ulster, not just for the battles he fought. The prominence given to the Siege of Derry and the Battle of Newtownbutler among the Williamite events are further examples of this localisation, as examples of local resistance. The Williamite campaigns could be, and were, used to inspire resolve and steel in the opposition to Home Rule. The developments in banner paintings ran parallel to the debates among Unionists over the legality and morality of raising the paramilitary Ulster Volunteer Force and organising military opposition to Home Rule.

The biblical and religious imagery can also be understood within this framework of localism. Religious symbols and Old Testament stories, a central element of the iconography of the Freemasons, had been used by the Orange Order since its form-ation. Hitherto these had been publicly restricted to a few, abstract, coded expressions of the faith; but now they were made more elaborate and explicit. Historical figures such as Luther and Wycliff, Protestant martyrs like Latimer and Ridley, and biblical characters such as Moses, Samuel, David and Goliath, Naomi and

Ruth were represented for their metaphorical value, and as exemplars of the Unionist plight. Clear analogies could be drawn between the Ulster Protestants and the Israelites; biblical and religious history could be used as a guide to practical action (Buckley 1985–6). The religious values were no longer simply expressed through Imperial ideals and the 'Crown and Bible': these ideals were now embodied in the memory of radical Presbyterian preachers and grounded in the very bricks and mortar of neighbouring churches. The Imperial connection remained important, but local religious leaders and politicians were fêted with equal reverence.

In the extended period of heightened political debate over the long-term constitutional status of Ireland, the banners of the Orange Order were an important part of the political discourse of Unionism. Depicting a wide range of contemporary local heroes, they drew clear connections between the historical past and current concerns, and stressed the importance of action as well as words. In all these instances the changes emphasise the emerging identity grounded in a sense of place: a community defined by its history of independence, a tradition located in Ulster and intending to stay in Ulster, come what may. As a part of this unprecedented expansion of visual displays, wall murals appeared for the first time in the years immediately preceding the First World War:

> The usual arch at Albertbridge Road, on Malcolm Street has been replaced by a large painting of King William on the side of a house at the corner of Malcolm Street. The painting has been draped with purple, garlanded with evergreen and surmounted by loyal and patriotic mottoes, Union Jacks, portraits of the King and Queen and Orange leaders, and, above all, the inscription "God Save the King". A somewhat similar idea has been effectively carried out on the gable of a house on Beersbridge Road near Clara Street. (*Belfast Telegraph (BT)* 12.7.1911).

Murals were soon an established feature of the Twelfth decorations in 'several districts' of the city. Most paintings depicted King Billy, but Sir Edward Carson was portrayed on at least one wall (*NW* 13.7.1914). These paintings were a direct development from the arch-building tradition, an ancestry that was embodied in the content of the painting itself. The variety of images and slogans within a single form was typical of the increasing complexity of arches in the pre-war period, while the inclusion of an evergreen garland is a direct reference to the traditional and still widespread practice of basing arch designs on floral devices. In the attempts to increase the complexity of the displays the one area left still to explore was the temporal. Arches were still erected in the days immediately preceding the Twelfth, and were removed soon after; but by painting on the walls, displays of loyalty could remain in place the year round. The atmosphere of friendly rivalry within the loyalist community and the broader political debate encouraged this elaboration of images. The painting of a mural would not necessarily prevent an arch from being erected, but it would be a permanent reminder to neighbours and others that this street was not just occupied by fair-weather loyalists. In the years when opposition to Home Rule was being most intensely demonstrated, by mass mobilisations, the signing of the Ulster covenant, the formation of the Ulster Volunteer Force and the illegal smuggling of arms, the ideals of the Ulster British identity were being elaborated and visualised on the streets and walls of Belfast and elsewhere. Parades, arches, banners and murals were all key elements in the expression and consolidation of Ulster Unionism: they were as significant as the political speeches and writings of the leadership. The commemorative parades and displays were the locale at which the political leadership of the Unionist Party and the popular mass of the Orangemen annually reaffirmed their allegiance to each other, to Ulster and to Britain.

From the Somme to Stormont

The threat of armed resistance to the British state was lifted with the start of the war and the mass mobilisation of both Protestant and Catholic Irishmen into the British Army. For unionists the formation of the 36th (Ulster) Division from the ranks of the UVF exemplified their faith in their British identity. Unionist resistance to Home Rule was further bolstered by the contrasting actions and experiences of republicans and unionists in 1916. The Easter Rising in Dublin was regarded by unionists as a stab in the back to Britain, an action that stood in stark contrast to the tragic, but heroic, slaughter of the Ulster Division at the Somme in July 1916, this willing sacrifice being the strongest possible indication of Protestant loyalty and their irredeemable Britishness. Opposition to Home Rule was no longer couched solely in references to

seventeenth-century battles or in abstract politico-religious ideals;
it was securely anchored in the events of the recent past. If Derry
and the Boyne had proved the willingness of the Ulstermen to
fight for their faith, then the Somme was a symbol of their
willingness to fight (and die) for King and Country. After 1918,
the World War, condensed into the single event of 'the Somme',
was introduced into Orange mytho-history as a contemporary
equivalent to 1690. The ultimate sacrifice made by so many
Ulstermen provided further justification for their resistance to
Home Rule and enhanced their determination to remain part of
the United Kingdom. The connection between the two battles was
paraded for the first time on the morning of 12 July 1919, when
Hydepark LOL 1067 unveiled their new banner portraying King
William on one side and the 'Battle of the Somme' on the other.
The elevation of the Somme into the iconography of the Orange
Order confirmed its near-sacred status in popular memory.

The first murals painted after the war were a similar mixture
of the established designs and references to the war: at Hornby
Street a painting depicted the *'Mountjoy* breaking the Boom'
overlooked by an imperial Britannia; at Victoria Street the painting
of King Billy was surmounted by an Ulster Red Hand symbol;
and at Carnan Street the depiction took the form of a memorial to
those killed in the war: the Red Hand and Union Jack flags flew
over a mourning figure, and underneath the memorial was the
motto 'For King and Country' (*BT* 11.7, 12.7.1919).

The unionist stance was vindicated by partition. The Orange
Order was so deeply embedded in the fabric and ideology of the
new 'Protestant state for a Protestant people' that in fifty years
of Stormont government, all but three Cabinet Ministers were
Orangemen, while the first Prime Minister James Craig
(in)famously declared 'I am an Orangeman first and a politician
. . . afterwards' (Buckland 1980:20). Orange commemorations
flourished under the Stormont administration, and the now
legitimised Ulster British identity was publicly celebrated each
year, as the Twelfth became the ritual of state in all but name. In
contrast, nationalist commemorations and displays were banned
or restricted to the margins of society. The Orange parades grew
to enormous size: 100,000 Orangemen were reported to have
walked in Belfast in 1926, with a further 50,000 people looking on
(*NW* 13.7.1926). Street decorations flourished, and numerous King
Billy murals and memorials to the war were painted on the streets

of Belfast: Sir Henry Wilson, the Unionist Chief of the Imperial General Staff, Edward Carson and Sir James Craig all appeared on murals in the 1920s and 1930s. They were also widely depicted on the Orange banners among portraits of those earlier heroes who had opposed Home Rule or promoted the Orange Order: Disraeli, Chamberlain, Colonel Verner, Edward Saunderson, William Johnston and others. But arches were the dominant visual display. Designs became ever more elaborate, and in 1939, as war approached, the tradition reached a climax in a riot of extravagant displays: in Berlin Street, Abraham prepared to sacrifice his son in the centre of a floral suspension arch; in Malvern Way the *Mountjoy* formed the centrepiece; in Brown Street the fabric suspension arch, six sections deep, contained portraits of the King and Queen; in Scott Street a mock brick structure was erected; and in Cable Street a triple arch in a modern, industrial style depicted King Billy on the top (*BNL* 12.7.1939).

In many ways the inter-war period represented the climax of Orange commemorative displays. Alongside the visual exuberance, the loyal orders extended their public presence by expanding their parading calendar. The years following partition saw the formalisation and consolidation of Royal Black Institution parades on the last Saturday in August; of junior Orange parades at Easter from the 1930s; and of a range of Apprentice Boys parades across the province. Year in, year out the loyal orders marched unimpeded across the north, confirming Northern Ireland as a place apart.

But the Second World War seems to have defined a break scarcely less significant than did the earlier Great War. While Unionist political dominance continued in Northern Ireland, fractures began to appear in the old certainties. In the early 1950s a number of challenges were mounted to the rights of Orangemen to parade where they would (although these were swiftly dealt with at the time, on two occasions this necessitated Cabinet changes); and the 150th anniversary of Emmett's rising was marked by nationalist parades and celebrations. These perhaps mark the reappearance of a more positive cultural and political assertion of identity among nationalists; while at the same time it has been suggested that by the 1950s enthusiasm for the old traditions was flagging among the loyalist working classes.

Although arches continued to be erected after the Second World War, the decorations never matched the profusion of styles and inventiveness of the inter-war years, and the custom steadily declined. By 1964 only one arch was reported in east Belfast (*BNL* 10.7.1964). Nor were any substantial additions made to the Orange pantheon on the banners after the flurry of new designs following the First World War and partition: the catalogue produced by Bridgett Brothers in 1930 included practically all the historical, religious and imperial images that are currently paraded, and many contemporary banner designs are clearly close copies of Bridgett's original work. By the 1950s mural painting was almost non-existent: in 1960 there was only one painting in good condition in Belfast, a King Billy mural in Silvergrove Street that had been first painted in 1938 and was redone that year (*BNL* 9.7.1960). Other paintings in east Belfast, on the Ormeau Road and in the Shankill, were 'so faded that only the poorest outline was visible'.

Post-war austerity has been cited as one reason for the decline in decorations. Arches had become a major communal investment that would be expected to last for a number of years: the new arch erected on Sandy Row in 1964 had a span of 40 feet and cost £1,000 (Orange Order 1970). Raising the money for these structures required planning and organisation; but post-war urban renewal and slum clearance programmes had begun to break up long-established, tight-knit communities that had kept up these traditions. As people were encouraged to move out of the inner-city areas to satellite estates and towns, there were fewer individuals willing and able to erect the displays. Bill Rolston suggests that popular support for loyalism was steadily eroded with the decline in the traditional industries, while the growth of the welfare state undermined inter-class Unionist unity and systems of patronage and self-confidence. As the loyalist consensus, built up during the Home Rule resistance, began to fragment, the 'beginnings of unionist uncertainty were reflected in the decline of traditional cultural expression' (Rolston 1991:27). From the mid-sixties these changes were represented by the appearance of a more liberal Unionism, apparently willing to make reforms and shed some of the siege mentality of the past.

However, though there does seem to be evidence for decline in some areas, Orange culture had been a dynamic process for over 150 years; during that time it had redefined itself on a number of occasions, adopting and developing a number of visual forms to represent its current ideological position; and its demise had been welcomed numerous times before. Cultural expression had flowered most strongly in periods and places of most tension and uncertainty, in County Armagh in the early nineteenth century and Belfast after 1900. It had also lain dormant and declined in intensity before, notably in the mid-nineteenth century, only to revive at the next crisis. Mural painting, which clearly did decline after the 1940s, was after all the most recent and most geographically restricted of the cultural traditions in the North. It is less clear when one considers the experience outside the city whether unionist traditions did suffer real decline.

While some facets of loyalist commemorative exuberance clearly had stagnated after the 1930s, it would be mistaken to assume a more widespread *anomie* from the evidence of Belfast alone. In Londonderry the summer celebrations commemorating the Relief of the Siege appear to have grown steadily in popularity in the post-war period (there is a question over the veracity of the numbers quoted in the papers, but even with this caveat the general principle of growth stands). The first anniversary after the war attracted some 12,000 people; but by 1960 an estimated 40,000 people watched the 5,000 Apprentice Boys who paraded the city, and the following year the parade was described as one of the biggest this century (*BT* 11.8.1945; *BNL* 15.8.1960, 14.8.1961). It was also important for politicians to be seen on the big parades: Lord Brookeborough, the Northern Irish Prime Minister, was among 500 individuals who joined the Apprentice Boys in 1960; the liberal unionist Prime Minister Terence O'Neill joined the parade in 1965; and in 1968 his future replacement James Chichester-Clark and the Official Unionist Party leader-to-be, Harry West, were among a number of MPs who attended. By this time the parade had become so big that the route had to be extended by half a mile to stop those at the head and the tail of the march from meeting on the circular route (*BNL* 12.8.1968). This all suggests that it is simplistic to argue for a wholesale decline in unionist cultural traditions after the Second World War. The Relief celebration was thriving, even expanding, and clearly remained an important occasion for Unionist politicians to affirm their allegiance to the spirit of the Apprentice Boys and the Union. The large numbers of men and boys who joined the organisation each year show that this was still an important feature of Orange popular culture and of unionist identity.

Walking into Trouble

Londonderry has long been the most potent symbolic place in
Ulster for unionists, and the story of the siege remains the most
powerful metaphor of Protestant sensibilities in Ireland (Buckley
and Kenney 1995). The narrative is used to illustrate the need for
decisive action, for unity in adversity; and it can be used as a
justification for resistance to the law. It is also used as a warning
of the danger of compromise and to justify the fear of the traitor
within. Parading the walls of Derry is not just about maintaining
tradition and celebrating loyalist culture, it is also about reaffirm-
ing the principles on which Protestant power was structured in
Ulster: never trust the enemy within, exclude them from power
and authority. But Derry is also a city in which Catholics have
long been the majority of the population. Under Stormont
gerrymandering of the local government wards ensured that
Unionists retained control of the city council. The city therefore
had a special significance for the nationalists too: it was a symbol
of their second-class status in Northern Ireland.

The liberal unionism that came to the fore in the 1960s suggested
that there was a possibility of reforming the northern state, and
demands began to be made for equal civil rights for the Catholic
population. The Northern Ireland Civil Rights Association
(NICRA) was initially a broad movement that used non-violent
resistance, direct action and protest marches to draw attention to,
and show support for, its demands (Purdie 1990). While the use
of protest marches was drawn from the example of the American
civil rights movement, it confronted head-on the loyalist belief that
parading was largely the prerogative of unionists. In August 1968
NICRA supporters marched from Coalisland to Dungannon to
draw attention to discriminatory housing policy in County
Tyrone; but the parade was prevented from entering the town
centre by a crowd of loyalists, who categorised it as a nationalist
demonstration 'intent on invading Protestant territory' (Bardon
1992:653).

When another march was planned for Derry on 5 October, the
Apprentice Boys promptly announced that they would be holding
an 'annual parade' over the same route and at the same time. This
was a tactic that had been widely used by loyalists in the past as a
means of preventing nationalist parades, and the government duly
banned both parades. Nevertheless about 400 people, including a

number of Stormont and Westminster MPs, turned up for the parade. Violent clashes broke out as the police used batons to disperse the marchers, and rioting flared sporadically in the city through the next day: 77 civilians and 4 policemen were injured. In spite of widespread criticism of the handling of the events, the Northern Irish government defended the police action and accused NICRA of being a republican and communist front (McCann 1980; Purdie 1990).

Although the parade failed in its objective, support for the civil rights movement grew, and a number of concessions were won, including the replacement of the elected city Corporation by an appointed commission. In November another march was prevented from going through Armagh when Ian Paisley and a group of loyalists, armed with clubs and other weapons, occupied the city centre; and in January a march from Belfast to Derry by the People's Democracy group was ambushed at Burntollet Bridge, where the marchers were attacked by loyalists. The police failed to protect the marchers, and a number of the assailants were later identified as members of the B Special Reserve. After marchers had finally reached Derry a group of RUC reserve officers ran riot through the Catholic Bogside area. Next morning, barricades were erected for the first time, and a gable wall proclaimed 'You Are Now Entering Free Derry' (McCann 1980:53).

The barricades were soon removed, but a week later another civil rights march in Newry erupted into rioting. The Prime Minister, Terence O'Neill, offered a package of reforms to the Catholics; but these only served to antagonise fellow unionists, and in April 1969 he resigned. There was widespread violence on and after the Twelfth parades in July; but the climax to a year of increasing tension and polarisation over the right to march was in Derry on 12 August. Widespread calls to have the Apprentice Boys parade banned were ignored, and violent exchanges between nationalists and loyalists soon began. As the police tried to move into the Bogside they were met with petrol bombs and bricks; CS gas was used, but the battle continued.

At 4.15 p.m. on 14 August, after two days of continuous fighting, the British army was called on to the streets and the RUC were removed. Hundreds of people had been injured in Derry; but in Belfast people were being killed in the clashes. On 15 August, troops arrived on the Belfast streets (Bardon 1992). There was a honeymoon period of some months, during which time the British army were welcomed and accepted in Catholic areas. However, the violence rumbled on, and when the marching season began at Easter 1970, Orange parades in Belfast provoked sustained rioting in both Protestant and Catholic areas, and, with the IRA now active, gun battles and bombings were widespread. In spite of the increasing chaos, when a three-day blanket ban on parades was announced in early July, John Bryan, the Grand Master of the Orange Institution, declared it to be 'unthinkable' to ban Orange parades and that it would bring Ulster 'to the edge of a revolution' (*BT* 4.7.1970). The Twelfth parades were finally allowed to go ahead after Prime Minister Chichester-Clark had declared on a BBC Panorama programme that they were not provocative (*BT* 7.7.1970). Although these passed peacefully, no chances were taken with the Apprentice Boys parade in Derry, and in late July a six months' ban was imposed on all parades, the only time such celebrations had been stopped since the Northern Ireland state was established.

This cycle of parades in 1968–70 did not cause the Troubles, but they proved critical in opening up the fracture zones in Northern Irish life that had been obscured and ignored for so long. Protestants felt that the right to parade was their prerogative and their heritage, while for the Catholics the Orange parades were an affront and a constant reminder of their second-class status. The annual Apprentice Boys parade round the city walls and the ceremonial burning of the reviled traitor Lundy[1] from a position overlooking the Bogside drove home the point that, despite the Catholic majority, Derry would remain a Protestant city. They were not only excluded as Catholics from loyalist parades, but they were also stopped from holding their own events. For while loyalists insisted on their inalienable right to parade wherever and whenever they wished, this right was not extended to Catholics. Civil rights parades did not fit into the traditional polarities; but by challenging the authority of the Protestant state and demanding equal rights for the minority they became immediately liable to be categorised as Catholic and nationalist. After the Coalisland to

---

1. Lieutenant-Colonel Robert Lundy was the military governor of Derry at the beginning of the siege; his equivocation in dealing with the Jacobite forces and fears that he planned to surrender the city led to his overthrow by the civilian defenders in April 1689. To be called a 'Lundy', a traitor to one's own people, is still a withering insult today. An effigy of Lundy is burnt every December, at the parade held to mark the 'Closing of the Gates'.

Dungannon parade in August 1968 had been excluded from the centre of Dungannon, Bernadette Devlin stated: 'I do believe that then for the first time it dawned on people that Northern Ireland was a series of Catholic and Protestant ghettoes' (quoted in Bardon 1992:653). This situation did not just happen by chance. It was maintained, practically, by the very systems of discrimination that were beginning to be challenged, and symbolically, by the practice of parading. The civil rights parades were instrumental in clarifying these divisions and drawing the attention of a wider audience to them. These parades became as contentious as the political reforms, as they became a visible symbol of the Catholic nationalist challenge to the state.

Parades have continued to be held throughout the Troubles, and in fact they have increased in number. The loyal orders continue to dominate the parading tradition; but since 1968 nationalist and republican groups have also more readily taken to the streets to assert their rights. Parading remains the most prominent means of asserting collective identities and claiming political dominance over territory. But it is no more a static tradition than it has ever been: the Troubles have also witnessed the development of many new practices within the broad culture of parading – the increasing prominence of 'blood and thunder' bands at loyalist parades, the appearance of loyalist paramilitary iconography and displays, the assertion of republican parading rights, the public commemoration of events and martyrs of recent years, the flowering of mural displays in the nationalist areas, and the refocusing of murals in loyalist areas. Parades and the associated visual displays have been a vibrant feature of political life in the north of Ireland for over two hundred years. These displays have always flowered most powerfully at times of crisis: is it any wonder that they have continued to flourish over the past twenty-five years?

Re-route Sectarian Marches, Ormeau Road, Belfast, June 1995

Part II

Two Communities

Band Girls; Derry, Our Lady's day, August 1993.

Colour Bearer; Donegall Pass, August 1995.

Waiting for the Boys; Derry, August 1993.

Following the Bands; East Belfast Somme Parade, July 1993.

Orangewomen, Rossnowlagh, Co Donegal, July 1993.

In Northern Ireland the two confessional communities have remained distinct: culturally, socially, politically and to a great extent geographically. Protestants and Catholics are largely endogamous communities; and although the towns, villages and dispersed rural settlements are to some degree mixed, many individual streets or estates in working-class areas are designated or acknowledged as identified with one faith or the other (MacFarlane 1989; O'Dowd 1993; Vincent 1989). At the 1991 census the population of Northern Ireland was 1,577,836: 38.4 per cent of the population declared themselves as Roman Catholics, while 50.7 per cent were Protestant. However, the local proportions of Catholics and Protestants vary from area to area: the Protestant community remains dominant in the eastern counties of Antrim and Down, while Catholics are numerically dominant west of the River Bann and in the border areas. But a sense of antagonistic difference is not in any way immutable: in many parts of Ulster the two communities live side by side and in relative harmony (Buckley 1982; Leyton 1974; MacFarlane 1986a,b).

Belfast has developed into a mosaic of estates and districts that are predominately defined in terms of the sectarian divide. East of the river Lagan, Belfast is overwhelmingly Protestant (McAuley 1994); the west of the city is largely perceived by outsiders to be synonymous with the nationalist Falls Road (Conroy 1988; Sluka 1989), but it also includes the staunchly loyalist Shankill Road. The north of the city is a heterogeneous mixture of small groups of streets, each with a distinct identity (Beattie 1993; Burton 1978); while the south is a mix of working-class Protestant areas and middle-class districts. Although these divisions can be traced back into the early history and development of the city (Beckett *et al.* 1983), the periods of violence around partition and since 1968 have seen a hardening and formalising of the separation of the two communities. In 1911, 41 per cent of Catholics and 62 per cent of Protestants lived in streets in which 90 per cent of the population were of similar faith. By 1969 this had increased to 56 per cent and 69 per cent respectively, and by 1972 to 70 per cent and 78 per cent (Boal 1982).

These divisions have been consolidated by the Troubles. But more than that, the informality of earlier divisions, which allowed a steady, if partial, re-integration in periods of peace, has been transformed by a series of permanent divisions, or 'peace lines', so that sectarian division of the working-class areas has become institutionalised as part of the fabric of the city. The peace lines have evolved from crude barricades or rolls of barbed wire into carefully planned and aesthetically landscaped brick structures (Jarman 1993; Quinn 1994). The rebuilding of an extensive wall dividing Springmartin from New Barnsley in west Belfast began the day the IRA ceasefire was declared; around the same time a 'peace fence' was erected through Alexandra Park in the north of the city. While the peace process has seen many of the dividing gateways in the city and the border crossings re-opened, the divisions between residential communities remain. Although these peace lines have been built to separate Protestant from Catholic, they also help to fragment the two communities internally. The geographical disruption and road closures have meant that many circumferential journeys can no longer be made easily. People travel along radial routes into the city centre and out again. The older networks of contact between areas have been closed down. Furthermore, there has been an extensive movement of population out of the city centre and out of Belfast altogether to suburban satellite towns (Boal 1995). The core city has suffered a decline in population since 1971 from 350,000 to 279,000. Many of the old-established communities have been demolished and fragmented as people have been relocated in suburban estates (Jenkins 1982, 1983; Wiener 1978). Taking this change together with the massive decline in the industrial and economic base, the old certainties of life in Belfast have been catastrophically removed.

This changing city has perhaps been more acutely experienced by the Protestant working class, not because they have suffered more than the Catholic community but because they expected more (Goldring 1991). They had been encouraged to believe in the idea of a Protestant state for a Protestant people and in Belfast as the capital of their country. But the city was never just a collection of streets, factories, shops and buildings: it was always partly a place of the imagination, which could only ever really be realised in the act of movement (de Certeau 1984). Benedict Anderson (1983) has suggested that one of the important stimuli to the idea of a national identity among the colonial regimes of

South America was the constant movement of administrators, whose travels encouraged the formation of a geographically bounded place. In Belfast, the very existence of the city as a single place, and the personal sense of belonging to the larger community, is brought about through the act of walking together in an act of commemoration and celebration. As the city has grown and fragmented, the very idea of Belfast as a place, and the unity of one's own community within it, has been maintained and confirmed by personal experience of it: a city which is most readily experienced by the annual cycle of parades. Parading is confrontational and oppositional in the way that I have traced through its history; but it also forms part of the process of mapping the city, inscribing an identity into the physical geography and reconnecting the fragmented parts into an idealised whole.

Building the Boney; Roden Street, July 1994.

Lundy the Traitor; Londonderry, August 1992.

Souvenir Stall; East Belfast Somme Parade, July 1993.

Preacher; Scarva, July 1994.

Chapter 5

The Glorious Twelfth

The Twelfth of July is the most important date of the year for Ulster Protestants. Each year the Orange Order organises 18 major parades to celebrate the victory at the Boyne in 1690. The Order is a male organisation (although there is a small women's Institution), a brotherhood that is open only to Protestants. With an estimated membership of 40,000, the Orange Order is the largest fraternal organisation in the north of Ireland, and it remains at the heart of Ulster loyalism (see Bryan 1996 for analysis of the Orange Order). The Order has a hierarchical structure; but much of the power is decentralised, and practical activity is carried out at a local level. Private lodges, the lowest level of the hierarchy, are organised around churches, places of residence or workplaces. An individual can apply to join any lodge he chooses, but family, social or residential connections usually determine the choice that is made. In the urban areas this may mean that each lodge is a relatively homogeneous body with no great social differentiation; but in the rural areas membership may be socially diverse, a feature which has been useful in maintaining vertical alliances within the Protestant community (Harris 1972). Each lodge has a range of officers: Worshipful Master, deputy Master, secretary, treasurer and chaplain, which are often rotated around the membership on an annual basis. Members meet and pay fees on a monthly basis at an Orange Hall, which can be found in most towns and villages. Meetings are functional affairs to discuss business matters, fund-raising and planning for the annual commemorations that are the main activity of the loyal orders. The officers of private lodges meet together at district level to organise church and mini-Twelfth parades, and the districts are in turn organised at county level: the Belfast districts form one county, those of the City of Londonderry another, and the six others follow the county boundaries.

The Order has had fluctuating fortunes during the Troubles: it is seen by many as an anachronism in a modern state, and an uncomfortable reminder of the sectarianism that underpinned the formation of Northern Ireland. Its demise had been expected, if not confidently predicted; but it has survived, and in the 1990s seems to have stabilised its earlier decline. Most Unionist MPs, and many local councillors, still feel it is important to be a member of one of the loyal orders, and can be seen on parade during the summer. Having said that, the Order has declined considerably in importance from earlier in the century, when the membership was estimated at perhaps 100,000 strong and it was at the very heart of the unionist state. In the urban centres it is now a predominantly working-class organisation, although membership is more diverse in rural areas; and it remains a pervasive body throughout Ulster Protestant society, cutting across boundaries of place, class and wealth. Changing patterns of industrial production and employment have also meant that its importance within systems of patronage has declined from the earlier years of the century (Bew, Gibbon and Patterson 1995; Farrell 1980). An Orangeman is often seen as the epitome of the Ulster Protestant; but the decline in membership indicates that the Order is no longer regarded as highly as it once was. For many it is no longer a respectable body: it is now much less disciplined, less dignified; in local parlance, it is 'rougher' (Buckley and Kenney 1995).

While it has long been acknowledged that many Catholics have a strong dislike and even fear of the Twelfth, and leave the north when possible, many Protestants also take the opportunity to go on holiday at this time. Catholics and nationalists publicly denounce the Orange Order as a sectarian, anti-Catholic, anti-nationalist, divisive force within the north, and privately many Protestants, especially middle-class Protestants, would agree with them, although they would be reticent about publicising their views. Other, younger and more militant, Protestants see the Orange Order as too conservative, too cautious and too passive in defending Ulster's interests. While they would be critical of the Order, they would nevertheless take part in the celebrations.

To return to my opening statement, the Twelfth is still the most important date for Ulster Protestants: even though many are critical of the body that organises the events, they continue to take part in them; others refuse to voice criticism and remain invisible; and the nationalist community acknowledges the significance of the occasion and usually quietly puts up with things. It is quite possible, therefore, to present the Twelfth as an uncontentious, carnival-like event, as many Orangemen would like to; but this would be to ignore the diversity of the attitudes that are often subsumed within the celebrations. In this chapter I focus on the role the Orange celebrations play in creating a sense of community among the Protestants of Belfast. In the next chapter I discuss the way parading is used to affirm the Protestant position across the north, how and why parades create antagonism within the nationalist community, and how nationalists have responded.

The Belfast Twelfth

The Belfast County parade is one of the biggest events of the Ulster marching season, and the culmination of much intense preparation and activity over the preceding weeks. This involves erecting decorations, building bonfires and holding smaller parades and commemorations throughout the city. Therefore, rather than analysing the Twelfth as a single day of commemoration and celebration, it needs to be considered as an extended ritual process, of variable length and complexity. In this chapter I discuss how the Protestant community is re-created and reaffirmed each year through these events, and, in particular, how the scale of the event helps to accommodate differences within that community, the culmination being to present a public semblance of unity that is structured upon a diverse range of interpretations of the key symbols of Ulster loyalism. By spreading the commemorations over an extended period all sections of the community have an opportunity to engage in the re-enactment, and public unity is built from the bottom upwards rather than imposed from the top downwards. The scale and complexity of the political community in Belfast necessitates this extended germination, and this in turn helps to retain all opinion within the flexible and expandable boundary of loyalism. This process will be illustrated by describing the build-up to the Twelfth in the Sandy Row area of the city through the summer of 1994. Sandy Row is a working-class area in south Belfast adjacent to Great Victoria Street and Dublin Road, the main southbound thoroughfares into the city. It is a local shopping centre, largely consisting of two-storey Victorian properties. Much of the housing has been redeveloped in recent years, although a large area at the northern end, off Great Victoria Street, is now a car park. Bounded on the north and east by the city centre, on the north-west by railway tracks, and in the south by the Lisburn Road, Sandy Row is a geographically tightly defined community that retains a strong sense of identity and distinctiveness. Apart from the shops, the prominent buildings are the four-storey Victorian Orange Hall and the recently reconstructed and enlarged Rangers Supporters' Club. Facing each other at the Donegall Road junction, these two buildings exemplify the cultural parameters of many working-class Protestant men.

Flags and Boneys

Public preparations begin towards the end of June, when the arch is erected in front of the Orange Hall. An arch was first recorded in Sandy Row in 1835, and the current version is the most imposing of the few that are still erected in the city. The orange and blue structure spans the width of the road, and in the evening the designs of King William and other Orange symbols are illuminated by numerous small lights. Red, white and blue bunting is strung across the main shopping area and in some of the residential streets. Flags are flown the length of the street on shops and houses, and are displayed in many shop windows. The red and white Ulster cross is prominent, and so too is the unofficial, Independent Ulster flag, while only a few buildings fly the Union Flag. Every few years the kerbstones on the main thoroughfare are repainted red, white and blue; this is also the time for painting and repainting murals, although no new ones appear this year in Sandy Row.

All the decorations are completed for the mini-Twelfth parade on 1 July. This is a local version of the main parade, timed as a commemoration of the battle of the Somme. It is a popular event that draws large crowds of spectators on to the streets. The Orangemen, in full regalia and carrying their flags and banners, are accompanied by local bands as they set off along Sandy Row. Halting briefly for the District officers to lay a wreath on the local memorial, their route takes in Sandy Row, and the Donegall Pass, Roden Street and Village areas in a figure-of-eight route that finishes back at the hall. The parade takes about two hours to

complete. While this is a commemoration, the Orangemen simultaneously mark out the extent of Protestant South Belfast as
they walk to the boundaries that separate the adjacent loyalist
communities from their nationalist neighbours. These boundaries
are now distinctly defined by buffer zones, empty spaces, major
through roads and prominent murals; but these divisions are
symbolically reaffirmed by the act of processing. Marking the
boundaries also serves to facilitate the symbolic unity of the four
distinct geographical communities in the Sandy Row Orange
district. The local allegiance to a sense of community, which
through the rest of the year serves to maintain a sense of difference
between these areas, is put to one side (Holloway 1994a,b; see
Chapter 10) as the parade reaffirms an essential unity of faith.
Similar mini-Twelfth parades are held in other areas of the city in
the run-up to the Twelfth (and increasingly in other towns across
the north). The first of these, in north Belfast at the beginning of
June, marks the beginning of the Belfast Orange parading calendar.
Collectively these district parades map out and affirm the integrity
of the main loyalist areas of Belfast prior to the symbolic reinte-
gration of these scattered communities as a single entity on the
Twelfth. Together they encompass most loyalist residential areas
of the city within their perambulations, and they practically
inscribe the Orange claim that Belfast is their city on to the very
streets themselves (Werbner 1991). In reasserting the traditional
Orange right to parade where they will, the mini-Twelfth parades
provide the secure foundations for the domination of the heart of
the city on the Twelfth itself.

The parade declares the essential unity of a community that is
spread disparately over a diverse, but bounded, geographical area.
It publicly reveals and gives physical expression to an otherwise
fragmented imagined community. But, the community having
made its statement, this unity of purpose once again disappears
from view: preparations continue, and much of them in public;
but there is little public activity as such. Orangemen, bandsmen,
bonfire builders, and also the women, whose invisible work is no
less necessary to a successful Twelfth, prepare for their part in the
celebrations independently of each other. There is no central
organisation overseeing this larger process, although individual
activities and groups are of course organised. Preparations happen
informally, and to a great extent depend on the number of people
able and willing to get involved. Therefore the scale, the range

and the quality of the celebrations vary from year to year and from area to area. The scale of flags, decorations, murals and bonfires may depend on the actions of no more than a few men.

The main visible activity at this time is in gathering and protecting wood for the local bonfire. Countless fires are built across the city in preparation for the 11th night. Pallets, railway sleepers, tyres, old furniture and any burnable debris are gathered at the chosen site. Each locality gathers and builds its own fire; and, with local competition over who can erect the biggest stack, there is a threat and fear that outsiders will try to burn the assembled timber before the event. So most wood appears, and the fire is built, in the few days before the 11th. During this time the pile is always protected: young boys stand guard through the night, with a makeshift shelter offering protection from the rain. The fire-builders are assisted by boys of all ages, the youngest kids being content to play with the small smoky fires and embers that are a constant feature of these sites; but girls are rarely attracted to them, or encouraged to join in. The finished fires can in some cases be awe-inspiring in their height and apparent precariousness. They often reach twenty feet or more, and only the amount of wood available and the ingenuity and skill of the builders constrains the scale. In recent years the Sandy Row fire has been built on the corner of a car park at Hope Street. Before that, empty land next to the Orange Hall had been used; but, as with all bonfires across the city, traditional sites have to be given up to the demands of redevelopment or safety, and the fire-builders are forced into a nomadic quest for space. Usually another derelict plot is available; but fires are sometimes built in the road, or closer than desirable to buildings: houses and shops get damaged as plastic gutters and signs melt, murals get blackened or destroyed, street lamps are burnt, telephone poles are set on fire and wires brought down, and grassy play areas are scorched. Within broad limits the inconvenience and potential danger is tolerated. The fire is an essential part of the Twelfth celebrations, and as such has a primacy in many people's eyes over more mundane concerns.

As well as the mini-Twelfth parades, the Orangemen also parade to church. The Sandy Row men join the other Belfast districts in the Ulster Hall for the Somme Anniversary Service at the beginning of July; and on the Sunday before the Twelfth they walk to a local church for the Boyne Anniversary Service. No banners are carried at these events. For the Boyne service a Union

Flag, an Ulster Cross and the Orange Standard head the single column of three ranks of perhaps 400 men and a single accordion band. Few people gather to watch: without the brash music, the banners and flags, church parades lack the attractions of the main commemorations; they are essentially private events for the Orange Order that move through public space, rather than being public occasions *per se*. This distinction between church parades and public commemorations is enhanced by the fact that, alone of all varieties of Orange parade, they are held on a Sunday, a day that is devoid of public or commercial activity within the Protestant community. When the Twelfth falls on a Sunday the parades are postponed until the next day. Church parades focus attention on to the religious principles that underpin the institution and provide its unifying core – principles that are frequently occluded in the public sphere. But just as the church parades hold little attraction for the public, they are also often poorly supported by the membership. In spite of the religious base of the Orange Order, the secular celebrations are the most popular.

On the eleventh of July the final touches are put to the bonfires. From eleven o'clock people gather around the fire sites, young men and women with carrier bags full of cans of beer, families with young children and babies in prams, older people who have seen it all many times before, a few tourists. Chip shops and fast food vans do a roaring trade; two small groups of evangelical Christians hold services on the pavement, trying to convince passers-by of the errors of their ways, but generate little interest. As a prologue to the main event a small fire made of left-over wood is lit by the younger children. This quickly gets out of hand and engulfs a group of advertising hoardings, whose images are gradually eaten away by the flames. Later the boards themselves crash to the ground, to cheers from the crowd. The main fire is lit on the dot of midnight to welcome in the Twelfth. The fire starts slowly; but as it spreads around and up the stack the crowd is forced to retreat across the road. As the flames eat their way up the pile of sleepers and pallets, attention is focused on the Irish tricolour at the top: a great cheer goes up as this is engulfed in flames. Once the flag has been burnt and the peak of the fire has passed, the crowd rapidly fades away: some get some sleep before the big parade, but many of the younger ones move elsewhere to party the night away.

The Big Parade

Orangemen and their bands assemble at the Orange Hall around eight o'clock in readiness for a 9 a.m. departure. Here they break ranks and, leaning flags and banners against the walls and scattering drums over the pavement, talk, smoke and in some cases crack an early beer. A steady drizzle falls; the sky is a darkish shade of grey, and there is no wind to clear the air. Popularly, a sunny Twelfth confirms that God is Protestant: but this year he is definitely a 'taig' (Catholic). Many Orangemen carry umbrellas as a matter of course; but most of the younger bandsmen, attired in brightly coloured uniforms, take the rain as part of the day and are quite wet by the time the parade starts. The stereotypical dark suit and tie, with a bowler hat and umbrella, remain the appropriate dress for many Orangemen; but the one article of clothing that is essential is the sash (worn over one shoulder) or collarette, which carries the member's lodge number and badges, noting the wearer's present or past office in the lodge (Treasurer, Chaplain, Past Master, etc.). Sashes are usually orange and purple; but blue, crimson and white are also common colours. All members of a lodge wear the same style and colour.

Each Twelfth numerous small boys make their first appearance on the Orange stage, accompanying fathers or grandfathers in the ranks. Some hold the ribbons of the banners to stop them blowing about too much. Boys from as young as 4 or 5 years old also appear in bands: carrying cymbals or miniature drum major's staffs they walk as far as they can. Women also parade in small but growing numbers; but they never seem as relaxed as the men, as if they know they are intruding on a male event. Younger girls are largely kept to the sidelines: a few accompany their fathers, but not in the same number as young boys, and although girls often form the colour party or play in many of many of the bands, they are forced to adopt male dress and roles for the day. Most women settle for an informal supporting role, by cheering their men from the sidelines.

At 9 a.m. the Orangemen set off down Sandy Row for the fourth time in recent days. The Somme Memorial is acknowledged with the usual solemnity; they pass the bonfire; still smouldering from the night before; turn left on to Great Victoria Street, and parade through the city centre before turning up towards the Shankill. At Peter's Hill, they pass the small nationalist Unity Flats estate, which is blocked off by vehicle-mounted screens attended by army personnel who stand guard attentively as the Orangemen pass by. The parade cuts through to Carlisle Circus, where the brethren from other Belfast districts assemble for the start of the main parade. Here the junction with the Antrim Road is also closed and screened off, and further down Clifton Street the north end of the Unity estate is similarly closed. Although the residents make no protest and remain invisible, they are effectively imprisoned within their estate until the procession has left the city centre.

At 10 a.m. the main parade begins, led by the Belfast County officers and the Burdge Memorial Standards (a Union Flag, and the Orange and Purple Standards of the Institution); these are followed by a colour party carrying the flags of the countries in which Orangeism flourishes. The standards are protected by six Tylers, who walk on the outside of the colour party carrying unsheathed ceremonial swords. The first of the many lodges then follow behind their district bannerettes; they parade in numerical order by warrant number. Each year a different district leads the parade. This year the recently combined numbers 7 and 8 districts from north Belfast head the parade, followed by numbers 9 and 10 and then 1 through to 6. District No. 6 arrives from east Belfast to join the main procession at Royal Avenue; No. 9 District, from west Belfast, joins at North Street, while No. 10 District, from Ballynafeigh, parades down the Ormeau Road and joins the main body at Donegall Square.

The ritual reunification of the dispersed Protestant communities of Belfast culminates at this point, the seat of local civic authority and centre of the city. The decentralised symbolic communities that had been mapped out by the many mini-Twelfth parades are joined together as a single body. Having inscribed their presence over the loyalist areas of the city, the separate threads are combined at the City Hall as the Belfast Orangemen occupy and claim authority over the streets of the city centre. In the build-up to the Twelfth the city centre remains devoid of party displays or decorations; but on the Twelfth all other activities are abandoned for the day, shops and businesses are closed, and the city is claimed by the Orangemen as theirs and theirs alone. The city of Belfast is clearly marked as Protestant.

At the City Hall the county officers lay a wreath at the Cenotaph. Having made their commemoration to the war dead, they rejoin the main body of the parade, which now begins the long walk to the Field. Each band acknowledges the Cenotaph by marching to a single drum's beat or in silence; but as soon as they have passed the memorial the bands burst into full voice, and traditional loyalist anthems are mixed in with military marches, film music and interpretations of modern pop songs. While there are a number of accordion bands on the parade, flutes and drums are the most popular instruments. Behind the drum major or colour party, a row of side drummers, a bass drummer and several ranks of flautists, sometimes thirty or more in number, march out in regular step. The aggressive 'blood and thunder' flute bands dominate the Belfast parade, and concentrate on marching and party tunes with a strong percussive beat, which they play from memory. Most bands are independent of the Orange Order and hired just for the day. Many are critical of the loyal orders and are closer to the loyalist paramilitary groups; but by participating in the Orange parades the bands affirm their support for the general unionist position, although without necessarily conforming to the Orange ideals.

Some tensions exist in this relationship: the bandsmen often flout rules and regulations controlling the forms of regalia that can be carried on Orange parades. Like the Orange lodges, the bands carry distinctive regalia to proclaim their public identity and their ideological allegiance; some of these include the emblems of the loyalist paramilitary groups, the UDA, the UVF and the Red Hand Commando, which appear on flags and bannerettes or emblazoned on bass drums; such displays are not formally permitted at Orange parades, but they appear each year. To an extent the autonomy of the bands has become an accepted part of unionist public unity; but in private the paramilitary regalia have been regarded as an unwelcome intrusion, disrupting the public image of an erstwhile religious organisation.

While it may be possible to banish the more extreme regalia from the parade, it is more difficult to control the many sectarian anthems that are beaten out with a gusto and regularity that delights the crowds. A parade without bands has little appeal for spectators, and the rhythm of the drums helps pass the miles to the Field; this is why most lodges continue to hire a band, even if they disapprove of some aspects of their displays. The parade is awash with noise over the entire route, as the seventy or eighty bands maintain a steady stream of tunes. Each band plays at its own preferred volume, regardless of neighbouring bands, so that at any one time spectators are likely to be able to hear three different tunes, one from the band that has just passed, one from the one in front of them and one from the one approaching. Most spectators stay at one spot to watch the parade pass; but many of the blood and thunder bands are accompanied by a crowd of friends and girlfriends, who walk along the pavement, cheering and encouraging the bandsmen and joining in with some of the tunes. Friends also help with important business of supplying refreshments; soft drinks are usually consumed on the route, but beers are expected at the Field. Accompanying supporters are usually seen with carrier bags full of cans of lager.

Despite the rain, thousands of people line the route to Eden-derry. They stand two or three deep in places, while the kerbside is claimed by an array of picnic chairs, household chairs and assorted other seats. Elderly people and children occupy most of these, while the rest of the family and friends stand around, sheltering from the weather under umbrellas or a variety of headgear. Few shops are open on the Twelfth (and no bars), and so picnics and drinks are brought out on to the streets. Burger stands, sandwich stalls and ice-cream vans dot the route, and every church on the Lisburn Road seems to be selling teas and sand-wiches. The spectators listen to the music, wait for husbands, fathers and relatives, and look out for old friends, who have perhaps not been seen since the last Twelfth. Although the parade is a formal occasion, Orangemen readily break ranks to shake hands and acknowledge friends as people call out from the roadside, even stopping off for a quick word before rejoining their lodge. The procession takes about two hours to pass any one spot; but as soon as the final lodge and the police escort have passed the crowd breaks up and returns home until it is time to greet the men on their return in the afternoon.

It is a long haul to the Field. The six miles of the Belfast route are by far the longest of any, and many of the men will have walked some miles to reach the official start of the parade. The last lodge will not arrive until after 2 p.m., some 4 hours after the head of the parade left Carlisle Circus; and by the time they return home some men will have walked 18 or 20 miles in the day. The first half involves a steady climb up the Lisburn Road, replicating (supposedly) the route King Billy took from Belfast in 1690; but the final couple of miles are downhill to the Lagan valley and along leafy lanes to the Field.

The Field affords an opportunity to rest and recuperate: some lodges bring caravans or marquees to provide a modicum of comfort, and in recent years more and more lodges have coaches waiting to take them to a restaurant or bar for a meal. But for many there is little option but to kill time. Musical equipment is discarded in a pile; banners are often used to protect drums or lie crumpled on the damp grass. For the two-hour break they are forgotten, and time is spent talking and resting. Fast food stalls offer their limited range of burgers and chips. An evangelical preacher, whose church had preceded the Orangemen, vainly attempts to attract attention. A few stalls offer a selection of loyalist trinkets: tapes, badges, flags and hats. Fortunately, the rain has largely stopped by mid-morning, and the weather is now pleasantly mild.

At the lower end of the Field the officers and dignitaries hold a Service of Thanksgiving and a Public Meeting from a covered platform. The meeting approves a series of resolutions on loyalty, faith and state, and allows leading members of the Order (who are often politicians as well) to comment on current affairs. The resolutions and the speeches made from the platform are widely reported on the news and in the papers, where extensive quotations are recorded; but they are almost totally ignored at the Field. Of the estimated 20,000 men on parade, barely 50 took part in the service; a few more stood idly by listening to the speeches; and even the presentation of the band awards drew little interest. Belfast is not unique in this matter; a similar level of interest in the platform is shown at all loyalist events.

At 4.15 p.m. the Orangemen leave the Field in the same order in which they had arrived. The return lacks the precision and efficiency of the outward march: bandsmen and Orangemen are often late returning to the Field or simply never arrive, preferring to join the parade *en route*. The return parade is more celebratory: alcohol has helped to relax the mood of both crowd and marchers. Some bands adopt funny costumes or paint their faces with Union Jacks; a variety of hats or headgear is substituted for the tam o'shanters of the uniform. This year the biggest response was for a band wearing Mexican sombreros and false moustaches (a reference to the recent Irish defeat by Mexico in the World Cup). The spectators crowd into the road, narrowing the space for the walkers; and by the time the parade arrives at Sandy Row at the bottom of the Lisburn Road, the road is reduced to barely half its width. The security presence here is the most concentrated since leaving the city in the morning; but the police remain in the background, watchful yet unobtrusive. The crowds call out to friends and cheer the bands; middle-aged women have licence to be more outrageous than most – a group of 'Orange Lil's', wearing Union Jack clothing, join in with the parade for a few yards, accosting, flirting and dancing with the men. The paraders respond to the welcome of the crowd: the bass drummers strike up as loudly as they can with the favourite loyalist anthems; the drum majors perform flamboyant, acrobatic staff twirling, throwing their heavy batons twenty feet into the air and then catching them cleanly to roars of approval; the younger Orangemen, now down to shirt sleeves, exert their final energy and display their bravado by jigging along with the heavy banners, leading their brethren in a snake-like dance along the road.

At Shaftesbury Square the parade begins to break up: No.10 District return to Ballynafeigh via Donegall Pass, and the Sandy Row lodges separate to end their Twelfth at the Orange Hall. Other districts will break ranks and head their separate ways home before the remnants of the parade finally end back at Carlisle Circus. It is shortly after 7.30 p.m. when the Sandy Row lodges end their day's walking. As the parade passes and the spectators drift away the pavements and gutters are awash with paper, cans and bottles, the debris of the celebrations. The cleaning up operation begins immediately: by the following morning the city is spick and span.

In Conclusion

The Twelfth of July parade is an act of commemoration, a time to perpetuate and celebrate the memory of a three-hundred-year-old battle when the Catholic King James was defeated by the Protestant King William and the Protestant Ascendancy was established. This Ascendancy is reaffirmed across the north each Twelfth of July, as the past struggles are recalled through a performative re-enactment. Each year the events of July 1690 are replayed, the march to battle and back now condensed into a single day. For that day the Orangemen constitute themselves as a replica army, and their parade mimics the departure to, and return from, war. The Order displays itself as a mirror of the military structure of regiments and companies; each group of men headed by their officers and their standardised, and almost identical, ceremonial regalia, accompanied by the martial music of the young bandsmen in their brilliant costumes. As the contemporary community re-lives the events of the past they become contemporary events: the performance is no longer restricted to a symbolic meaning, the enactment has real effects in real time. The sombre mood of the morning, with the ardours of the march in front of them, contrasts with the joyful, drunken exuberance of the return to the city in the evening, elated by the success of the (battle)field. The tension and expectation of the departure is resolved and released with the safe arrival home. The victory is confirmed for another year, and the Ascendancy assured. For the performance to be disrupted or cancelled would be to transform history, to rupture the simultaneity of past and present and make the future uncertain. The act of performative commemoration completes a circle between the past and the present, and thus makes the future certain.

In spite of the emphasis on the militaristic base of Protestant life, the performance highlights other aspects of the community's identity which remain vital to its sense of unity. The Orange structure of egalitarianism, as a fraternity of brethren, is made visible in the form of the parade. There is little formal distinction between the marchers, between lodges and between districts. Each one of the marchers is the equal of all the others. Each of the different districts is represented as an equal, each takes its turn at both the head and the rear of the parade. The discipline and hierarchy of the army is strengthened because it is entered into freely and based on mutual respect and common purpose. Bourdieu (1977) and Foucault (1977, 1981) have shown how the disciplined body can serve to concentrate and focus more abstract ideological ideals, all the more powerfully for being entered into unknowingly, the imposed discipline of the prison less successful than the insidious subtlety of the domestic routine. The rituals of the marching season, which include both extensive and intensive periods of performative display and discipline, are a period when the collective focus is on the idealised community, and the community collectively embodies and dramatises its past glories and future aspirations.

While the overt focus at this time is on the performance of the men on parade, there is still a role for those members of the community who are excluded from the walk. At the departure the men are cheered on their way by the women, the children and the elderly, who remain behind, but are proud to witness their men depart. They will be on the streets later to see them return. These people may appear to be excluded from the actual parade, but they retain a key role in the community: they may seem little more than a passive audience, but they too are confirming their role. They are witness to their men's courage and fortitude; they too are forced to make sacrifices; they will maintain the community in their absence: they are providers and nurturers, and thus have their part in assuring the future. The ceremonies of remembering therefore extend beyond the pure act of commemoration and engage with more mundane features of daily life. The performance helps to confirm the importance of traditional and 'natural' divisions of labour, the essence of what it is to be male and female, adult and child within the Protestant community, and thereby defines that community in opposition to the other. These embodied memories can then be carried over into the daily routine.

The Twelfth of July commemorations physically reconstruct and reaffirm the unity of the fragmented loyalist population of Belfast. This unity is achieved through the process of creating and displaying a community whose defining values are expressed and internalised both through an extended ritual performance and, as we shall see below, through an elaborate visual display. This performance is extended over a lengthy period, not because of the complexity of the message being conveyed, but to allow it to be expressed in as many different ways and by as many different interest groups as possible. This extensive ritual process also helps to embed the values and memories that are displayed at the key moments into the routine of daily life. The ideal community is momentarily realised during the parade on the Twelfth, when the imagined Protestant community of Belfast is made visible and physical, in total and uninhibited control of the public spaces of the city.

This unity is created in opposition to those who are excluded from the day's events, the Roman Catholic population, who are allowed no part in the proceedings, and are in some cases virtually imprisoned for the day, as daily routine is put on hold. Anecdotal reference is often made to the fact that in the past, before the Troubles began, Catholics would often come on to the streets to watch the parade pass. But these people could never participate in any way as Roman Catholics, but only in the non-sectarian and individualised role of 'good neighbours'. The unity of the Twelfth can only ever be a unity based principally on the Protestant faith. The visibility of the Protestant is enhanced by the total invisibility of outsiders: no reference is made to the Catholics in the images on the parade, and their houses are physically concealed from the marchers. On the Twelfth they do not exist. The day is an occasion when the city of Belfast is not only host to the reunited Protestant community, but becomes a totally Protestant city. Belfast is not unique in this: the complex web of parade routes and preliminary events that built up to the Twelfth is also played out across the rest of Ulster, similar parades held across the six counties extend the unity to all Protestants. The nationalist community in their turn also commemorate their heroes and parade to assert their political visibility and affirm their continued presence within Northern Ireland. It is the wider practice of parading that will now be considered.

Craigavon Protestant Boy; Ballmoney, Easter 1995.

Lambeg Drummers; Portadown, Twelfth 1993.

Bass Drummer, Bridgetown Republican Flute Band; Belfast Internment Parade, August 1995.

Sam; Ballymoney, Easter 1995.

Chapter 6

The Endless Parade

While the Orangemen parade through Belfast, their brethren are holding similar demonstrations across the north. Each year the Orange Order holds Twelfth parades in eighteen locations, and the small Independent Orange Order, a product of a split in the early 1900s (Morgan 1991), hold their own event. The Twelfth is the centrepiece of the marching season, and the climax of the Orange parades, but the Order is only one of a number of similar bodies that organise parades in Northern Ireland. On 13 July the parading tradition is taken up by the Blackmen from Counties Armagh and Down, who host a large parade and gathering at Scarva, Co. Down, reputedly on the route that King Billy's army took on its way south. The Black parades continue through August, until their main demonstration on the last Saturday marks the traditional end to the parading calendar.

Some members of the Orange Order will have begun their association as children, as members of the Junior Orange Order, but most join an Orange lodge as adults. Most men then progress rapidly to membership of the Royal Arch Purple Chapter, a body that has little in the way of public identity and is scarcely distinct from the Orange. They are then eligible to join the Royal Black Institution (RBI), or, to give it its full title, the Imperial Grand Black Chapter of the British Commonwealth, which is regarded by many as representing the more middle-aged, middle-class, respectable and religious side of Orangeism. Alongside membership of the Orange and Black some men also belong to the Apprentice Boys of Derry which, with a membership of around 12,000 men, is the smallest of the three main orders. The three senior loyal orders are responsible for organising the major annual parades that commemorate the Williamite and Somme anniversaries. They also organise a wide range of smaller parades, and these have increased in number to such an extent that the period from Easter to the end of August is now known as the marching season. The marching season is dominated by the parades of the loyal orders; but there is also a distinct nationalist parading calendar that is part of the wider culture of parading, and this will be considered later.

The Orange, The Black and The Boys

The build-up to the Twelfth that I have described in the Sandy Row area of Belfast is replicated across the north. In the two or three weeks prior to the anniversary of the Boyne all Orange lodges will parade once or twice to church services, and many towns hold mini-Twelfth parades around the time of the Somme commemorations on 1 July. In recent years these have become increasingly popular, and more districts seem to announce a preparatory parade each year. These are usually evening events, and amount to little more than a relaxed stroll around the host town, a warm-up for the big parade. They are social rather than commemorative occasions: they draw large crowds on to the streets, and attract visiting lodges and bands from nearby towns and villages. Apart from the Twelfth these are the only occasions when the banners are publicly displayed.

While the focus of attention is on the Ulster parades, Orangemen also parade in Britain and Ireland in this period. On the Saturday before the Twelfth, the County Donegal Orangemen host a parade at the small seaside resort of Rossnowlagh. This is primarily for lodges from the Republic; but large numbers of Orangemen come from Northern Ireland, making a symbolic gesture of solidarity to those brethren that were abandoned to the demands of pragmatic politics in the 1920s, when nine-county Ulster was partitioned to ensure a permanent Protestant majority in the new northern statelet. The same weekend some Orangemen and bandsmen make the journey over to Scotland, where a number of Orange parades are held in the Strathclyde region. On the return they are accompanied by Scottish bandsmen, and sometimes Scottish Orange lodges, who come over to parade in Belfast and elsewhere on the Twelfth. Many bands and lodges have built up long-standing connections in Scotland, which are renewed each year. English Orange lodges hold an annual parade in Southport on the Twelfth; but many members prefer to come over to Ulster for the parades.

The reciprocal network of affiliations that are extended the length and breadth of the north on the Twelfth are thereby further extended, to include brethren in Ireland, in Scotland and in England.

The Twelfth signifies the climax of the Orange Order parades, and many people spend the next day recovering from the walking and celebrating. But 13 July also marks the first of the major Black parades, when up to 50,000 visitors come to the parade and Sham Fight at Scarva in County Down. In contrast to the exertions of the Belfast Twelfth, this is only a short parade, and if the weather is fine the day has the feel of a large picnic in the countryside.

Although Orange and Black parades are broadly similar in form and style, there are significant differences, which highlight the complexity and variations both within the loyal orders and from area to area (see Cecil 1993; Larsen 1982). The Black parade is a much more stately affair: it is little more than a short walk through the village, which is taken at an easy pace and is far less dominated by the military rhythms of the Belfast Twelfth. There are fewer of the noisy blood and thunder bands at Scarva, and instead the music is provided by a wide selection of bands: accordion, pipe and a range of part-music and silver flute bands. These styles of bands are usually dominated by women and older men: the musicians often play from sheet music, while the music is softer and more melodic, with more hymns and fewer party tunes. Although accordion bands do still parade in Belfast, the pipe bands no longer attend: the walk is too long and the bands are too slow. In contrast, the pace of the Scarva parade is set by the pipe bands, who always turn out dressed in full highland costume.

The parade therefore sounds different; and it also looks different. The displays of national emblems are usually less pronounced, and paramilitary regalia are rare: the visual displays of the Black banners give less emphasis to the military history of Protestantism, and are heavily dominated by religious themes (see Chapter 8). These differences can be seen as contrasts between the more elderly and religious orientations of the Black and the working-class secularism of many Orangemen. They also represent some of the differences between urban and rural areas: rural Orange parades are more like Black parades, with a wider range of bands and more Biblical imagery, while the blood and thunder bands also bring their paramilitary style to the Belfast Black parade.

The Belfast Twelfth and Scarva signify the two poles of 'Orangeism': the urban event, dominated by the young, secular, and working-class, is 'rough' and noisy, while the rural parades are representative of elderly, middle class, religious, respectable values (Buckley and Kenney 1995). But these distinctions are always matters of degree: both parts are always present at the major parades; they are the two halves of the Orange community; it is neither just religious, nor purely secular and sectarian: it is always both. One of the most surprising features of the Orange tradition is that it still manages to retain this diversity of features within a single organisation, within a single event, and that it has not been subject to schism and fragmentation in the way that the Protestant Church has. In fact virtually all sects within the Protestant faith are able to come together within the framework of loyalist parades. This is possible because that framework, while nominally religious, is principally about a collective national identity, constructed and maintained in the face of a threatening Other.

The Twelfth parades also traditionally marked the beginning of the summer holiday period, with factories and industry closing down for two weeks. As a result there is a break in the marching. The season recommences in mid-August with the Relief of Derry commemoration, organised by the Apprentice Boys, and more Black parades. The Apprentice Boys are based in the city of Londonderry; their main purpose is to commemorate the events of the siege of the city in 1688–9. To do so they host a small parade each December to mark the Closing of the Gates and the beginning of the siege, and another on the Saturday nearest 12 August to mark the Relief of the city (Derry Day). This latter is one of the biggest events in the parading calendar: it draws members, bands and supporters from all across the north, as they come to Derry for the day to remember 1689, to walk the walls, and to renew friendships. On the same day the Blackmen of County Fermanagh commemorate the battle of Newtownbutler in 1689, when the Enniskillen garrison defeated the approaching Irish army, an event that in turn assisted the final relief of the siege of Derry (Macrory 1988).

The final major parading day of the season is the Last Saturday of August, when the Royal Black Institution hold six county demonstrations (Black Saturday). This day does not herald any specific anniversary, but rather marks a ceremonial end to the summer marching season. These are only the largest and most prominent of the parades: woven in amongst these anniversaries are numerous smaller events that often pass unnoticed except by those immediately involved. These begin with an Apprentice Boys parade on Easter Monday and end with Reformation Day church services at the end of October; in between, each of the local branches of the loyal orders will hold a number of church parades, as well as parades to unfurl banners and to dedicate halls, charity parades, and others.

How Many?

In 1995 there were 3,500 parades held in the north of Ireland: 2,581 of these were classified by the police as loyalist events, and 302 were nationalist (these will be considered in more detail in the next chapter); the remaining 617 were made up of such events as St Patrick's day parades, the trade union May Day parades and those organised by bodies such as the Boys' Brigade and the Salvation Army. In spite of the insistence on the importance of parading as a tradition, with all the implications of continuity and lack of change that that word suggests, police records show (Table 6.1) that there has been a steady increase in loyalist parades over the past ten years. The figures also show a vast imbalance between the number of parades that are held by the two dominant communities: loyalist parades outnumber republican ones by around 9:1. I want therefore to address three issues that these statistics raise: firstly, Why are there so many parades? – even given the number of anniversaries and local parades already discussed above, the numbers seem excessive; second, Why are the numbers of parades increasing?; and third, Why is there such a difference between the number of loyalist and republican parades?

The description of the main anniversaries of the marching season only scratches the surface in addressing the number of parades that are held each year. If we return to the description of the Belfast Twelfth, it is clear that not only are there a number of smaller parades in the days preceding the main event, but that there are also many small parades on the Twelfth itself, as lodges and bands assemble at their local hall prior to parading to join the main event. There is no requirement to seek permission to hold a

Year	Total	Loyalist	Republican	Rerouted
1995	2883	2581	302	22
1994	2792	2520	272	29
1993	2662	2411	251	12
1992	2744	2498	246	16
1991	2379	2183	196	14
1990	2713	2467	246	10
1989	2317	2099	218	14
1988	2055	1865	190	10
1987	2112	1863	249	11
1986	1950	1731	219	9
1985	2120	1897	223	22

Source: Royal Ulster Constabulary Chief Constable's *Annual Report*. (No statistics were published prior to 1985.)

Table 6.1. Total number of parades between 1985 and 1995

parade – it is regarded as a civil right (although not an unproblematic one); however, under the 1987 Public Order (Northern Ireland) Order, parade organisers must notify the police of their intentions to hold a parade, and indicate the route and the probable number of participants, at least seven days beforehand. This is done by filling out a detailed form known as an '11/1'. In most cases this is a formality: the police do not give permission or sanction the parade, although if in their opinion they think the parade may cause serious public disorder they can impose constraints (on music, on flags, etc.) or order that the parade take a different route. Most parades take the route they wish, with a minimum of constraint. Each parade organiser therefore fills in an 11/1; and each completed 11/1 signifies a statistical parade.

Each of the main parading days will involve a large number of individual parades. Members of the loyal orders rarely depart for, or arrive at, a venue in a quiet and inconspicuous manner. In many cases a lodge or a band gather in the morning at the lodge master's or the band leader's house; they may then parade to the local hall to meet other local lodges, and collectively they will parade to the main assembly point. In other cases the lodges parade through their home area before boarding a bus that takes them to the main venue. Some lodges or bands may have taken part in three different parades before the main event has started. Each major event always involves a large number of these small feeder parades, and, whether it includes 10 men or 10,000 men, statistically each parade is treated the same. Although there are eighteen main parades on the Twelfth of July, the total number of notifications, and therefore legally recorded parades, on the Twelfth in 1995 was 547. Over 20 per cent of all loyalist parades were held on a single day. Similar large numbers of parades will be held on Derry Day and on Black Saturday: the marching season therefore is not evenly spread. The large number of loyalist parades is in part a reflection of both the scale of the organisation and its decentralised nature. There is no part of the Orange hierarchy that oversees, or restricts, these parades. Some areas seem to parade more often than others; but there is no formal means of constraint – the decision to parade to another parade is a purely local matter, although one that invariably invokes the idea of tradition.

Providing an explanation for the steady growth in the number of parades is rather more difficult. However, one must be aware that tradition is a vague, and sometimes elastic, concept, especially when it is used as political weapon and when there are no clear records available. Nor do the police statistics provide much help. They do not indicate whether the growth is a regional factor or specific to one organisation, or represents an increase in one particular type of parade. The decentralisation of the loyal orders means that no central records are kept of the total number of parades, while individual members often have no more than a very general idea of the total number of parades in their own areas. Few people are willing even to admit that parade numbers are growing to any extent, and, on the contrary, many loyalists feel that their parading traditions are under threat. Nevertheless, I will offer some suggestions to account for the increase. The decentralised nature of the loyal orders is probably one factor in the growth in the number of parades in recent years. In the past the elaboration of loyalist parades and displays has occurred largely in response to perceived political threats: parading was a way of displaying and affirming communal strength and local dominance. In recent years, and perhaps particularly since the signing of the Anglo-Irish Agreement in 1985, Protestants have felt their constitutional position, and therefore their sense of national identity, more threatened than at any time since partition. One response has been to parade more frequently in local areas, and also to organise more parades for more events: mini-Twelfth and Somme anniversary parades seem to have been two particular growth areas. Another growth area may be in the number of feeder parades to main events, especially as the loyalist communities have become more dispersed in the greater Belfast area: for instance, there has been a steady increase in the total number of parades on the Twelfth in recent years – these have risen from 361 in 1990 to 547 in 1995. It is difficult to account for this increase except as an expansion of local practice.

Another prominent factor has been the emergence of a new type of parades that are organised by the bands themselves, and that fall outside the auspices of the loyal orders. Band parades are held on each Friday and Saturday evening and on many Saturday afternoons throughout the summer months (Bell 1990). These are a distinct part of the wider loyalist culture of parading, but are not related to any formal commemoration. Instead, they are social events: the host band uses the event to raise money, while the visiting bands compete with each other for a range of trophies and prizes that are adjudged to them on their marching and musical abilities. The successful bands are those that go to lots of other parades, and only by visiting other band parades are they likely to attract bands to their own parade. A more recent extension to these social events has been the development of commemorative band parades: these are held both to honour the memory of local paramilitaries and on Armistice Day in November to commemorate the First World War UVF volunteers. Both of these types of event illustrate the close links between some of the bands and the paramilitary groups. While they are not a part of the formal commemorative cycle, these parades nevertheless add another layer to the network of affiliations that is mapped out across the province, and add more figures to the statistics.

Parading is often claimed to be a specific feature of Orange or loyalist culture, and a parade an expression of Orange culture. The implication of this statement is that parading is not a feature of nationalist culture. But the discrepancy between the number of loyalist and nationalist parades can also be related to the broader political history of Ireland. The imbalance of power in the north has historically been used to constrain nationalist and republican parades, while loyalists have come to regard parading as a key element of their culture and an expression of their inalienable civil rights and liberties. Loyalists expect to be able to march where and when they will in their country; but they regard nationalist parades as a threat to public order. Loyalist parades are inevitably presented as cultural and traditional rather than political, while nationalist, and in particular republican, parades are seen as political and therefore provocative and confrontational. Traditional parades are presented as unproblematic and uncontentious, whereas political parades need to be carefully policed and constrained. The opportunity to demand and to exercise the right to march is thus a symbol of the distribution of political power in Northern Ireland. Tradition is invoked wherever possible, while the language of politics is avoided.

Although parading continues to be claimed as the prerogative of the loyalist community, nationalists also have a long history of parading. The nationalist parading bodies, the Ancient Order of Hibernians (AOH) and the Irish National Foresters (INF), as well as the republican movement organise an extensive range of parades throughout the marching season and, as we shall see in the next chapter, in recent years the republican movement has readily taken up the practice of parading as an element of its own culture of remembrance. But it is almost easier to regard these as two distinct marching seasons – a nationalist commemorative calendar that runs in parallel to the loyalist one. The two cycles are only ever vaguely connected: although the loyalist parades over the Easter weekend were begun in the 1930s to counterbalance the republican Easter parades, few people are aware of this, and they are now an accepted part of the loyalist tradition. In practice the marching season consists of two groups of interlocking but distinct cycles (see Table 6.2): loyalist and nationalist groups neither share nor contest any commemorative occasions. Furthermore, the two communities rarely ever parade on the same day: most loyalist parades are held on a Saturday or on a weekday evening, and only church parades (which are treated by Protestants as an extension of the act of worship) are held on a Sunday, which is idealised as a purely religious day. In contrast, Sunday is used by Catholics as the principal day for religious observance, recreation and public demonstrations. Morning Mass is followed by an afternoon of sports, and, on the appropriate occasions, by public commemorations and political demonstrations. The two cycles of commemorations never coincide: the two communities parade on distinct and mutually exclusive anniversaries, and on different days of the week; and furthermore, they rarely even parade over

Date	Loyalist	Nationalist
January 29		Bloody Sunday
March 17		St Patricks Day
Easter Sunday		Easter Rising
Monday	ABOD	
Tuesday	Junior LOL	
May 1st Sunday		Hunger Strikes
June 10	Portadown M-12	
3rd Friday	N. Belfast M-12	
20		Wolf Tone
4th Saturday	W. Belfast M-12	
July 1	Somme Commemorations	
Sat. before 12	Rossnowlagh (Donegal)	
	Scotland	
Sun. before 12	Orange Church Parades	
12	Twelfth – 19 venues	
13	RBI – Scarva	
August 1st Sunday		INF Annual Parade
2nd Sunday		Internment Parades
12	ABOD – Siege of Derry	
	RBI – Newtownbutler	
15		AOH – Lady Day
Last Saturday	RBI – 6 venues	
October		
Last Sunday	Reformation Day	
	Church Services	
December 18	ABOD – Closing Gates	

˙Including all the major parades but with an over-emphasis on Belfast
for the Orange Order mini-Twelfth (M-12) parades.
The exact dates often vary from year to year; most are held on the nearest
weekend.

Table 6.2. The Annual Cycle of Parades in Ulster˙

the same routes or through the same towns. However, the
cumulative effect of the (seemingly) continuous routine of
alternating loyalist and nationalist parades is to raise tension and
to sour community relations, particularly during the most intense
cycle of parades in midsummer.

The Geography of Parading

The significance of parading in the politics of Northern Ireland is as much about geography as it is about history. For loyalists parading is a means of displaying faith and pride in one's culture, and exercising the right to parade is also a means of confirming that Ulster is British. Nationalists on the other hand see loyalist parades as triumphal expressions of superiority, as coat-trailing and an indicator of the continuing differences in communal civil rights. Both perspectives have a validity. Parades are expressions of culture, displays of faith *and* acts of domination; and they are intimately linked to the wider political domain. They work both as a part of an internal dynamic and to consolidate difference. Kertzer (1988:23) has argued that the simultaneous enactment of ritual activities is a widely used mechanism through which peripheral groups are symbolically connected to the centre of political power. Geographically or socially marginal groups mirror the displays of the political or ritual centre, and thereby are able to affirm their place in an idealised unity (see also Vogt and Abel 1977).

In Northern Ireland, the Protestant ideology of individualistic egalitarianism circumvents the need for a permanent centre. On the Twelfth of July and on the Last Saturday there is no unifying centre that determines either the ritual procedure or standards; rather, a multitude of decentralised events incorporate the whole province within their scope. The parades simultaneously connect the entire unionist population of Northern Ireland in the process of public commemoration. But they do so without valuing one group of people, one locality or one parade venue over another: each locality that hosts a parade is on an equal footing with the others. Belfast may host the biggest single event and attract much of the media coverage on the Twelfth; but the city never hosts a major Black or Apprentice Boys parade. All venues attract prominent public speakers from within the loyalist community; but the political heavyweights may choose, or be invited, to appear at any of the many venues. Ian Paisley parades each year with the small Independent Orange Order (although he is not a member), away from the centre of political importance in rural County Antrim. Furthermore, the decentralised nature of the organisation of the parades demands a constant rotation of the venues: this helps to consolidate the unity of Protestant Ulster by drawing a maximum number of people into participation. Because this custom draws on and reconfirms the egalitarian principles of Protestantism, it thereby confirms to the faithful that Ulster remains in essence a Protestant state for a Protestant people. The parades themselves commemorate military victories, but the process of commemoration has become interwoven with the threads of religious faith, and each year these are re-spun across the province.

The Twelfth of July generates the biggest parades and crowds, the most colour and noise as well as the most disruption and protests. It remains the highlight of the parading calendar, THE single event that marks the Ulster identity. The locations of the Twelfth parades are therefore shared out across the province, to include as many towns and villages as possible within the celebrations. The only place apart from Belfast to host an annual Twelfth parade is the staunchly Protestant town of Ballymena in the Democratic Unionist Party heartlands of mid-Antrim. Apart from these two fixed points, each of the six Orange county organisations has its own routine for planning the location and the number of parades in its own area. The 17 venues outside Belfast are divided as follows:

Co. Antrim	6
Co. Armagh	1
Co. Down	4
Co. Fermanagh	1
Co. Londonderry	2
Co. Tyrone	3

In County Armagh the parade rotates on an 11-year cycle around the principal towns of the county. Apart from Fermanagh, the other counties hold larger numbers of smaller parades at which participation is based at the lower district level of organisation. In County Down, for example, there are four parades in which the lodges from Newtownards, Upper Ards, Bangor and Holywood Districts from the north of the county walk together; the 15 Mourne District lodges in the south hold another parade; the eastern Districts of Lecale, Saintfield, Castlewellan, Comber and Bally-nahinch hold another; and the lodges from eight western Districts hold the fourth. By rotating the venues within each group of districts practical matters such as the organisational work and the cost of the day's commemorations are shared around. Large parades are shared around a greater number of venues, and these costs are incurred only rarely. In County Armagh the parade has been held in 12 different venues in the past 26 years, and no district has hosted the event on more than three occasions; whereas in the Mourne District, in which only a small number of villages are represented, the parade returns on a much more regular cycle.

Table 6.3 lists the venues of all the Twelfth parades, by county, in the 26 years of the Troubles. Like Co. Armagh, many towns and villages host the event on a regular cycle: these range from a parade every two years for Kilkeel in the Mourne district to one every 10 years for Ballyclare. The majority of cyclical parade venues host the event on a cycle of between four and eight years. Besides the practicalities that affect the rotating of parades, the scale of the distribution symbolically affirms Ulster's Protestant status. The insistence by the Orangemen that they have a right to walk anywhere in Northern Ireland, and that Ulster is primarily a Protestant province, is annually put into practice, and over a period of years the entire six counties is encapsulated within the recurring and expanding trace of 'traditional' routes. Most towns and villages, regardless of the relative proportions of Protestant and Catholic inhabitants, will eventually host a parade, which will thereby confirm their symbolic 'Protestant' status.

Orangemen claim that being able to walk along traditional routes is an essential feature of their civil rights. Any challenge to this is seen as symptomatic of the creeping influence of Dublin and of the threat of compromise over the status of Northern Ireland. The range of towns and villages that are regularly paraded implies that these rights are being actively maintained, and that nowhere is abandoned as an integral part of Protestant Ulster. In practice it seems more complicated. Some of these venues have not been walked on the Twelfth since the early 1970s, although they are maintained as traditional routes by hosting other parades. In County Fermanagh, an area in which the *Orange Standard* (the Order's monthly paper) regularly claims that Protestants are being hounded out of their farms in the remoter border areas ('ethnically cleansed', in their current language), one-third of the venues have not been used in recent years: the Twelfth parades have been concentrated in fewer, larger and safer towns. However, the Black parades in late August, which, until recently, have not tended to

ANTRIM, 33 venues

Aghalee	4
Ahogill	8
Antrim	6
Aughafatten	1
Ballinderry	4
Ballycastle	8
Ballyclare	3
Ballygelly	1
Ballymena	26
Ballymoney	9
Broughshane	6
Buckna	3
Bushmills	5
Carnlough	4
Carnmoney	2
Carrickfergus	3
Cloughmills	3
Crumlin	2
Cullybackey	10
Derriaghey	4
Dervock	1
Glenarm	5
Glenavy	2
Glengormley	1
Larne	6
Lisburn	4
Mosside	1
Newtownabbey	1
Portglenone	12
Portrush	1
Randalstown	4
Rasharkin	10
Stonyford	1

ARMAGH, 12 venues

Armagh	2
Bessbrook	2
Keady	2
Kilmore	1
Killylea	3
Loughgall	2
Lurgan	2
Markethill	3
N'townhamilton	3
Portadown	3
Richhill	3
Tandragee	2

DOWN, 37 venues

Annalong	6
Ballygowan	1
Ballyhalbert	1
Ballymartin	5
Ballynahinch	5
Banbridge	8
Bangor	5
Braniel	1
Carrowdore	1
Carryduff	1
Castlewellan	2
Comber	5
Crossgar	2
Donacloney	1
Downpatrick	2
Dromara	2
Dundrum	2
Gilford	3
Greyabbey	1
Groomsport	1
Hillsborough	4
Holywood	4
Kilkeel	14
Killyleagh	1
Kircubbin	1
Loughbrickland	33
Millisle	1
Moira	2
Newcastle	1
Newry	2
Newtownards	6
Portaferry	2
Portavogie	1
Rathfriland	3
Saintfield	3
Waringstown	1
Warrenpoint	4

FERMANAGH, 12 venues

Ballinamallard	22
Brookeborough	3
Derrygonnelly	1
Enniskillen	7
Irvinestown	1
Kesh	2
Lisbelaw	3
Lisnaskea	2
Maguiresbridge	3
Newtownbutler	1
Tempo	1

LONDONDERRY, 14 venues

Ballyronan	2
Bellaghy	1
Castledawson	1
Coleraine	7
Garvagh	3
Kilrea	4
Limavady	7
Londonderry	7
Macosquin	2
Maghera	2
Magherafelt	4
Moneymore	4
Portstewart	2
Tobermore	3

TYRONE, 22 venues

Augher	4
Aughnacloy	6
Ballygawley	7
Benburb	4
Beragh	3
Castlecaulfield	44
Castlederg	3
Castlederry	1
Clogher	5
Coagh	3
Cookstown	5
Dromore	3
Dungannon	4
Fintona	2
FiveMileTown	3
Killen	1
N'townstewart	5
Omagh	4
Pomeroy	4
Sixmilecross	2
Stewartstown	4
Strabane	1

Table 6.3. Location and Number of Twelfth Parades, 1968–1994

generate such strong emotions as the Twelfth, continue to be held across a wide range of venues. Smaller venues, such as Claudy, Co. Derry, Sion Mills near Strabane, Moy on the Tyrone–Armagh border and Dromore and Donaghadee in Co. Down, can maintain their traditional status by hosting Black parades on the Last Saturday. Once the wider range of parades and the complex patterns of sharing the venues around are drawn out, the settlements that are voluntarily excluded from the major events of the parading cycle are few indeed.

Nevertheless, there are some. Most of the places that have not hosted a major loyalist parade are on the margins of the province, and have no great symbolic significance to Orangemen. They are either geographically isolated or surrounded by towns and villages that do hold parades, and can thus be overlooked without causing an affront to Orange tradition. Such places include Cushendall and Whitehead on the Antrim coast; Strangford and Ballywalter on the Ards peninsula; Ardglass, Killough and Rostrevor on the South Down coast; Crossmaglen and Middletown on the Armagh border; and Belleek on the Fermanagh border. The towns of Coalisland in Tyrone and Dungiven in Co. Derry are the only other substantial places that have been (relatively) parade-free recently, although Dungiven was the site of major disputes in the 1950s (Bryan 1996; Farrell 1980). All of these are also towns and villages with an overwhelmingly Catholic and nationalist population, and this seems to be discreetly acknowledged as a significant fact by the Orangemen, in spite of the rhetoric of walking where they will. Similarly within Belfast, some nationalist areas that were once paraded, such as the New Lodge and parts of the Falls, have long been abandoned. Part of the concerns of the loyal orders over the growing nationalist protests at their parades is that the areas where they are no longer able to walk freely will only increase. The fight to maintain traditional routes in areas with a large Catholic population is an attempt to deny or to ignore the demographic and political changes that have been taking place in Northern Ireland in the past few decades.

Although some nationalist towns or areas do seem to be acknowledged as inappropriate venues by the loyal orders, an overwhelming or dominant Catholic population need not be regarded as a deterrent if the Order regards it as part of a traditional Orange route. Keady in Co. Armagh and Pomeroy in Co. Tyrone, both of which have an estimated 95 per cent Catholic population, have hosted controversial Twelfth parades in recent years (*Belfast Telegraph* 11.7.89). In 1991 a judicial review was held at the last minute on an RUC decision to authorise the parade through Pomeroy, an event that occurs every 7 years. After permission to allow the parade was finally given, the local Orangemen agreed to amend their route slightly to avoid an area that was described as 'predominately nationalist' (*BT* 11.7.91, 12.7.91). Still, a massive security operation was mounted to protect the estimated 10,000 marchers. In most similar cases the RUC have been prepared to authorise Orange parades even in the face of stiff local opposition, and have emphasised the Order's own arguments that the practice is traditional (a distinct legal category until 1987) and that it is not meant to cause offence or that the parade will not take very long or cause much disruption. On such occasions an appeal is often made to the memory of previous parades that have passed peacefully or to nostalgic recollections of those days, before the Troubles, when Catholics enjoyed watching the Orangemen pass by. Until recently only rarely have the opponents' arguments been upheld, and usually some form of compromise that favours the Orangemen has been enforced.

Parades in Conflict

This is not an unchanging scenario, however: the disputes in Keady and Pomeroy marked the beginnings of a more serious contest over the right to parade, which has counterposed this civil right with the right not to suffer unwanted parades. The dispute reflects how parading is seen from two distinct perspectives. As I have described, the unionist community see the parades as an expression of their civil rights, a celebration of their culture and a confirmation of their constitutional status; whereas nationalists regard the (seemingly) constant parades as triumphalist reminders of their second-class status. The earliest signs of the present dispute began with disputes over loyalist parades in Castlewellan and Downpatrick in the early 1980s and in Portadown in 1985 and 1986 (Bryan, Fraser and Dunn 1995). These resulted in a change to the law, and some restriction on the rights of traditional parades; but the balance of political will remained with the Orangemen, as the cases of Keady and Pomeroy illustrate. However, since the

ceasefires of 1994 the issue of the right to parade has become a
major political issue.

Residents' groups opposing Orange parades began to appear
in 1995, in Belfast, Bellaghy, Derry and Portadown, and over the
next year similar groups were formed in other nationalist towns
and villages. They have demanded that parades be re-routed away
from their areas, or that the loyal orders seek the consent of the
residents before trying to parade. The loyal orders have generally
been unwilling either to change the route of their parades or to
negotiate with the residents, whom they regard as little more than
a Sinn Féin front. Mediation has largely been unsuccessful and
compromise rare; instead, the dispute has brought to a head the
divergent attitudes of the two communities (see Jarman and Bryan
1996; Montgomery and Whitten 1995; Pat Finucane Centre 1995,
1996). In July 1996 the decision by the police to ban an Orange
church parade from walking along the nationalist Garvaghy Road
in Portadown led to several days of loyalist road-blocks and
rioting. When the police reversed their decision in the face of even
more massive public disorder, the nationalist community reacted
in a similar way. The dispute polarised the two communities in a
way that had rarely been seen before, even during the height of
the Troubles; the political middle ground disappeared; and there
was widespread speculation of a return to paramilitary violence.
In the event the two sides pulled back, although the protests
against parades continued, and the dispute escalated on a slow
fuse with a campaign of consumer boycotts, intimidation, sporadic
arson attacks, increases in residential segregation, the picketing
of Catholic churches and a general rise in tension. The government
belatedly announced a review of the law and decision-making
process surrounding the rights to parade; but this was regarded
by many on both sides as too little, too late. As I write, the review
body is just beginning its work.

The crisis illustrates the continued symbolic and political
significance that is given to the right to parade, to particular parade
routes, to the importance of parading for geographical and
communal identity, and the difficulties of balancing conflicting
perceptions of those rights. But it would be wrong to see 1996 as
merely a cyclical re-enactment of 1969 – many things have
changed: too many for some, not enough for others. In 1996 it was
a confident and assertive nationalist community that confronted
the loyal orders, and although they were angry at what was seen

as the playing of the Orange card in Portadown and the capitulation of the state to the threat of violence, nationalists are more
readily able to assert their own communal identity than a generation ago. While the loyal orders feel threatened by the demands
to give up or change their traditions of parading, the nationalist
community have readily asserted their own rights to parade. A
little-publicised feature of the Troubles has been the way in which
the nationalist community, and in particular the republican
movement, have used public parades to assert their growing
power and to extend their tradition of commemorations; we turn
to these parades next.

Watching I: Edenderry, Twelfth 1995.

Watching II: Lower Falls, Internment Parade August 1993.

Watching III: East Belfast Somme Parade, July 1993.

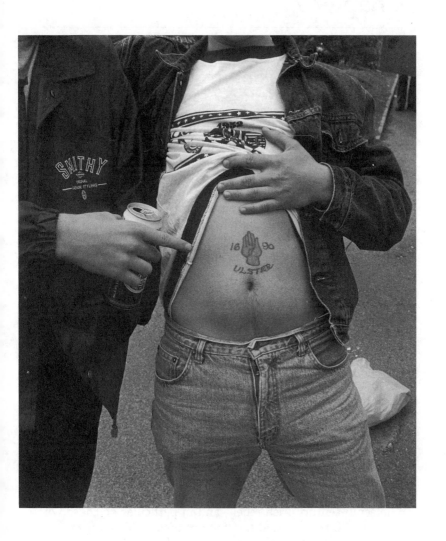

Watching IV: Londonderry, August 1992.

Chapter 7

Our Day Will Come – Parading Irish Nationalism

Protest parades supported by members of the Catholic community were the spark that set off the Troubles in 1968. They proved contentious because they made explicit and challenged the divisions within Northern Irish society. However, these civil rights parades were not the only public events supported by the nationalist community: commemorative parades are still a prominent feature of the Catholic and nationalist social calendar, although they rarely achieve the same scale of publicity as the loyalist parades. Three bodies organise nationalist parades: the Ancient Order of Hibernians, the Irish National Foresters and the republican movement. The AOH and INF date back to the nineteenth century; they are survivors of the widespread network of fraternal societies that was found among working people in Ireland (and Britain) at this time (Buckley n.d.; Buckley and Anderson 1988). Both groups are broadly nationalist and support the ideal of a United Ireland, but neither offers any support for the current armed struggle of the IRA. Instead they ground their ideals in the nationalist practices and heroes of the past. The visual displays of the AOH espouse the ideal of an Irish nationalism inseparable from the Roman Catholic religion and valorise the military heroes of the sixteenth and seventeenth centuries who fought their wars premised on distinctions of faith, which pre-dated a politicised national identity. The INF in turn draw on a later tradition, on the aims and ideals of the eighteenth- and nineteenth-century Irish rebels, and in particular on those who were able to transcended the 'faith of their fathers' for broader political ideals. Both groups operate today as interest groups within the constitutional political field, and although they may appear marginalised within the dominant political discourse about the future of Northern Ireland, they provide an important indicator of the variations of emphasis within contemporary nationalism. Sinn Féin, in contrast is a legal political party and, as the most public face of the republican movement, is openly involved in public commemorative parades in a way that other political parties are not. The republican movement is broader than Sinn Féin, and includes individuals and groups who distinguish themselves from the party. Republican commemorations are often organised under the auspices of the broader movement or by named local groupings, rather than advertised as a Sinn Féin event. Their commemorations acknowledge a debt to late-eighteenth-century Irish Nationalism, and emphasise the roots of their movement in the events of Easter 1916; but the majority of their public commemorations are linked to events that are the product of the contemporary Troubles and are seen as a continuation of the unfinished tradition.

The Hibs

The Hibernians are the nearest Catholic equivalent to the Orange Institution; they are sometimes described as 'Green Orangemen'. Membership is restricted to Roman Catholics, and much of their public ritual, regalia and displays are similar in form and style to Orange practices. The Hibs claim an ancestry dating back to the sixteenth and seventeenth centuries (*Hibernian Journal* 1967), but the contemporary organisation began in the USA and established itself as the defender of rural Catholic interest in the middle of the last century. For a time the AOH remained a secret organisation, and membership was forbidden by the Roman Catholic Church. This ban was only lifted in 1904; but by 1901 the AOH already had an estimated 8,000 members, with the bulk of its support coming from Ulster. Under the influence of Joe Devlin, Nationalist MP for West Belfast, the Hibernians grew rapidly,and became a powerful, conservative force within constitutional nationalism. They organised and managed a wide range of social events and insurance schemes, and this helped to consolidate their base in urban Ulster. However, after the Easter Rising of 1916, support swung away from constitutional nationalism towards Sinn Féin, and with partition the influence of the AOH declined rapidly. The friendly society side of its work continued; but with the establish-ment of state insurance schemes in both Ireland and Britain the role of the AOH declined further still. In Ulster it has survived as an extra-parliamentary body that has espoused an increasingly conservative and Catholic nationalism (Boyce 1991; Foy 1976; Hepburn 1996; Phoenix 1994).

In recent years the AOH has picked up in numbers, and now claims around 12,000 members for its benefit services. Active membership remains strongest in Counties Antrim, Derry and Tyrone, and in the Irish border counties of Donegal, Cavan and Louth. Many branches have a hall or club that is used for social functions, and thereby continues to provide a necessary resource in many towns and rural areas. AOH divisions are largely made up of older men, although a younger membership continues to be drawn in through participation in the marching bands, which remain a part of the Hibernian structure. These bands have developed in a different direction from loyalist bands: instead of the paramilitary iconography and uniforms they have adopted the styles of American marching bands. They are often fronted by a dozen or more young women or girls, who wear majorette-style uniforms and twirl pom-poms. These lead a small band of accordionists or flautists, while an often elderly bass drummer beats out a gentle rhythm. Many of the tunes are similar to those played at Orange parades, but their performance has none of the machismo of the loyalist bandsmen.

AOH divisions hold church parades at various times of the year, but their main parades are held on St Patrick's day (17 March) and, Our Lady's day (15 August). In recent years the Hibernians have held a single parade in Northern Ireland, and sometimes one in County Donegal, on each day. The style of the parades is broadly similar to rural Orange parades, but the major difference is in the scale of the events: Hibernian parades are small affairs, although they still attract an enthusiastic audience. They tend to be restricted to the afternoon rather than lasting all day, and usually they involve only a short walk to a Field and then a brief platform ceremony, without any religious service (mass is taken privately in the morning), before breaking up into a social event. There is no return march. At Draperstown, in March 1993, the procession took barely an hour to walk from one end of the small town to the Field at the other end, and the platform proceedings were being completed as the final band arrived. A republican band who attempted to join on the end of the parade arrived only as most people were leaving the Field. The rest of the afternoon was spent in drinking and socialising in the bars on the main street. Through the 1950s and 1960s, before the Troubles began, Hibernian commemorations were used to make major political speeches from the platform; but nowadays, although mild calls for peace and unification are made, the platform is rarely used for major statements, and anyway the Hibernians are no longer a significant political force.

At the beginning of the Troubles, in 1971, the AOH imposed a voluntary ban on their members parading, which was only lifted in 1975. However, it was never fully supported by members. On St Patrick's day 1971 a new banner was unfurled at Ballerin, Co. Derry, amid protests at the decision to cancel the formal parades, and some form of public commemoration was held each year while the ban was in force (*Irish News (IN)* 18.3.1971). In 1974, AOH divisions paraded in at least seven venues, and the following year when the ban was lifted parades were held at twenty centres across Antrim, Derry and Tyrone (*IN* 18.3.1974, 18.3.1975). In 1978 an estimated 10,000 people attended the parade in Kilrea, and heard the resolution call for 'the peaceful reunification of Ireland' (*IN* 16.8.78). Since this time the scale of the proceedings has dropped to, at most, 20 divisions parading at a single location. Hibernian parades have generally remained peaceful and uncontentious, although sporadic clashes occurred at the August parades through the 1980s when the republican hunger strikes and the Anglo-Irish Agreement generated greater tension. An uninvited band dressed in paramilitary-style clothing were blamed for disturbances at Draperstown in 1980, and again at Magherafelt in 1984 and at Ballerin the following year. On each of these occasions the trouble began as the RUC moved into remove 'offensive' Irish tricolours. As a response numerous tricolours were carried on the parade in 1986, and one was flown from the platform. The AOH may be a conservative body, but the tricolour remains a potent symbol. In that year the platform speakers renewed their call for a United Ireland; but they also spoke against violence and for improved relations with the Protestants (*IN* 16.8.80, 16.8.84, 16.8.85, 16.8.86).

As already illustrated, the segregation of the two communities extends to the practice of parading, and the Hibernians have been largely reduced to marching in the gaps left by the Orangemen. Despite their conservatism, the Hibernians were often regarded with antagonism by loyalists, and their parades were accepted only in areas with a strong nationalist presence. Of the 21 AOH venues since 1969, 11 have not hosted a major Twelfth parade since the Troubles began (Table 7.1). These 21 venues are overwhelmingly in Derry and Tyrone, the western counties of Ulster. The AOH have not paraded in Fermanagh since the Troubles began, and only once in County Armagh and twice in County Down, and these were all in recent years. While this pattern also reflects the strengths of the Hibernians, whose membership is strongest in the west of the province, where Catholics are in a majority, it is also part of their strategy of trying to stand outside the conflict and trying not to provoke trouble. This has only worked to an extent, for when Hibernians have been felt by loyalists to be stepping out of their own areas and parading in or near loyalist towns, trouble has ensued.

In 1979 violent scuffles broke out when loyalists protested as AOH members used Larne as a point of arrival for their parade at:

Draperstown (Derry)	6 (0)
Coalisland (Tyrone)	4 (0)
Dungiven (Derry)	4 (0)
Maghera (Derry)	4 (2)
Toome (Antrim)	3 (0)
Carnlough (Antrim)	2 (4)
Kilrea (Derry)	2 (4)
Magherafelt (Derry)	2 (4)
Rasharkin (Antrim)	2 (10)
Swatragh (Derry)	2 (0)
Ardboe (Tyrone)	1 (0)
Armoy (Antrim)	1 (0)
Ballerin (Derry)	1 (0)
Ballycastle (Antrim)	1 (8)
Bellaghy (Derry)	1 (1)
Blackwaterstown (Armagh)	1 (0)
Cushendall (Antrim)	1 (0)
Derry	1 (7)
Downpatrick (Down)	1 (2)
Dungannon (Tyrone)	1 (4)
Feeny (Derry)	1 (0)
Garvagh (Derry)	1 (3)
Newry (Down)	1 (2)

Table 7.1. Venues of Major AOH parades since 1969 (Twelfth of July parades in same period in brackets)

Carnlough; a Hibernian band was stoned when passing through Portglenone in 1982; and at Garvagh in 1985 the AOH coaches, were stoned after the parade (*BT* 15.8.79; *IN* 18.3.1982, 16.8.85). Scuffles and stone-throwing again broke out in Armoy in 1989, as loyalist women heckled the first Hibernian parade in the town for thirty-five years (*IN* 16.8.89). Loyalists were clearly unwilling to see nationalists of any hue parading through their towns. But more recently, with the Hibernians marginalised by republicanism, their parades have not attracted the opposition of previous years, and they have been able to march in a wider range of locations. County Armagh was used as a parade venue in August 1987 for the first time since the Troubles began, and in the last few years the AOH have returned to parading in some of the larger towns, albeit those with a large nationalist population. Downpatrick was the August venue in 1992 and Newry in 1994, while in 1993 they were able to hold their first-ever parade in Derry, a city with a large AOH membership and social club. The AOH parade was held the day after the Apprentice Boys celebrated the raising of the siege of Derry; but both parades passed peacefully.

The Foresters

The Irish National Foresters Friendly Society was formed in 1877 after a split within the Ancient Order of Foresters by a group of 'more nationally-minded' members (Buckley 1987:53). The precipitating incident was concern over the continuation of their annual parade (John Campbell, pers. comm.). By 1911 they were the largest friendly society in Ireland, and were widely established in smaller towns and rural areas, where they provided sickness benefits and funeral expenses. In 1919 they had at least nine branches in Belfast and many more in Ulster, where membership was strongest in the southern counties of Armagh, Down and in east Tyrone, a bias that continues today. The Foresters are a nationalist organisation: their 1921 annual convention pledged allegiance to the Dáil and the Irish state. They are non-sectarian, but membership is restricted to those who are Irish by birth or descent, and this has meant that they largely draw on the Catholic population. The names of the branches in Dublin and the north of Ireland in existence in 1919 shows that they drew inspiration extensively from the pantheon of heroes of Irish nationalism:

Sarsfield, Parnell, Brian Boru, Napper Tandy, Thomas Russell, Robert Emmett, William Orr and John Mitchel all had branches named after them, and Catholic saints and religious leaders were also extremely popular.

The partition of Ireland and the introduction of state insurance schemes has affected the size of the membership, but the organisation continues to provide insurance and, as with the AOH, many branches of the INF have their own halls and run social centres. The Foresters also uphold the tradition of friendly societies as parading bodies – perhaps the last to do so. In the 1960s they were a more integral part of the broader nationalist movement and paraded in Belfast on St Patrick's day and at Easter commemorations. Local parades are still held on St Patrick's day; but their main parade is held at the time of their national convention, at the end of July or the beginning of August. This convention usually alternates between venues in the north and in the Republic. In recent years these parades have been held at Ballyholland, Co. Down in 1995; Hilltown, Co. Down in 1994; and Lurgan, Co. Armagh in 1992. INF parades are similar in scale to those of the AOH, with some 15 branches represented by their banners. Their regalia and bands are comparable to those of the Hibernians, and the parade is a similar short affair, although it is held earlier in the day and the route takes the members to a local church for Sunday mass in the midst of the weekend convention.

The Hibernians and Foresters parades are very similar in style, form and scale, but they draw on two distinct strands of ideals and attitudes within the nationalist community. This variation is not apparent from the rhetoric of the parade as a performance, but only becomes apparent through consideration of the visual displays of flags and banners. As with the loyalist groups, an analysis of the parades as parades can only tell part of the story. These parades appear similar to their Orange counterparts, of which they seem to be little more than a simplified or atrophied version, since they are performed on a small scale and reduced to a single location. But these nationalist parades no longer evoke the war-like rhetoric of the Orange parades: the drums do not beat as fiercely, the uniforms have none of the paramilitary overtones, and the parade does not re-present or re-create the battle march. Orange and Green parades are similar in style; but they are not mirror images, since the rhetoric of the respective performances is different. They nevertheless draw on common practice, which serves to reaffirm the unity of a scattered community and to map that identity over a wide terrain. Although this sense of communal territory is much reduced in size compared with the Protestant ideal, it still exists in those spaces that loyalists acknowledge as outside their domain. It is a parallel spatialised identity interlocked with, but rarely intersecting with, Protestant Ulster. In some cases – Derry and Lurgan are recent examples – both communities have paraded through a town or city in the same marching season, but not on the same day; and they never occupy the same routes, the same streets or the same public spaces. The loyalists claim the central area, and nationalists are forced to skirt the boundaries. Even when the town comprises equal proportions of both communities, there is a division and segregation rather than a sharing of space. And, as we have seen, nationalists are not welcomed if they attempt to parade outside their designated areas. Loyalists are only prepared to cede space on the margins of the Protestant state.

The Rising of Republicans

Constitutional nationalist parades have proved to be largely uncontentious in recent years, but republican commemorations, which perpetuate the memory of people who opposed the very existence of the Northern Irish state, have regularly provoked the wrath of loyalists and have been subjected to heavy policing and security constraints. The importance of groups like the Hibernians and Foresters has declined as the republican movement has become more prominent in public street protests and commemorations; and, while the AOH have avoided challenges to loyalists over the issue of parading, republicans have been keen to seize on the issue to confront the inequalities between towns and streets where loyalists are allowed to parade and where nationalists are not. The recent Hibernian parades in Derry and Downpatrick must therefore be viewed within the context of more militant action by supporters of the republican cause, who insist on their equal right to parade where they will.

There are five major annual republican commemorations. The birth of Theobold Wolfe Tone, a leading figure in the United Irishmen rising of 1798, is celebrated in June at Bodenstown, Co. Kildare; the Easter Rising of 1916 is commemorated with parades throughout Ireland; Bloody Sunday, 30 January 1972, is marked by a parade in Derry; the 1981 Hunger Strikes by parades in early May; and the anniversary of the introduction of Internment in 1971 is commemorated each year on the second Sunday of August.

The Easter Rising is the most important of these commemorations: this event led to the formation of an independent Irish state, but also left the problem of a partitioned island. Sinn Féin and the IRA claim the inheritance of the leaders of the Easter Rising and the right to complete the process of removing the British state presence in Ireland. The day commemorates the heroic failure of 1916; but by extension it also commemorates all those men and women who have died for the ideal of an independent Ireland. The Rising began on Easter Monday, 24 April 1916, when a heterogeneous group of Catholic nationalists, revolutionary socialists and Fenian republicans took over key buildings in Dublin and proclaimed an Independent Irish Republic. It failed to attract mass support, and the city was heavily bombarded by the British forces for nearly a week before the rebels surrendered. The widespread destruction hardened public opinion against the rebels and, although the Rising had generated more determined resistance than previous attempts to oust the British in 1798, 1803, 1848 and 1867, it appeared to have achieved no more success. However, the British Government were determined to make an example of the leaders, and at dawn on 3 May Padraic Pearse, Thomas MacDonagh and Tom Clarke were executed. Over the next ten days, twelve more of the rebel leadership were shot (Beckett 1981; Jackson 1947; Kee 1989b; Lyons 1973).

This prolonged cycle of executions transformed the public reaction to the Easter Rising: they generated immense sympathy for the dead and anger at the British government, both in Ireland and across America. Martyred to the cause of an independent Ireland, the executions produced what Ruth Dudley-Edwards has called the 'triumph of failure' (1977). In 1918, at the first post-war General Election, Sinn Féin, which had previously been an insignificant political force, won 73 of 105 Irish seats, and the constitutional nationalist Irish Parliamentary Party was almost wiped out. After independence, the Rising and its leaders were widely commemorated and celebrated as the inspiration of the new state. In the newly created Northern Ireland, small commemorations were held in nationalist communities, but widespread public displays of support for Irish nationalism were not welcome. The 1922 Special Powers Act and, from 1954, the Flags and Emblems Act were used to constrain nationalist displays; but bans were often ignored. Instead, the parades were effectively confined to strongly nationalist towns like Newry or Armagh or to the Falls Road, where the tricolour flew freely out of sight of unionist eyes.

At the 50th anniversary in 1966, parades were held in towns across the north, and at a special commemorative rally in Belfast an estimated 50,000 people lined the route to watch the representatives of the Trades Council, trade unions, the INF, the Gaelic Athletic Association, numerous nationalist clubs and members of the Old IRA parade to Casement Park (*IN* 18.4.1966). Since the onset of the Troubles, Easter has became more closely identified as a republican, rather than a more generally nationalist, commemoration. In Dublin, the state has scaled down its support for the occasion; but it remains the most widely observed anniversary, and is marked by parades and assemblies all across Ireland. A divided Ireland is symbolically reunited each Easter as people parade simultaneously across the country to remember 1916.

In Belfast the main parade, organised by the National Graves Association, is held on the Falls Road on Easter Sunday. Republicans assemble in the early afternoon at the junction of Beechmount Avenue and the Falls Road for the parade to Milltown cemetery. The area is decked with orange, white and green bunting; but the main visual impact is made by two murals that flank the assembly point. The larger of these depicts a manacled hand clenching an Easter lily over a map of Ireland; above it a phoenix rises from a flaming GPO, and in the corners are the shields of the four provinces of Ireland. The mural surrounds a small plaque commemorating local IRA volunteers who have died in the Troubles, while on the back yard wall are the unacknowledged words of Padraic Pearse: 'The fools, the fools, they have left us our Fenian dead, and while Ireland holds these graves, Ireland unfree shall never be at peace.' This quotation is taken from a speech that Pearse made in 1915 at the funeral in Dublin of O'Donovan Rossa, and prophetically refers to the importance of the rebel dead as a continuing inspiration for the living to continue the struggle for Irish unity. Each Easter the commemoration of the sacrificial execution of the leaders of the Rising condenses within it a general acknowledgement of all those who have given, and continue to give, their lives for Ireland.

The parade itself begins around two o'clock. The walk, of about a mile, up the Falls Road to Milltown cemetery takes half an hour. A large crowd of onlookers gather at the departure point and a smaller number of people watch the procession, a few thousand strong, pass by. The parade is led by a colour party wearing uniform black jacket, trousers or skirt and white shirt. At the head is the Irish tricolour, followed in the second rank by James Connolly's Starry Plough, the sunburst flag of the *Fianna*, the republican youth wing, and a blue flag with a gold trim bearing the words *Óglaigh na hÉireann*, the Irish name of the IRA. Finally, the flags of the four provinces of Ireland. No other flags or banners are carried. The colour party is followed by a pipe band, and several other bands march within the body of the procession. At the republican plot in Milltown there are two memorials: the original cross was erected in 1912 to commemorate the Fenians of 1867; next to it is the contemporary County Antrim memorial. Two interlocking blocks, which form a cross when viewed from above, list all IRA volunteers and Sinn Féin members from the area who have been killed in the various campaigns since 1916, along with the names of known dead of the United Irishman rebellion of 1798, two men killed in the 1803 rising, and the Fenians of 1867. In front of the memorial a small platform is erected for the speakers; people assemble around the republican plot, careful to avoid adjacent graves. Reporters and camera crews occupy much of the space near to the platform.

The proceedings follow a form that dates back at least as far as the 1966 anniversary, and probably to well before this (*IN* 11.4.1966). A general introduction and welcome is followed by a reading of the 1916 Proclamation of Independence and then a decade of the Rosary. Wreaths are then laid by, or on behalf of, Sinn Féin, the IRA, republican prisoners, the Gaelic Athletic Association and the National Graves Association. This is followed by the playing of a lament by a solitary piper, as all flags are slowly lowered. The proceedings end with a number of speeches: Easter is used not only to encourage the resolve of republican supporters but also to make public statements in response to the broader political situation. In 1993 Tom Hartley, the Sinn Féin chair, focused on the desire for peace and stressed the need for dialogue as a means to this end. In 1994 Gerry Adams spoke as part of the moves towards peace following the Downing Street Declaration of December 1993, and in 1995 Martin McGuinness spoke in Belfast for the first time. Speeches are also made by a representative of the IRA: these reiterate their support for Sinn Féin and their resolve to continue the armed struggle. The speaker is hidden from view, but the numerous RUC officers in the vicinity make no attempt to stop the speech or to intercept the speaker; nobody attempts to take photographs during the speech, and all television cameras are conspicuously turned away from the platform.

The commemoration ends up with a request for people to depart quietly and with respect, but also with a reminder to ignore the 'other parade' coming up the Falls Road to the cemetery. This is a reference to the Easter commemoration of the Workers' Party which follows the Sinn Féin event. The Workers' Party were the product of a split in the republican movement in 1969. The Official IRA favoured a more political approach to the conflict, while the Provisionals claimed the inheritance of the armed struggle (Bowyer Bell 1989; Coogan 1987). The Workers' Party still claim their right to the inheritance of 1916, and hold a similar style of parade to their memorial in Milltown, although their commemoration is a much smaller affair. They follow the same array of flags as Sinn Féin, lacking only the *Óglaigh na hÉireann* flag, and hold a ceremony with a similar mixture of acts of remembrance and political rhetoric. The other smaller republican groups, Republican Sinn Féin and the Irish Republican Socialist Party, hold similar events on Easter Sunday.

Orange commemorations, celebrating collective triumph, maintain a public unity even though diverse opinions and ideals are on display; but the nationalist movement, whose commemorations are rooted in bitter memories of sacrifice and failure, has been unable to maintain any formal unity. As one group has voted for compromise and agreed to work within the available political framework, another group has always been ready to claim the inheritance of the armed struggle and the right to transform the system through violence. Divided in their strategy for the future, they have also become divided in their claims to the past. But the Easter anniversary also illustrates how it has proved more difficult to reject the symbolism of Irish nationalism than the tactics: even conservative groups must acknowledge the powerful presence of the armed struggle, even though they no longer publicly celebrate it. This tendency has been accelerated during the Troubles, as constitutional groups have sought to distance themselves from the tactics of the IRA while retaining a claim on nationalist history.

Each of the nationalist groups has tended towards independent and exclusive public occasions while maintaining their claim to a common heritage. Although neither the Ancient Order of Hibernians nor the Irish National Foresters publicly commemorate the Easter Rising, they retain references to it on their banners carried on other parades. Amidst the portraits of Saints, Popes, early Irish heroes and nineteenth-century constitutionalist politicians, the Rising retains a foothold for the military tradition within all fractions of the nationalist movement.

Easter remains the most prominent and widespread commemoration in the republican calendar; but the practice of celebrating the desire for national and political aspirations through commemoration of sacrificial death is much more widespread. As well as the major anniversaries, numerous smaller events are held across Ireland throughout the year as republicans gather to remember individuals who have died in the struggle for Ireland. These local commemorations extend the tradition of the Easter memorials, and the contemporary struggle is thus personalised and exemplified through the actions of individuals. The frequent repetition of public remembrance ensures that the resolve to continue the struggle is maintained. To give up or to compromise without achieving substantial gains would mean that these men and women had died in vain. The ritual of the Easter commemoration and the names on the County Antrim memorial allude to a sense of an unbroken chain of struggle, which extends from the rebels of 1798 through to the most recent IRA volunteer interred in Milltown – a continuum that each generation must honour and extend until Ireland is free.

The 1981 Hunger Strikes have been adopted into the collective republican memory as the modern equivalent of the Easter Rising. The prolonged repetition of deaths between May and August was a traumatic experience that was spread across the entire nationalist community, both spatially and politically (Feldman 1991; O'Malley 1990). As well as firing the embers of bitterness, the new republican martyrs became a spur to a new course of action once the potential power of the ballot box had been realised with the election of Bobby Sands as MP for Fermanagh and South Tyrone (Clarke 1987). All the dead Hunger Strikers have their own local commemorations, but the event is remembered specifically through Bobby Sands, the leader of the strike and the first to die. Sands has become the clearest symbol of the determination of the republican community to continue their struggle to the end.

In contrast, the other major commemorations of recent history, Internment and Bloody Sunday, celebrate a more generalised and depersonalised nationalist community. They have come to signify the defiance and resolve of the Catholic population as a whole, and exemplify collective strength drawn from adversity rather than individual sacrifice and resistance. The British government introduced internment on 9 August 1971 in response to the increase in violence and to unionist pressure. Over 300 Catholic men were imprisoned without trial or charge on suspicion of being involved in the paramilitary violence (De Baroid 1990; McCann 1980). But instead of clamping down on violence, the crudely blunt instrument of internment was

> a disaster as a police measure, alienating many of the still neutral Catholic middle class, in no way damaging the structure of the Officials or the Provos, and to an increasingly fascinated world revealing the sectarian nature of justice – British justice supposedly – in Northern Ireland. As a symbolic victory for the Loyalists it was an equal disaster. Their good advice had led Northern Ireland into open rebellion and chaos and general disrepute (Bowyer Bell 1989:381).

Widespread protests followed, and on 30 January an estimated 10,000 people joined an anti-Internment demonstration organised by the Civil Rights Association in Derry. Their route into the city centre was barricaded by the British army. Some of the demonstrators sought to break down the barriers, and a flurry of stones and bottles was met with rubber bullets. Then, without warning, members of the Parachute Regiment opened fire with live rounds, and within a few minutes 13 unarmed civilians were shot dead. Another man died later from wounds received (McCann 1992). Internment and Bloody Sunday confirmed to the nationalist population that the British government was no longer a neutral player. It was clearly seen as on the side of the unionists. These actions were perceived as random attacks on the Catholic community as a whole, rather than aimed specifically at republicans or those politically involved. Innocent men were arrested and held without charge, and, it was later accepted, many were tortured (McGuffin 1973, 1974). Those who protested against this injustice were summarily shot dead. To add insult to injury, the British

Government have continued to offer justifications for their actions rather than apologies. These two events were central to the widespread alienation of the mass of the Catholic population from the British army and the Government, and as a result of Internment and Bloody Sunday membership of the IRA and support for the republican movement grew rapidly.

The first anniversary of Internment established what was to become the customary pattern for the day – a march along the Falls Road, followed by a political rally, while the evening degenerated into rioting or stone-throwing. By 1975 Sinn Féin had taken over the organisation of the Belfast rally, a parallel process to the republican take-over of the Easter commemorations and, for many years, St Patrick's day. As the scale of the violence increased the republican movement became the principal focus for all nationalist protest. Internment parades were moved to the Sunday nearest the anniversary, and the event was used to publicise the wider political demands of the republican movement. Calls were made for the withdrawal of British troops and support for the Republican prisoners in their campaign for political status was repeated annually; members of NORAID from the USA regularly attended; GLC councillors came from London; and armed members of the IRA made regular appearances.

But from the mid-1980s the style of commemoration was changed: the West Belfast Community Festival was organised in the week before the rally with the intention of generating positive emotions rather than the customary violent reaction to soldiers and police. The festival has since developed as a wide mixture of political debates and meetings and concerts of music, drama and dance. The commemoration of Internment has became part of a broader celebration of the 'culture of resistance' and an exhibition of the strength and vitality of the nationalist community (Sluka 1995).

As part of this wider transformation, the Internment anniversary was used to challenge some of the constraints placed on the location of republican events. In Belfast the main nationalist commemorations had been historically confined to the extended network of Catholic estates in west Belfast, centred on the Falls Road. Road-blocks and army patrols secured all roads in and out of the nationalist area, which was effectively segregated from the larger city for the day. Republicans were allowed to celebrate in public, but only in what were regarded as their areas, not in the city as a whole. The city centre remained a no-go area. From 1990 determined efforts were made to carry republican parades and demonstrations into the heart of the city, and in August 1991 a march from east Belfast was able to parade past the City Hall *en route* to the Falls Road. In 1993, in spite of protests from unionist politicians, the main Internment day demonstration was allowed to rally in front of the City Hall for the first time (*An Phoblacht* 12.8.1993). This parade began at Twinbrook, the south-west extremity of the nationalist area and the home of Bobby Sands, and gradually accumulated more people as it wove its way along the axis of nationalist Belfast, through Andersonstown and down the Falls Road. It was led into the city, previously the preserve of loyalist parades, by Sinn Féin leaders Gerry Adams and Martin McGuinness, and the rally was held directly in front of the statue of Queen Victoria. Throughout the late eighties the Internment rallies had only been attracting crowds of 3,000–4,000; but Sinn Féin estimated that a crowd of up to 15,000 attended the rally in 1993. The heart of Belfast having once been breached, City Hall has now become the annual venue for the Internment rally.

Easter remains the pre-eminent commemoration of the republican community, but the Internment celebrations have developed into a new form of commemoration. Rather than remembering acts of individual sacrifice, of violence and death, Internment has come to be focused away from the past and instead directed towards the future. The commemoration of collective outrage has been transformed and transcended into a festival that celebrates the collective strength and vitality of the wider nationalist community; it balances the memory of violence with music and drama. Easter and the Hunger Strike parade focus on the determination to continue the fight and the readiness for self-sacrifice, while Internment has become a time to celebrate the creative aspects of society that allow the republican movement to look forward with optimism. This division can be dated at least back to last century, when the more overt revolutionary politics of republicanism were enmeshed with the cultural nationalism of the Gaelic revival, with its emphasis on the creative spirit of the Irish. The more violent political tactics of the twentieth century have tended to overwhelm these aspects of the republican movement, which have only surfaced with any verve in parallel with Sinn Féin's greater emphasis on their electoral political campaign.

Two Forms of Remembering

Republican and loyalist organisations have a broad similarity in their use of public parades for commemorative events, but there is a substantial difference in the structure and form of the parade between the two communities. In contrast to the military-style presentation of loyalist events, with their rigid separation of participants and spectators and the division of participants into distinct, independent groups, the republican parades are much more open affairs. There is little formality, no structured dress code, and no separation by gender or age. Anyone can participate in a republican parade. People join in as individuals and as supporters of a common ideal, rather than as part of a formal group. Although both commemorations include brash paramilitary-type bands, republican parades do not move with the same militarised step as those of the loyalists. Instead, they have a more relaxed and informal air about them. The crowd that follows the colour party includes large numbers of women and girls and even babies in prams, who are largely excluded from participating in Orange parades. Loyalist parades are essentially triumphal expressions of a collective determination, a celebration of strength in unity and in brotherhood, while republican parades commemorate the continued resolve in defeat and the determination to carry on the fight. The followers mourn the dead, draw strength from their sacrifice, and show that their heroes did not die in vain. This suggests something of the two historical traditions that are being drawn on in the contemporary commemorative practices: women are always sidelined by the march to war, but are always prominent at the resulting funeral ceremonies.

The loyalist style of parades, and those of the AOH and INF, can be traced to the paramilitary traditions of the Volunteers in the late eighteenth century. These were formalised and redefined in the emerging and combative sectarian politics of the nineteenth century to emphasise the power and unity of the community. Republican commemorations draw more heavily on the tradition of the funeral procession, which dates from the same era but has a less readily documented history. The Catholic Ribbonmen paraded in large numbers at funerals in the 1830s (Garvin 1981:42), and Freemasons also paraded on such occasions: one masonic lodge in Comber, County Down paraded at over 70 funerals between

1808 and 1845 (Simpson 1926:83). Funerals and memorials to well-known political figures have often been turned into major public events, and have mobilised the Catholic population more readily than simple commemorative parades. Setting the foundation stone for the O'Connell memorial in Dublin in August 1864 served as a proxy funeral, 17 years after the death of the Liberator. Enormous crowds were attracted to the centre of Dublin, and riots broke out in Belfast as Catholics were attacked as they returned home (Boyd 1987). The return of the body of the exiled Young Irelander T. B. McManus provoked a mass demonstration of patriotism in 1861, in stark contrast to the lack of support for their attempted rebellion in 1848. Half a century later the political mobilisation of nationalists for the funeral of O'Donovan Rossa, in August 1915, enabled Pearse and the Irish Volunteers to lay public claim to the inheritance of the Fenian tradition (Kee 1989a, 1989b). In the aftermath of the failed Rising, the funerals of republican hunger strikers Thomas Ashe, in Dublin in 1917, and Terence MacSwiney, in Cork in 1920, provoked major displays of support for the republican ideal. Over 30,000 people followed Ashe's coffin through Dublin (Kee 1989c).

More recently, this tradition has been extended to IRA funerals. The funeral of Bobby Sands in 1981 was the biggest demonstration of all, as an estimated 100,000 people lined the route from his home in Twinbrook to Milltown cemetery (Beresford 1987). This tradition of honouring the fallen hero has been the most consistent means of mobilising public support for the nationalist or republican ideal. It is this practice that underlies the Easter commemorations in Belfast. In contrast to the celebratory commemoration of a military victory that structures the loyalist parades, the emphasis within the republican movement is on honouring its dead: those who died at Easter 1916, on Bloody Sunday 1972 and during the Hunger Strikes of 1981.

While drawing on an entwined tradition of commemorative ritual, current practices serve to emphasise two opposing senses of communal or ethnic identity and destiny that are grounded in an essential and exclusive sense of difference. This is made most explicit in the commemorations of the Somme and Easter, the two recent events that are most widely used to symbolise the divergent aspirations and senses of identity between the Protestant–Unionist and Catholic–Nationalist communities. The Somme commemorations confirm that Ulster is Protestant and British, and Catholics are excluded as Catholics, since all the loyal orders remain exclusive to Protestants. The Easter parades are, theoretically, open to anyone who wants to walk: nationalist and republican groups proclaim a non-sectarian and universalist ideology, and welcome supporters of all faiths (apart from the AOH, which is a specifically Catholic body).

However, in practice the Easter parades are scarcely less exclusive than the Somme parades. In a society where every aspect of life is potentially indicative of one or the other community, the structure and form of the Easter commemorations indicate a distinctly Catholic activity. The location and timing, as well as the more obvious religious symbols of the commemoration, the rosary and the easter lily, enhance the identification with a religious anniversary. These features were continued by the republican movement when it claimed the inheritance of the event. The religious sense of Easter is also connoted in the name for the events of 1916: it is not called a rebellion, a revolution or even an uprising, but simply The Rising. The Rising in Ireland coincides with the rising of Christ after the Crucifixion. The event is commemorated on Easter Sunday, as part of the Christian calendar, rather than on a Monday or every 24 April, as part of the secular calendar. This conjunction substantiates the performative rhetoric of the commemorations, by drawing on long-standing and deeply felt religious codes for legitimacy.

Easter is commemorated and personified through the identities of the individuals who signed the Proclamation of Independence, who were executed as martyrs to the cause of Ireland and who today are honoured as vainly concealed, secularised modern-day saints. Recent republican murals devoted to the hunger strikes drew quite clearly on religious iconography, and in particular *Pietà*-type imagery when depicting the plight of the men in the H Blocks. Their leader, Bobby Sands, like the seven signatories of the Proclamation before him, has become abstracted into the idealised hero figure, whose life and death represents the embodied virtues of the nationalist ideal. In this he follows in the path not only of Pearse and Connolly, but also of Wolfe Tone, Robert Emmett and the Manchester Martyrs before them, whose memorials can be found in provincial towns throughout the south as martyrs to the cause of Ireland. The personal suffering and willing sacrifice of these individuals gives them moral authority over, and leadership of, the community of followers.

In contrast to this focus on individual heroes, the loyalist commemoration of the Somme is enacted through remembering and honouring the entire community of individuals involved. Although occasional references are made to the Ulster Protestant soldiers who received the Victoria Cross during the First World War, essentially the event is viewed as a collective sacrifice. Immediately after the war some Protestant leaders were celebrated above others, and Carson is still widely lionised; but other figures of this era receive scant recognition nowadays. The individuals who fought and died may be remembered locally or on lodge banners; but, as with the numerous Orange worthies, they are no more than first amongst equals. For the Protestants authority remains invested in the community of the faithful, collectively.

Forgetting Similarity, Remembering Difference

Loyalist and republican traditions are rooted in a common ground and two distinct pasts. A shared history is used and re-worked both to enhance the identity of each community and to mark it as emphatically different from the other; they mirror each other and gain internal strength from their mutual opposition. The broad view of these commemorative practices can be used to emphasise the similarity of such features as the parades, music and visual displays, while many of the details serve to stress the distinctiveness of two identities rooted in opposing religious and political ideals. The events of 1916 are commemorated in a way that builds on and strengthens their existing concepts of Protestant/Unionist and Catholic/Nationalist identities. But no less important an aspect of public commemorations are those inconvenient features of the past that do not help to substantiate the preferred reading, those events and details that contradict widely held assumptions or at least provoke awkward questions, and thereby rub against the grain of official and popular understanding and memory. These are the events, or facts of history, that are written out of the dominant literature, erased from public commemorations and forgotten by popular memory. Ireland is no different from other countries in this matter. The importance in stressing the Catholic nationalism of Ireland or the loyal Protestantism of Ulster is to maintain an entrenched resolve behind the barricades of an essential identity, and has meant greater emphasis has been placed on the differences between the two communities than on exploring what exists of a shared past.

The Easter Rising and the Battle of the Somme are important in so far as they emphasise the irreconcilably different aspirations of Protestants and Catholics. While the Protestant community were sacrificing their young men against German guns, the Catholic rebels were acknowledging the support of 'our gallant allies in Europe' as they rose up to stab Britain in the back. Alternatively, the Irish nationalists were following heroic precedents in their legitimate aspirations to a God-ordained, independent nationhood, which had been constantly thwarted by the threats of violence by an undemocratic minority, who merely wished to maintain their discriminatory privileges.

However, when one considers some of the ignored facts about the war years, the simple symmetry of the polarisation is difficult to sustain. On 20 September 1914, just two days after the Home Rule Bill had become an Act of Parliament, John Redmond, leader of the Irish Party and of the nationalist Irish Volunteers, encouraged the organisation's 170,000 members to support the war effort. The 10th and 16th Divisions were recruited from the nationalist population and sent to England for training. In Ulster in 1915 Catholics volunteered in proportionately equal numbers to Protestants, and by autumn 1915 81,408 Irishmen had volunteered for the British Army. Some 27,000 were members of the Ulster Volunteer Force and 27,000 members of the Irish Volunteers. Only a minority of the membership of either the Ulster Volunteer Force or the Irish Volunteers ever joined up; but altogether over 200,000 Irishmen enlisted in the British forces during the war. Seventeen Catholic Irishmen won Victoria Crosses in the first 15 months of the war (Kee 1989b; Morgan 1991).

In Ireland, however, until the last few years the war has only been commemorated by unionists: some memorials were erected in the south, but not with the public prominence they received in the north. The building of a National War Memorial in Dublin dragged on through the 1930s:

> Today, the Irish National Memorial is in a sorry state . . . the bleak granite, decapitated columns, broken-down hedges, rotted pergolas, damaged fountains and empty pavilions are aptly evocative of a long-abandoned battlefield. Neglect verging on desecration symbolises the

persistent indifference to the War and its legacy of successive administrations, anxious to guard the people from historical awareness lest they remember too much (Leonard 1988:67).

An official change of attitude has meant that the memorial has recently finally been repaired and completed, although the war is still not regarded as an appropriate event through which one should remember one's Irish identity.

The events of Easter 1916 have eclipsed the nationalist and Catholic contribution to the Great War, and remembrance of that contribution would only undermine the unity drawn around the independent Irish state, and obscure the clarity of the sense of distinction between Britain and Ireland. The sanctity of the memory of Easter 1916 is such that Charles Haughey's Government provoked outrage among republicans when the official 75th Anniversary commemorations were reduced to a minimal level (Ní Dhonnchadha and Dorgan 1991). This reaction refuses to confront the facts that support for the republican cause only became substantial after the defeat of the Rising, and that in the north republicans were largely unimpressed with Dublin's plans for their role in the Rising, and did nothing. Sinn Féin claimed over 70 per cent of the parliamentary seats in 1918, but they still gained less than 50 per cent of the vote, while Catholic Belfast remained supporters of the constitutional nationalist position (Morgan 1991).

But the nationalist contribution to the war is no less an inconvenience for the loyalists, who would ideally include all Catholics within the rebel camp, and see themselves as the paragons of Irish loyalty. In turn this position, which emphasises the sacrifice of 1916, allows them to forget or ignore the uncomfortable facts of 1914. To forget that, in the weeks preceding the war, while the Irish Party was working through Parliament for Home Rule, loyalists had been on the verge of an armed rebellion against the Government; that they were unwilling to accept the will of the democratic majority in Parliament; that they had imported arms from Germany to support their effort; and that they had provoked a mutiny amongst the British army officers in Ireland in support of their cause. The Protestant tradition of opposing locally unpopular Government decisions by the threat of armed rebellion is scarcely less time-honoured or widely documented than that of the nationalist community; but that opposition has always been clouded by fervent expressions of loyalty. Social memories do not draw on some unquestioned mass of empirical facts, but sift through the confusion of the past for evidence that serves to substantiate existing beliefs. Public commemorations help convert those selective details into unquestionable history. In Ireland popular memory and written history both forget the awkward, grey areas and mutually sustain the social truth of irreconcilable difference and antagonism between Protestant and Catholic.

Part III

Displaying Faith

Arch Opening; Ian Paisley at the Thompson Family Farm, July 1993.

Gerry Adams and Martin McGuinness; Belfast, Internment Parade, August 1993.

Security Forces, Hunger Strike Commemoration, Falls Road, May 1994.

Banners and flags are a central part of the colour and display of the parades. The banners are only brought out once or twice a year for the main events, but flags are normally carried at all parades to display national allegiance (Bryson and McCartney 1994). At Orange parades the Union Flag and the Ulster Flag are most widely carried, although each Order has its own flag, and military flags from the Home Rule era and the First World War are frequently displayed. The Irish tricolour and the flags of the four Irish provinces are usually carried at nationalist parades, and the papal flag is also carried by the AOH. But it is the banners that illustrate the nuances of the national identity and make the most visual impact. At the Belfast Twelfth, 100 or more banners are carried by the Orange lodges, and many bands are led by a colour party carrying smaller bannerettes. At nationalist and republican parades flags and banners are just as much in evidence, although in smaller numbers. The form and style of contemporary banners is an inheritance from the work of George Tutill, who professionalised banner-making in nineteenth-century England (Gorman 1986). The firm of Bridgett Brothers of Belfast have been the most significant painters and designers of banners for the Ulster groups. Although Bridgett's closed in the late 1980s, their legacy lives on: many of the contemporary banners painters learnt their trade at Bridgett's or utilise their original designs. The subject of the main image is chosen by the purchaser, but the painter has a strong influence on the overall appearance. Sometimes an old or damaged banner is used as a template for the replacement; as a result many of the images have changed little in style or in content over this century. But new images are also regularly demanded: a local building or a recently deceased member may be chosen to grace the new banner; sometimes customers only request a general theme and leave it to the painter to interpret their wishes by drawing on his experience. The painters will use a range of original images: sometimes they start from a photograph of a building or an individual, sometimes from prints or paintings; for religious themes pictures from a Children's Bible are valuable resources. A large part of the painter's skill is to summarise complex stories and focus their meaning into a single salient event or into an easily recognisable image, to balance the need for a pleasing image with the desire to convey a specific message. The original image is not simply copied directly, but functions as the starting-point from which the banner painter will then interpret his customer's desires by repositioning or removing characters and working with the shadows, shading and colour to effect the best translation from one medium to the other.

The standard size of a banner is 7´ x 6´. Most are made from silk. The central image is enclosed within a frame varying from circular to shield-like in shape, with a different image painted on each side. The name of the lodge or division and its warrant number run across the top, and along the bottom may be an appropriate motto or quotation, or a reference to the lodge's geographical location. Enclosing and surrounding these are heraldic-styled floral or leaf designs. The central design is sketched on paper before being transferred on to the silk, which is stretched on a wooden frame to keep it taut. A white ground is painted on first, and then several undercoats are added before the final image is gradually built up. Painting is done in stages, and can take several weeks, since time is allowed for areas to dry before adding the next layers. Sometimes gold leaf or aluminium foil is used to add extra sharpness and brightness to the background of the images and the heraldic scrolls. This adds to the cost; but on a sunny day the banner will shine with an extra brilliance. The painter works on several banners at once, each at a different stage of completion. Once all the painting is completed a silk border, about eight inches wide, normally in a contrasting colour to the main silk background, is sewn around three sides, and the top is edged with hoops from which the banner is suspended; a fringe and retaining ribbons complete the work.

On parade the banner is hung from a cross bar, suspended between two wooden poles. These poles are topped by ornamental metalwork: many Orange poles depict a five-pointed star in a circle; the Black preceptories favour a compass and square; the Hibernians commonly carry either a Celtic cross or an ornate Catholic cross; while among the INF the Irish harp is common. Both loyalist and nationalist organisations also allude to the military origins of this displaying practice by topping the poles with a small decorative axe head or a pike point. Two men are needed to carry a standard banner, supporting the poles in a leather harness worn around the neck. If it is windy, young boys may hold the retaining ribbons to prevent the banner blowing freely; but this turns the banner into a sail, and they are often allowed to fly in the wind. If the banner is protected from wind damage and carefully dried before it is put away it may last for anything between 25 and 40 years. Many banners are not treated with the respect required for this length of life: they tear while blowing freely in the wind; they are laid out on the grass prior to a parade; they are sometimes used to cover and protect instruments at the lunch break; and they are rolled up wet at the end of the day. Notwithstanding this casual treatment, many banners still reach an old age, and many are brought out on parade despite being frayed, cracked and patched.

The first public appearance of a new banner is when it is unfurled. These are small ritual occasions, sometimes held in a church, sometimes in the open, at which the banner is dedicated to God and the work of the local branch of the institution is reflected upon and praised. In the weeks preceding the major parades there are numerous banner unfurlings that help to further focus local attention on the build-up to the big event (see Jarman 1997 for discussion of the unfurling ritual). The unfurling ceremony serves to announce the presence of the group of men as a public entity. Although lodges can and do walk on parade without any form of distinguishing regalia, they are effectively invisible in doing so. Without a banner to display at public events the men are a nameless group of individuals, lacking a collective identity and lacking a history: it is the banner that announces the name of the body, its geographical base, its political and religious orientation and, from its warrant number and sometimes from the image born on the banner, its history. Banners have been described as comparable to regimental flags in being both a focal point and a rallying point. It is only with a banner that the group of individuals are incorporated as a single body with their own identity, which enables them to represent themselves on parade to a wider public; without the banner they would be anonymous, and the parades would have no more form than a large crowd. It is the banners that give order and structure to the parades.

The dedication of a banner or of a replacement is an opportunity to announce and celebrate this existence within the community that has brought it forth. While all fraternal organisations have initiation ceremonies for their membership, these are private affairs, and the exact details of this process often remain secret (Buckley 1985–6). It is only with the appearance of a banner that these bodies cease to be secret organisations and announce their formal existence. The unfurling is the occasion when this hitherto private gathering of individuals declare their existence in public. When the collective body of brethren display their unity and parade their existence among their friends and neighbours and through their neighbourhoods, it makes the distinction and marks their transformation from a secret organisation to an 'organisation with secrets'.

After their unfurling, banners are rarely on public display more than once or twice each year; and when they do appear it is as one of a number of similar banners. At each parade a large number of different images will be displayed, and although these will be dominated by a central theme or core image (Ortner 1973) that is repeated many times at random throughout the parade, it will also include a number of images with no apparent connection to either the event being commemorated or the core image. Banners and images appear in a random order that does not allow any formal linear narrative to be developed, and yet many of the images clearly relate to the same period or series of events. Each organis-ation has different rules for the structuring of its parades: in Derry a different parent club of the Apprentice Boys is responsible for the commemorations each year, and has the honour of leading the parade; in Belfast the ten districts of the Orange Order rotate the lead position annually, and within each district lodges march in order of warrant number. The banner images are of no importance in this matter: on parade there is a random intermingling of the all the images. Although not everyone watching or participating in each parade may know the significance of each image, the core images are well known, and their over-duplication through the procession is constantly juxtaposing them with lesser subjects. The display thus builds up a series of equivalences.

There are few constraints as to what may be depicted on a banner: the loyal orders do not allow living people to be portrayed, but this is the only restriction of which I am aware.[1] This constraint

1. William Pirrie, a partner in the Harland and Woolf shipyards, was depicted on several Orange banners when he backed the formation of the Ulster Liberal Association in 1906, and indicated less than fullsome support for the union. As a result of his change of politics, the Orange Order passed a resolution banning the representation of living figures on their banners.

is important, however, and, combined with the long life and cost of the banners, it means that it is impractical to use this particular medium for campaigning activities or the like. Therefore what is portrayed by the display of banners is a 'history': a commemoration and celebration of past heroes, glories and sacrifices displayed as a morality and exemplar to the living. Or rather, a number of variations of a celebratory remembrance, for the range of images varies at each parade and from year to year. As the range of banners is continuously being added to, each year witnesses a slight variation of the public re-presentation of these local histories. As well as regional variations of emphasis within each organisation, loyalist and nationalist groups display their history as a feature of a wider political ideology. This means that the various parades generate a number of histories, which may include contrasting versions of the same events or periods of history.

Buckley (1985–6) sees these images functioning as mnemonic devices for the members themselves, referring back to the stories told to them in their initiation, but having only a much more restricted meaning for the 'casual observer'. However the committed member of any parading organisation sees very few of the banners on display: most of the walk involves following his own banner, with brief glimpses of those immediately in front. The banners as a display demand the 'casual observer', who is in any case rarely a neutral or disinterested onlooker, but part of the broader silent majority of support. But one also needs to recognise the importance of the commemorative events themselves for the broader community, and see how images on the banners create the wider context in which these celebrations have meaning, in which the meaningful histories of Ulster are created. Few of the myriad events of Irish history are publicly commemorated in any way: many minor events and personalities of Irish and Ulster history remain in the public eye solely on the banners. Most of the stories that are displayed are based around the one or two key events or figures that enable the viewer to locate the secondary subjects within more general but clearly positioned historical schemata. It is only on these occasions that the wide range of historical events and personalities are gathered together and the full sweep of history is laid out for display.

Most banners have at least one image that relates to the main concerns of the organisation; but often the second subject depicts an event, place or person of specifically local relevance. The core images may become over-duplicated; but events and individuals of purely localised significance are displayed to a wider audience. The seemingly random order in which the images appear and the lack of any coherent narrative helps to equalise events of apparently vastly different significance; but it also condenses several hundred years of history by denying and refusing any sense of temporal order or the passage of time. The juxtaposition of events like the battle of the Boyne and the battle of the Somme creates an equality of value between events of the recent past, still recalled by the living and remembered in oral histories, and those of the distant, almost mythological, past. History and time are condensed into a single concept of the past, an entity constructed of categories of events: sacrifice, martyrdom, betrayal, faith. This past has not ended, but rather continues to structure the feelings, expectations and fears of those acting in the present. These pasts can be added to and extended with the commemoration of new local heroes, whose modest faith and sacrifices are publicly recalled each year, as their images are paraded through the streets of Ulster.

Getting Ready I: Derry, Our Lady's Day, August 1993.

Getting Ready II: Newtownbutler, August 1993.

Chapter 8

Trust In God, But Keep Your Powder Dry

The images and themes on the banners of each of the loyal orders are linked in their subject-matter and complement each other. The various displays create a multi-layered representation of loyalist memories and aspirations, in which no two parades are identical. Because banner designs are chosen to highlight a narrow range of themes of common interest, all the parades of a single fraternity appear very similar to each other. Orange parades are sometimes described as an endless display of banners portraying King William III, a description that glosses over the variety of images and the complexity of the overall display. Furthermore, because there is a common interest and often a common membership, there is a degree of overlap of the images and subjects on Orange and Black banners, and distinctions between the different groups or areas are often blurred. But despite the common themes, the different parades are not simple duplications of one another, although each is a variation on a common theme.

This chapter discusses the banners of the two largest bodies, the Orange Order and the Royal Black Institution, and of the loyalist marching bands. The banners of the Apprentice Boys of Derry, the Junior Orange Order and the Independent Orange Order bear many similar images, although with differences of focus: respectively, they address the events surrounding the Siege of Derry; convey morals and stories pertaining to youth; and offer a fundamentalist version of Ulster history. For reasons of space these will not be discussed in this study.

In Glorious Memory – Orange Order Banners

The most widespread and important image on Orange displays depicts King William III (King Billy) in his military uniform, holding his sword aloft and riding a white horse across a river. This has become THE emblematic image of loyalism. Its use is not constrained to a ritualised context: it appears on a wide range of everyday and souvenir objects, ranging from tea towels to mugs, plates, tee-shirts, posters, tattoos and mural paintings. King William even appears on banners at football matches. He is the identifying icon of Ulster Protestants. But the Orange banners are about more than King Billy, although he remains at the heart of the displays. This analysis is based on the images on several hundred banners that I photographed at parades between 1990 and 1996. I have categorised this diversity of images into six main subject groups:

1. Those related to the Williamite wars of 1688–91. In 1992, 91 out of 236 images depicted King William III (hereafter KW3) or aspects of the Williamite campaign. This group represents 38.5 per cent of all the images, while one or another image of KW3 appeared on 69 per cent of all banners.
2. The second largest group portrays religious imagery: 20 per cent of all images were religious. Some of these were biblical scenes, but the most important were the more formal and abstract symbols of Ulster Protestantism, the Crown and Bible, which appeared on 21 per cent of all banners.
3. A large number of banners depict buildings or places, in or with significance to, Northern Ireland. Many of these are churches (16 per cent of banners portray a church), which could also be included in the previous category; but they are also part of a strong emphasis on localism and grounding the loyalist experience in a sense of place.
4. Similarly, this stress on local interest is shown in the 21 per cent of banners that carry the portraits of deceased Orangemen. These are largely publicly unknown individuals, who were locally important members of the order.
5. An important, though small, category are the images related to non-Williamite historical events. Some of these banners depict events of specific importance to Ulster, such as the

Somme, while others depict people, like Martin Luther, who are important in the broader Protestant tradition.
6. The final group is a number of banners that relate directly to the relationship with Britain. Images of Britannia and the lion or portraits of recent monarchs are a long-standing feature of Orange banners.

Table 8.1 compares this breakdown from three perspectives. The range of images on display at a single parade, Belfast in 1992; a composite list of all images photographed in Belfast over the period 1990–96; and a similar composite of banners photographed outside Belfast. The 1992 parade provides an objective body of data in which the images were recorded as they appeared, while the two lists based on photographic material are entirely subjective. The number of Williamite images is under-represented in these lists: emphasis was given to covering the full range of subjects.

King Billy appeared on one in two banners and represented nearly a quarter of all the images on display. His standard portrayal is drawn from fine art originals: in particular, works by Jan Wyck from the 1690s and a painting by Benjamin West done in 1778 (Loftus 1990). The Wyck paintings depicts KW3 on a rearing white horse in the foreground of the canvas; he is facing the viewer and has his back to the battle scene, which serves as little more than a contextualising backdrop. In West's painting, William is portrayed leading his troops into the heart of the battle; his sword is drawn and used to point the way forward. The banner painters use either of these two paintings, and sometimes incorporate elements of both into a hybrid version.

This formal composition, of the subject on a white horse in a heroic pose, was widely used throughout the seventeenth and eighteenth centuries. The National Gallery and the National Portrait Gallery in London have several similar paintings and engravings of various royals, aristocrats and gentlemen on white horses. These include portraits of the Duke of Monmouth by Jan Wyck *c.*1675 and the Duke of Marlborough by Sir Godfrey Kneller *c.*1706, both of whom also included King William among their subjects. In each of these, the subject is shown in contemporary costume or the uniform of a soldier, while background scenery or details contextualise and focus the portrait. The whiteness of the horse serves primarily to highlight the subject from the rest of the

Groups	1992	All Belfast	Non-Belfast
WILLIAMITE			
KW3	82	107	89
Relief of Derry	5	9	5
Mountjoy	–	2	2
Battle of Aughrim	2	2	1
Duke of Schomberg	1	2	1
Battle of Newtownbutler	1	1	–
Total	91	123	98
RELIGION			
Crown and Bible	25	29	24
My Faith Looks Up to Thee	9	13	7
Jesus	6	6	8
Biblical Stories	6	13	36
Other Religious Symbols	–	–	11
Total	46	61	86
LOCAL PLACES			
Churches	19	20	6
Orange Halls	6	7	2
Other Buildings	12	16	2
Industry	2	4	3
Total	39	47	13
PORTRAITS	26	31	12
HISTORY			
Battle of the Somme	5	7	13
Protestant History	9	19	5
Signing Ulster Covenant	3	3	1
Latimer and Ridley	3	4	8
Martin Luther	2	3	–
Total	22	36	27
BRITAIN			
Monarchs	7	8	2
Britannia	3	4	6
Secret England's Greatness	2	5	10
Total	12	17	18
Miscellaneous	–	3	6
Total Number of Images	236	318	260
Total Number of Banners	118	174	162

Table 8.1 Orange Institution Banners

painting, as it does in West's Battle of the Boyne, where the eye is immediately drawn to King William by his white mount.

This realist approach was only one possible portrayal of the victorious monarch. Other early representations of King William, such as the statue erected in Dublin in 1701 and the later ones in Bristol, Hull and St James's Square, London, used the image of a Roman emperor or general as the model. It was this portrayal of King Billy as the epitome of the classical ideal of heroic leadership that was at first used in popular commemorations, and it was not until much later, at least a century after the Battle of the Boyne, that the current image became widespread (Loftus 1990:18–25).

Belinda Loftus attributes the transformation, from the classical ideal to heroic realism, to the growing availability of reproductions of West's painting in the late eighteenth century. The change of representational style coincided with the emergence of a radical populist Protestantism, the formation of the Orange Order and the adoption by the lower classes of William as a symbol of their difference and distinction from the Catholic peasantry. Throughout the earlier eighteenth century many of the Williamite celebrations had been a more genteel, society affair of the Dublin Anglo-Irish upper classes, to whom the timeless, classical ideal of leadership was more attractive. The shift from bourgeois to populist commemoration over a period of decades coincided with widespread changes in aesthetic taste that favoured realism over the previously dominant classicism. The increasing commercialisation of production and marketing of works of art, especially through the sale of engraved copies, in turn made a wider number of copies available for public viewing. These changing social practices favoured the adoption of the heroic King William over the classical in popular representations.

While depictions of the battle scenes do occur on contemporary memorabilia and banners, the image is often simplified to the extent that William is abstracted from the specific historical events and, instead of the realism of the original paintings, is again depicted in an idealised manner. This ideal image portrays a figure alone on horseback, crossing a river or similar body of water, in a landscape of green fields or rolling hills under a blue sky. He is dressed in a red frock coat, with white breeches and thigh-length black boots; frequently he wears a sash or belt in royal blue and a soft hat with an orange or white plume. His white horse frequently has a royal blue saddle-cloth. This is an abstract, symbolic figure removed from any specific historical context. Although he retains the realistic dress of a seventeenth-century military figure, William has become the regal, heroic figure of an earlier genre of painting; his pose is that of a relaxed, unthreatened, natural leader, who connotes the aura of majesty: he is a man born to be King. The structured colour of his clothing, usually a combination of red, white and blue, signifies him specifically as a British monarch. He sits alone on his white horse, unchallenged and unchallengeable. His raised sword becomes less a sign of any forthcoming conflict than a simple symbolic affirmation of his status as leader, as a warrior-king. Portrayed alone in a landscape that is devoid of any sign of human agency, he is the undisputed master of all he surveys. His solitude further suggests a primordial position, a solitary figure in an unpopulated natural environment: this is no mere mortal, but an idealised culture-hero, who stands somewhere between man and god.

The colour of the horse is the most critical feature of any representation of King William for Protestants. The style and detail of the painting, the structure of the composition and the colour scheme for William's dress may vary, but there is no flexibility with regard to the colour of his horse. No definitive record exists about the colour of the horse that he rode at the Boyne, and in some early oil paintings he is depicted riding a dark horse. But for Ulster Protestants, no other colour except white is acceptable. In 1950 Belfast councillors vetoed the purchase of a painting of William by Jan Wyck because he was mounted on a brown horse (Loftus 1990:36). Much has been made of the significance of the whiteness of the horse. Loftus argues that it was a symbol of the Hanoverian monarchy in Britain, and Irish Williamites adopted the colour as a symbol of their continued allegiance to the monarchy. This may well have been a factor, since the Hanoverian monarchs were frequently represented on early Orange banners, and the riotous nineteenth-century Orangemen were keen to affirm their loyalty while disobeying the law; but it does not necessarily explain everything.

I have already noted how it was artistic convention to depict gentlemen and other self-important figures in the pose of a heroic warrior on a white horse. This in turn draws on an earlier tradition: in Uccello's 'St George slaying the dragon', *c*.1460, the hero was mounted on a white steed; this custom continued through Tintoretto's painting in the mid-sixteenth century to Moreau's

Raphael-inspired painting of the same subject of 1890. Depictions of St Michael battling against rebel angels show him on such a steed (Baddeley and Fraser 1989); and in a similar portrayal, sword raised and smiting the enemy, Santiago (St James) entered the iconography of Andean Peru as a Hispanicised and Christian incarnation of the Inca thunder god (Silverblatt 1988).

The custom of painting gentlemen on white horses drew on this wider tradition by which the whiteness of the horse reflected the status of the rider. The white horse thus becomes a symbol of the natural, spiritual purity of the heroic subject. The white horse remains as a symbol of purity and goodness: one only has to think of the westerns of the 1940s and 1950s, when white and black readily symbolised good and evil. The white horse has thus been widely used as a symbol of religious purity; it raises the status of the rider to one of Holy Warrior, defender of the faith. He has become God's right arm, and, bearing the sword of righteousness, his military battles are transformed into a Holy War.

Besides these broader European traditions, the white horse also featured prominently in Celtic mythology and custom as a symbol of leadership or magical status. Giraldus Cambrensis, writing in the twelfth century, reports of a people in Ulster who conferred kingship by ritual intercourse with, and the sacrifice of, a white mare (Gerald of Wales 1982:109–10). The midsummer festivals and the August festival of Lughnasa both incorporated horse-racing, horse-washing and fire purification: one recorded example of fire ritual involved a wooden frame with a horse's head that was covered in a white sheet (Frazer 1923; MacNeill 1962). The horse still retains a central symbolism in some surviving folk traditions, such as the Wren Boys in County Kerry, who parade with models of white horses on St Stephen's Day (MacDonagh 1983b). Macrory (1988:278, quoting Graham 1829) recounts a popular tradition that survived at least until 1829, that during the siege of Derry 'hopes of salvation were being sustained by a firm belief "that at midnight every night an Angel, mounted on a snow-white horse and brandishing a sword of bright colour, was seen to compass the city by land and water".' The magical, mystical white horse was also at the centre of 'Into the West', a recent feature film with a strong social critique of contemporary urban Ireland.

These multiple traditions seem to add to the potential depth of resonance of the symbol, each connection adding further layers of meaning. The continued insistence that King William rides a white horse must be seen as more than a late eighteenth-century legitimisation strategy, and instead viewed as part of the broader process by which the strictly realist historical representation is eroded, and a polysemic symbolic figure constructed in its place. The iconic figure includes within it mnemonic references to historical events; but it also addresses ideals of civil and religious authority, the form of legitimate action, and more abstract notions of good and evil. This symbolic King William is a composite figure, the individual as monarch, as warrior, and as religious leader. Once this range of concepts has become condensed within a single image, they can be elaborated through the broader display of images and icons during the performance of the parade. King William is not simply the most important image; he is also the pivot from which all the other images derive their valency. From this perspective, one must argue that the abstract King William of the banners is not just a simplified version of the figure portrayed in the battle scenes; he represents a completely different and much more complex individual, who is portrayed alongside the realistic heroic warrior king that is shown fighting the battle of the Boyne. The abstract William is the polysemic centrepiece that anchors all the other images on display. It provides the numerous points of contact that help to relay meaning and to weave the images together into a single elaborate text. On many banners, KW3 remains anchored and historicised by the references to the battles and events of the campaign of 1688–91: as such he is located as part of the historical narrative of the campaign whose seminal events are scattered randomly throughout the display. The vitality of the image emerges from this oscillation between the abstraction of the symbol and the concrete historicism of the heroic icon. He remains both a representation of empirical fact and an elusive symbol.

Numerous banners illustrate aspects of the events of 1688–91, but their emphasis is on William, the man, and his relationship with Ulster, rather than on the battles fought. Although they are scattered randomly through the length of the parade, rather than presented in a narrative, the events can be structured to recall the major themes of the Williamite campaign and describe the progress towards triumph. But story-telling does not seem to be the principal reason for the appearance of these particular images; they do not recount history so much as illustrate the relationship of King Billy to the Ulster Protestant people.

The narrative on the banners begins with William's arrival in England at Torbay in November 1688, and his coronation with Mary in London early the next year. These are the only things we are told of his background: he is an outsider who has been crowned King of Britain and Ireland. Much more is made of his time in Ireland: his arrival at Carrickfergus and his journey through Ulster *en route* for the Boyne. He is greeted by his troops on his arrival at the camp; he is shown leading his soldiers into battle and having a wound dressed. But the story seems to be less about military success than illustrative of William's character and moral status. His coronation emphasises his legitimacy as a true monarch; this is widely acknowledged by the warm greetings he receives during his journey through Ireland. His honest intentions are confirmed when he risks his life in and for Ireland, by leading his troops into battle and suffering the consequences by being wounded. The risk he took is emphasised by other banners that depict the death of William's general Schomberg at the Boyne. The depictions of his journey and battle scenes also humanise the atemporal, abstract hero figure in a manner that enables him to be held up as a practical example of what is to be expected of all true Ulstermen. The majority of the banners carry the timeless image of an idealised, heroic leader who epitomises the values of duty, action and sacrifice; but this mythicisation is tempered by the images that focus on the mundane, practical aspects of his life.

However, the Orange interest in William rests with his example in the fight to save Ireland from Catholicism, and no attention is paid to his life after the battle of the Boyne, or to any other features of his reign as King. The wider 1688–91 campaign is recalled in Ulster with the quatrain of 'Derry, Aughrim, Enniskillen and the Boyne'; but the three events that do not involve William are only represented on Orange banners in a minor way, and feed the wider discourse on the role of the individual and the nature of morally justified action, rather than celebrations of military triumph. Military victories reward moral superiority: the Relief of Derry, as the supply ship *Mountjoy* breaks the boom across the River Foyle, illustrates the need to maintain faith and resolve in the face of adversity; the battle of Newtownbutler in Fermanagh in July 1689 emphasises the importance of self-reliance and local resistance; and the rout of the Catholic forces at Aughrim in July 1691, a year after William had returned to England, focuses on the need to continue the fight, to go on the offensive to complete the victory, rather than allowing the enemy to remain a threat.

Apart from the Williamite events, the most prominent group of images are related to aspects of the Protestant faith. This group could have been larger if all the subjects, historical and spatial, that have some relationship to religion were linked together. The most popular, and the longest used, religious image depicts an open Bible lying on a red cushion. On the Bible lie a crossed mace and sword and a Crown; this group of objects is illuminated by a beam of light flowing from an 'all-seeing eye', an image that has been borrowed from masonic iconography. This painting refers to several important elements of the Ulster Protestant faith. The open Bible is accessible to all: it is unnecessary to have the mediation of a priest or a religious hierarchy to gain an understanding of biblical truth or to establish a relationship with God. This is one of the fundamental distinctions made between Protestantism and Roman Catholicism. Lay interpretations of the Bible, of morality, and lay justifications of action carried out in God's name are as valid as any.

The Crown and the symbols of royal power, the mace and sword, rest on the open Bible; royal authority, and all human authority derived from it, is contingent on support for the Protestant faith. There is no abstract royal authority separate from a religious authority. Finally, the Bible and the symbols of royalty are illuminated by the light from the eye of God, he who oversees all and who will be the ultimate arbiter. This also relates back to the Williamite images, since it becomes clear that his status as King derives not merely from secular acceptance or from moral righteousness, but from his Protestant faith. His Royal authority ultimately derives from his faith, an implication that is made clear on many of the Black banners, which bear the motto 'No Faith, No Crown'. Many of the Orange banners also carry phrases that emphasise this connection: 'Fear God, Honour the Queen', 'For the Throne is Established by Righteousness' and 'The secret of England's Greatness' serve to define the nature of, and constraints on, royal authority. This last slogan is reproduced on a number of banners that depict a painting of Queen Victoria handing a Bible to a kneeling Indian prince. The authority of the monarch comes from a Protestant faith; but it is the monarch's duty to defend and spread that faith wherever possible, to proselytise the heathen; spreading the faith in turn provides the basis for consolidating secular authority.

The key concern here is with the religious basis of royal authority; but this is depicted as a triadic relationship, which also includes the individual believer. It is also clear that the relationship between the three is not a linear hierarchy of God–Crown–Individual, as a mirror of the Catholic triad God–Pope/Church–Believer, in which truth passes downwards and service/obedience back up. Protestantism demands that the individual and the Crown stand in a similar relationship to God, and the authority of the monarch is conditionally accepted by the individual, not imposed on him. The motto 'Fear God, Honour the King' clarifies the duties of the individual within this covenant. This covenant or mutually binding contract has been seen as one of the distinctive themes of loyalist political thinking (Miller 1978). Protestants accept the authority of secular rulers provided the ruler acts within the terms of the faith. If the ruler is felt to be compromising the faith, then the contract is deemed to have been broken. If all Protestants have a right to interpret the faith and the contract for themselves, there are likely to be many views on what action is acceptable and justifiable. With the modern-day distancing of the monarch from the affairs of government, this concept allows loyalists to challenge or break the law, and even to threaten armed resistance to the will of the Queen's Government when they deem it necessary, and yet still proclaim their loyalty to the monarch herself.

A number of banners elaborate on the relationship of an individual to God. Over the motto 'My Faith looks up to Thee', a woman is depicted desperately hanging on to a cross amidst a stormy sea; a shaft of light shines through the cloudy skies on to the bedraggled woman, a ray of hope that God is watching over her in her time of trouble. This is a general commentary on the relationship of the believer to God, demanding that one trust in God and keep faith even when all seems hopeless, a theme that underlies many religious and historical images. But it can also be taken literally as the ideal female response: while male figures are shown taking decisive actions, women, who rarely appear on banners as individuals in their own right, are depicted passively clinging on to their faith – 'trust in God' is all these images offer. The banners offer no form of action legitimised by faith for women to take in their own interests. Faith gives women hope, whereas it inspires men to action.

This contrast runs through the images of historical events,

personalities and places that link the more universal interests of Protestantism with the local interests of Ulster. The images of Martin Luther, the signing of the covenant in Edinburgh, the mass drowning of Protestants in the River Bann during the Irish rebellion of 1641, Oliver Cromwell and Cromwell's forces taking Drogheda in 1649, all relate to the theme of Protestant faith and martyrdom, but also provide a wider framework for understanding the importance of the events of 1688–91. In terms of a narrative structure, we can see a series of events that involves a chain of contrasting actions and reactions: Luther's dissent and the Reformation leading to the burning of Latimer and Ridley; the violent rebellion of 1641, followed by the Cromwellian campaign to restore Protestant security; however in 1685 Margaret Wilson could still be martyred for her faith, since the threat persisted.

Collectively these events provide the prelude to, and the justification for, the popular resistance of Derry and support for the Williamite campaign. The images highlight the seemingly constant attempts by the Catholic establishment to destroy the Protestant reformation, and emphasise the need for vigilance and the legitimacy of any resistance. Protestant history becomes a spiral of action and reaction, in which the readiness to risk persecution and face death is balanced by a knowledge that these are legitimate fears that may need to be acted upon. All these images with a historical theme further illustrate the mutual intertwined relations between England, Scotland and Ireland, with Catholicism represented as a threat in all three countries at some time.

These concerns underlay the Protestant reaction to plans for Home Rule, in the years before the First World War. The campaign to oppose Home Rule, and by extension the British Government, is commemorated by banners depicting Edward Carson, the Unionist leader at the time, and the signing of the Ulster Covenant in September 1912, in which some 500,000 men and women declared a refusal to recognise Home Rule and vowed to oppose it. The idea of a covenant, a public avowal of unity and faith, recurs throughout Ulster Protestant history, and, as will be shown below, this receives its justification in Biblical antecedents. The paramilitary Ulster Volunteer Force, formed in 1912 to oppose Home Rule, are not commemorated on Orange banners, although they are celebrated on the regalia carried by many of the bands; but the *Clyde Valley*, the vessel used in a 1914 gun-running operation, is depicted. This rebellious prelude to crisis culminates in the battle of the Somme, which is commemorated on numerous banners, both via depictions of heroic troops storming the German lines and by portraits of Orangemen who died in the war. The pre-war crisis, in which the Ulster Protestants fought to remain part of Britain and yet also challenged the wishes of the government of the state, is the prelude to the events of the war, when their loyalty was finally expressed by willing sacrifice. Their actions are contrasted (in spirit if not in formal expression, for the Other is always absent from the discourse of the banners), by the actions of the Irish Republicans, who rose against the British state at Easter 1916 at a time when the Ulster Volunteers were fighting abroad. Republican treachery and betrayal are the constant counterpoint to unionist loyalty and sacrifice.

The remaining banners depict people, places and subjects that are of largely local interest: individuals and parish churches unknown outside their immediate locality, numerous minor examples of Ulster Protestant heroism or leadership. Most are memorable as members of the Orange Order or because they fought and died for Britain; but some depict more prominent personalities: vitriolic populist orators from last century, such as Dr Henry Cooke and the Revd Kane; early Orange leaders or supporters, like Colonel Verner and the Duke of York; politicians such as Carson and Disraeli; members of the Royal Family, Victoria, Prince Albert and George VI, or lesser members of the aristocracy who have a particular connection with Ulster. This local pride and rootedness is further valorised with paintings of local buildings ranging from Dan Winter's Cottage (the birthplace of the Order) to Belfast City Hall by way of numerous Orange Halls and parish churches, country houses and castles and industrial sites such as the Harland and Wolff shipyards. Orangeism, in spite of its iconography of Monarchs and Biblical Heroes, famous battles and the sacrifices of the martyrs, remains grounded in the mundane localism of the little-known people and places of the north of Ireland.

In spite of the numerous references to events in Irish history and in particular those related to Ulster, there are many exclusions. The banners offer an episodic history that concentrates on events that replicate the tragedies and heroism of the seventeenth century. The Somme is the last historical event that features on the banners. There are few references to the violence that followed the war and partition, and no overt acknowledgement of the contemporary

Troubles. An occasional Orangeman is described as 'Murdered by the enemies of the Empire'; another painting depicts three burning buildings and declares 'In memory of our friends who died because of their faith, 17 June 1922'; but neither banner explicitly recalls the circumstances. Lord Mountbatten has been portrayed on a banner since he was killed by the IRA; but there is no reference to the circumstances of his death. So the history of the Protestant people depicted on the banners is a partial one, one that is seen as an endless cycle of conflict, fear of betrayal and sacrifice, one that appears to have stopped in its tracks at the moment of its supreme expression of collective identity, the sacrifice of the Somme. The past becomes an object of veneration, and, having internalised the lessons of the past, the future is reduced to predictable certainty.

To Strike the First Blow – The Black Banners

The banners of the Royal Black Institution offer a different perspective on this theme of a collective identity that is rooted in a shared faith and a common threat by narrating history through biblical metaphor: the stories of Adam and Eve, Noah, Abraham, Moses, Daniel, David and Goliath, Elijah, and Solomon all appear frequently. Other banners depict symbols used by the organisation in its internal rituals; many of these symbols also refer to biblical stories, while others betray the organisation's ancestral links with masonic tradition. Anthony Buckley (1985–6) has analysed a selection of the banners displayed at Black parades in August 1982, and argues that the common theme running through the biblical stories concerns

> an individual or group of people who have found favour in the eyes of God confronting alien people . . . When someone has been chosen by God, and where in return he has been loyal to God, then he will in consequence prosper . . . This theme is the encounter between heathens or foreigners with God's chosen people (Buckley 1985–6:22).

He sees an obvious parallel between these themes and the attitudes of many Ulster Protestants to their own situation. Many of the stories concern the long struggle of the Israelites to live and rule in the land of their forefathers, and there is a long-standing, if rarely publicised, belief in the Ulster Protestants as the lost tribe of Israel, as God's Chosen People. This is an analogy that has implications for practical action and beliefs in contemporary Ireland. In contrast to religious teaching that emphasises that the faithful will be rewarded in the hereafter, the stories on the banners suggests that despite hardship and suffering the faithful will have their reward on this earth. This expectation of earthly recognition of righteous faith is a major tenet of Protestantism, and again distinguishes it from Roman Catholicism, with its promise of heavenly bliss (Weber 1985). This is a theme that runs through loyalist iconography and commemorations. The sacrifice at the Somme differs from the sacrifice of the Easter martyrs in so far as the one is celebrated for achieving its aims, while the other provides inspiration for future martyrs to take up the cause. The victory at the Somme therefore confirms the status of the Ulster Protestants as God's Chosen People: the covenant of faith that overrides pragmatic politics remains intact.

There are some other points that are worth drawing out of these general themes, and that link these ideas more closely to those expressed on the Orange banners. Firstly, the importance of the prophet or visionary: individuals who act or encourage others to act on the basis of a personal communication with their God. The stories of St John's vision and the visions of the prophet Ezekial exemplify the differences between Protestant and Catholic traditions: the direct relationship between an individual and God. While many of the contemporary 'prophets' may well be religious preachers of some sort, their faith and authority is not necessarily dependent on a religious hierarchy. This is illustrated by the banners that depict holy communication via an angel: offering succour to Elijah, appearing to Jacob, or simply descending from heaven with an open Bible in its hand. To communicate with God and to carry his message all that is required is faith, not special training in the priesthood. But, and this leads on to the second point, it is not sufficient simply to have faith: one must be prepared to act on one's beliefs as well. All the biblical characters cited earlier were prepared to do whatever God demanded of them, they were prepared to risk ridicule (Noah), to act against common morality (Jacob tricks his brother Esau, Abraham is prepared to kill his son), to betray one's own people (Rahab), and to oppose the lawful government when necessary (Moses, Elijah), if in so doing they were furthering God's desires. The most widely used image from the New Testament gives a similar example, as the Wise Men follow the star to Bethlehem.

Old Testament Stories		New Testament Stories	
Moses	35	Three Wise Men	16
Elijah	30	St John's Vision	4
David and Goliath	29	St Paul	2
Noah and the Dove	22	Jesus	1
Daniel	15	Good Samaritan	1
Adam and Eve	12	*Total*	24
Rahab and the Spies	9		
Joseph	8	*Religious Symbols*	
Abraham and Isaac	6		
Solomon	5	Cross and Crown	19
Jacob	4	My Faith Looks up to Thee	12
Angel and the Book	3	Bible and Cross	7
King Hiram	3	*Total*	38
Gideon and his 300	2		
Ezekial's Vision	1	*Other Images*	
Jephthah's Daughter	1		
Joshua	1	Arch and Symbols	28
Rebekah	1	Portraits	23
Ruth and Naomi	1	Places/Buildings	13
Total	188	Miscellaneous	10
		Williamite	2
		Total	76
		Grand Total of Images	326

Table 8.2 Subjects recorded on Royal Black Institution Banners
1991–95.

While the banners highlight the 'individual or group of people who have found favour in the eyes of God confronting alien peoples', they also demand that faith be prioritised at the expense of elements of human law, wisdom and morality. These banners use biblical authority to legitimise disobedience to civil authority, and show how it can be justified to take up arms. They emphasise the role of the leader or spokesman in provoking rebellion or resistance, and they confirm the right and justice of using physical force when necessary. This point is made frequently by the prominent image depicting David decapitating Goliath, framed by the motto 'He that would be free must strike the blow.' There are clear analogies in these images with the parallel status of King William on the Orange banners, for although David's status was derived directly from God, it was his readiness to display his faith and fight the seemingly superior opponent Goliath that marked the first step on his path to kingship.

The Black banners offer a biblical authority for the ideals expressed on the Orange banners. Just as the membership of the two bodies is similar, so the two groups of images provide solutions to the Ulster Protestant quandary from two distinct perspectives. One can resort to either historical fact or biblical narrative, but both will confirm that one must trust in one's faith and be ready and willing to act in one's own interests. Prophets and leaders may be important; but only in so far as they too are willing to act in the interests of the people. One must be wary of the Lundy, the traitor in the midst. The stories of the Old Testament, the history of the seventeenth century and memories of parents and grand-parents all confirm the same thesis, that faith without action or action without faith is insufficient, but the two together will win the day. Religion, history and politics become inseparably entwined in sustaining the identity of the Ulster Protestants. The Black banners emphasise the religious nature and ideals of the organisation; but they also provide a justification for the resort to arms that has so readily been raised in Irish history, that beyond the accepted civil law there is a higher law that permits, and even demands, both pro-active and re-active self-defence.

For God and Ulster – Band Bannerettes

Paramilitarism can be legitimised through the iconography of the Orange and Black banners, but neither organisation celebrates the recent or contemporary paramilitary tradition outside of what has been sanctioned by the state. It has been left to the more raucous 'blood and thunder' bands to introduce overt representations of paramilitarism into the visual displays of Protestant unity that are paraded across the province. Bell (1990) argues that the displays of paramilitary insignia and the affectation of paramilitary-style dark glasses and uniforms are little more than acts of bravado, and should be regarded as a display of youthful defiance at the sober and serious Orangemen, rather than as indications of active involvement. But the relationship is more complex than Bell would suggest: for instance, in recent years members of at least two bands have been convicted of loyalist paramilitary activities. In other cases bands are offered financial assistance for uniforms from paramilitary groups or are presented with flags by them. Some bands will carry paramilitary flags, some will not; many bands have names, such as 'Defenders' or 'Volunteers', that have paramilitary connotations. Blood and thunder bands dominate many Orange and Apprentice Boys parades, particularly in the urban areas: they offer a means through which the harder, more militant, edge of loyalism finds expression among the more traditional imagery of Orangeism.

Although they do not constitute an organised collective body, the bands are an important element of the visual display of the parades. Most urban bands are now independent of the loyal orders, and are therefore free to determine their own style of dress and music; but they still remain under the authority of the parade organisers, who have established rules of acceptable behaviour and styles, and who may, therefore, ban bands from parading or object to aspects of their display. The parade organisers stress their opposition both to the paramilitary groups and to expressions of support for them at Orange parades, but they are usually unwilling or unable to stop the bands continuing with their displays. Among traditional bands there was little call for an independent set of colours, and any display, commonly a version of King Billy and the band name, was carried on the bass drum. While this is still often decorated with name and designs, increasingly the independent bands vie with the lodges in the display of colours.

Bands do not parade with full-size banners, but they do often carry smaller bannerettes and may also carry a number of flags, although these are carried furled by the colour party: the Nelson Drive Flute Band from Londonderry carry up to six flags and a bannerette, but it is more usual for a band to carry about three flags. Most commonly these are the Ulster Cross, the St Andrew's Cross of Scotland and the Union Flag, all of which are widely carried by the loyal orders; but many bands also carry flags commemorating the Ulster Volunteer Force and the Young Citizens Volunteers and the battles they fought in the First World War. When the loyal orders commemorate the Ulster Volunteers of the First World War, they do so by focusing on the Battle of the Somme and the sacrifice of the soldiers willing to die for their country, rather than the memory of the organisation that the bands perpetrate. The name and insignia of the 1912 Ulster Volunteer Force was adopted, along with its motto 'For God and Ulster', by the first loyalist paramilitary group to appear since partition. Their emblems, and those of the other major loyalist paramilitary group, the UDA, are frequently found emblazoned on the walls of the working class areas of Belfast (see the chapter on murals below); the flags carried by the bands must therefore be considered as a declaration of support for the contemporary group as well as remembering the past.

As all flags are carried furled, the main display of paramilitary regalia is on the bands' bannerettes. Many of these do not directly refer to a paramilitary group by name, but simply adopt an emblem in a similar style. Typically this will depict the crossed flags of United Kingdom, Scotland and Ulster on either side of the Red Hand emblem of Ulster and surmounted by a crown. Both the UVF and the UDA feature the Red Hand of Ulster prominently in their visual rhetoric, and this appears frequently on band emblems. More explicit references to the paramilitary groups and former members can be found occasionally: Cloughfern Young Conquerers carry a Ulster Freedom Fighters bannerette; the Whitehill band from Bangor carry Red Hand Commando regalia. But UVF emblems, which can be legitimised as commemorative artefacts, are still the most visible presence.

While the displays of their elders are coded in historical or biblical references, it is perhaps not surprising that it would be the young working-class males who make the least subtle references to the contemporary Troubles and express the most explicit support for a violent response to the threats to Ulster's status. While this reaches its fullest expression on the streets of Belfast, their displays on parades are becoming increasingly bold and provocative. With their numerous flags and banners, in combination with the loud and raucous music of the flutes and drums, and the shrill colours of their uniforms, it is the bands that come more and more to attract the senses and dominate events. While the messages of support for violence are coded among the religious and historical banners of the Orange and the Black, the bandsmen make little pretence, and openly proclaim support for the paramilitary groups.

Sandy Row, Twelfth 1991.

Falls Road, Internment Parade, August 1993.

Chapter 9

A Nation Once Again

The banners of the loyalist organisations focus on different areas of interest, but these are essentially linked in their themes: Orange and Black approach Protestant identity from differing but complementary perspectives. The banners of the nationalist organisations display a much wider range of political orientations and approaches, even if, ultimately, they all espouse the same aim of a United Ireland. Two of the three groups concerned in this study, the Ancient Order of Hibernians and the Irish National Foresters, parade with banners of the same format as those of the unionist groups. Until recently such banners have not been carried at republican parades; instead, their banners have been of a much simpler designs and manufacture, and carried by hand rather than suspended from poles. This was perhaps more suited to the campaigning nature of their politics, in which quickly and cheaply produced banners were used to respond to changing political events and used to highlight diverse political campaigns. Republican banners have been largely restricted to slogans and names, rather than more elaborate displays; however, at the 1995 Hunger Strike commemoration in Belfast some half a dozen banners appeared commemorating the republican dead through portraits and additional designs that were in the more traditional format. It is early to judge as yet, but it will be interesting to see whether this trend continues over the next few years – whether, as the republican movement make more use of formal parades as a medium of celebration and commemoration, they also adopt the styles of banners that are currently used by the other parading bodies. At present the most dynamic element of contemporary republican iconography is on the mural paintings, which will be analysed in a later chapter.

For Faith and Fatherland: Hibernian Banners

There are a much smaller number of banners at Hibernian commemorations compared with loyalist parades; but they still include a diverse range of images. The majority of the banners carry religious images of some kind, with 65 per cent of the images depicting religious personalities or places, and the remainder featuring historical events, images related to the AOH or depictions of the Maid of Erin. One feature of the design of AOH banners that differs from those of the other parading fraternities is the inclusion of secondary images in the corners of the banners. These are often no more than representations of the symbols of the four provinces of Ireland; but a number of banners use this space to depict historical personalities. By incorporating and conjoining a wide range of historical figures within a single image in this way, Hibernian banners can display a more diverse message than the equivalent Orange banners.

The most prominent figure is St Patrick, who is credited with introducing Christianity to Ireland in the fifth century. He is portrayed ridding Ireland of snakes by driving them into the sea. A large church in the background and a Celtic gravecross symbolise that Christian order and authority is now firmly established and that civilisation and learning have replaced the old pagan belief, which are represented by the snakes. St Columba and St Brigid are two other early saints who are represented on the banners, while images such as 'the Old Cross at Ardboe', or 'Killevy Old Churches' similarly refer to the long history of Catholicism in Ireland. This is further emphasised by the captions that appear on many of the paintings: 'To God and Ireland True'; 'Faith and Fatherland'; and 'Faith of our Fathers Living Still'. All of which link the idea of a single and indivisible Irish nation with the establishment of the Christian religion and its authority. Figures such as Patrick and Columba appear not as exemplars of the ideal of the nation, but as the founders. Ireland is portrayed as coming into being at the time when Christianity arrived and established its dominance over the native traditions.

Besides the founding saints, the most important religious images are of Mary, mother of Jesus, and the Pope. Mary is named as both Queen of Heaven and Queen of Ireland, and although she is a relatively minor figure within the AOH religious pantheon she

Hibernians (36 banners)		Foresters (18 banners)	
St Patrick	15	Maid of Erin	13
Historical Figures	9	Historical Figures	11
Pope	7	Forester giving aid	3
Maid of Erin	7	Saints	3
Penal Mass	7	Churchmen	3
Symbols	5	Local Church	2
Saints	5		
Mary	5		
Local People & Places	4		

Table 9.1 Main Images on Nationalist Banners, 1992–95

remains the most important popular religious icon in Catholic Ireland (Taylor 1995). The Pope has always featured prominently on Hibernian banners; but the popularity of the current Pope, John Paul II, was further enhanced when he became the first Pope to visit Ireland in September 1979. This event is commemorated on the banner of Island Hill Division 399, which shows the Pope waving from the steps of an aeroplane; beside him is Cardinal O'Fiaich, and behind him, emblazoned on the side of the plane (and dominating the image) is the name 'Aer Lingus'. St Patrick, the Madonna and the Pope bracket the span of Irish faith and history; they define and confirm the essence of the religious spirituality of the nation, that Ireland was unified through adoption of the Christian faith, and draws her destiny and her strength from adherence to that faith. It is faith that has enabled the Irish nation to sustain itself through all its troubled history, and it is the interweaving of faith and historical destiny that is addressed by the other banners.

The physical presence of the Irish nation is embodied in the figure of Hibernia or Erin, who has remained a popular icon of Irish nationalism since the eighteenth century. Female personifications of Ireland appears in various guises (Loftus 1990); but, for the AOH, Erin is a passive, subjugated figure for whom her menfolk must be ready and willing to sacrifice themselves. On the banners she wears a pure white dress and is enclosed by a green cloak and, seated on a rock, she rests on a harp while an Irish wolfhound lies at her feet. Her outstretched left arm guides the eye to a church, a round tower, and behind that the sun rising over the horizon. Sprigs of shamrock form the border.

Collectively this image includes some of the most prominent symbols of Irish national identity. The shamrock has been an Irish emblem since at least the seventeenth century, while the harp has been used since the sixteenth century: Henry VII utilised the harp from 1534, and it was incorporated into the royal coat of arms of James I in 1603, where it remains today. It was used on a (green) flag by the Irish leader Owen Roe O'Neill during the rebellion against English rule in the 1640s (Hayes-McCoy 1979). The United Irishmen later adopted the harp surmounted by a Phrygian cap (the French revolutionary symbol of liberty) and the motto 'It is new strung and shall be heard' as their symbol. Today this emblem is still used by Sinn Féin on the masthead of their paper '*An Phoblacht*. Although the round tower and the wolfhound suggest the ancient past of early Christianity and natural fauna, they were only adopted as symbols of Irish national identity during the cultural revival of the nineteenth-century (Sheehy 1980). The round tower was brought to prominence by the nineteenth-century fascination with antiquities, and was eventually accepted as evidence for early Christianity in Ireland. The other prominent image incorporated in these paintings of Erin, the rising sun, also dates back to the Volunteer period. In turn it was adopted in the 1840s by the Repeal Association, who used it on their membership cards, while today it also features in Republican symbolism (Hayes-McCoy 1979:92; Sheehy 1980:28).

Although the image appears as a coherent whole, it has clearly been built up over time, with symbols from different periods added to the original figure of Hibernia. The finished version is a product of the reformist and romantic movements of the late nineteenth century, a symbolic jigsaw to give form to the emerging imagined national community of Ireland. As a composite image, the painting alludes to an idealised past when the indigenous culture and religion flourished free from outside interference, while the rising sun offers both hope and expectation for the future, freed from the constraints of the present. Sheehy (1980:69) summarises the aspirations of the wider nineteenth-century cultural revival, which, for Catholics at least, offered the hope of 'a return to a hazily perceived period when Ireland was free, Catholic (Protestantism was, after all, an English import) and an international focus for saints and scholars'.

These ideals are still projected through the images on the AOH banners. There are no references to plurality of faith: Protestantism is seen to offer nothing to the symbolic content of the nation. Ireland is portrayed as a rural landscape whose people are exemplified by a pure maiden. But this feminised Erin/Ireland is passive and acquiescent, and as such she appears in stark contrast to the pike-carrying Erin of the Volunteers. Weaponless, the seated Erin can only point to the rising sun, the future time when the Catholic Church or its agent will enable her to become a 'Nation once Again'. Meanwhile she must sit and wait, maintaining the 'Faith of her Fathers' while relying on her 'Illustrious Sons' to take the appropriate action. From this perspective Erin can be identified with Mary, mother of Jesus, who grieves over her dead son but is powerless to act on her own. She can only be a vehicle for God's will. The banner image is frequently underscored with the lines

> And then I prayed I yet might see
> our fetters rent in twain
> and Ireland, long a province, be
> A NATION ONCE AGAIN.

Although the implication is that it will only be through the help of prayer and divine intervention that Ireland will become a nation, the frequent references to her 'Illustrious Sons' elsewhere on the banners suggests that there is still a legitimate role for action, if it is taken to speed up this process. One banner (Div 378) challenges the resignation to an expectation of religious salvation to Ireland's problems: Erin stands with a broken chain hanging from her wrist and accepts a paper marked 'Catholic Emancipation' from Daniel O'Connell. This does not directly concern a separatist national struggle – O'Connell was an advocate of non-violent reform to British rule; but the picture is surrounded by portraits of Padraic Pearse, James Connolly, Tom Clarke and Thomas MacDonagh, signatories to the Proclamation of Independence in 1916, and also includes a portrait of Thomas Emmett, a leading United Irishman. This rather curious collection of 'illustrious sons' brings together on one banner the physical force tradition of Irish nationalism of Pearse and Connolly with the conservative and non-violent approach of O'Connell. The only points of contact are their Catholicism and their desire for an independent Ireland. However, linking them together through the figure of Erin admits to other possible courses of action in the cause of Ireland: although the risen Erin accepts O'Connell's gift of Emancipation, the advocates of more radical tactics remain ready in the background. This is the only Hibernian banner to include representatives of the recent physical force tradition. More appropriate to the AOH ideology are politicians like Joseph Devlin, John Dillon, T. P. O'Connor and John Redmond, who appear elsewhere. These were all leading constitutional nationalists who led negotiations for Home Rule from the 1890s until the outbreak of the First World War. Devlin, moreover, was the major influence in revitalising the AOH in this period and making it a force within the nationalist movement (Boyce 1991).

While the AOH does acknowledge the tradition of political violence, it prefers instead to highlight non-violent tactics. However, the banners that feature historical themes serve to emphasise the legitimacy, in specific circumstances, of the resort to arms. Many of the historical events that they portray depict counterbalancing perspectives to the unionist historiography of the Orange banners, and show a similar mixture of religious persecution and heroic resistance. The most prominent victim is St Oliver Plunkett, Archbishop of Armagh, who was arrested in 1679 at the height of a Catholic conspiracy scare during the reign of Charles II. Removed to London, he was tried and condemned for high treason in 1681. His politically motivated execution makes him a suitable subject as religious martyr, and a balance to the Protestant martyrs Latimer and Ridley (Beckett 1981).

However, there is a much greater emphasis on the heroic secular resistance during this period. The 1641 rebellion is celebrated in the person of the military leader Rory O'More on one banner, and the victory of Catholic forces under Owen Roe O'Neill at the battle of Benburb in 1648 on another. (Protestants in turn remember these years through the massacre at the River Bann and Cromwellian retribution.) These events were not so much an attempt to overthrow English power *per se*, but defensive actions to maintain the position of Ireland as both loyal and Catholic. The Williamite period is similarly commemorated as a time of rearguard action, through the figure of Patrick Sarsfield, commander of James's armies, who held off William's forces at the siege of Limerick in August 1690. This successful resistance forced the campaign into another season, and nullified the immediate success of the Williamite forces at the Boyne. Both communities therefore have their heroes and martyrs of the seventeenth century; both claim victories and both honour their heroic dead.

In contrast, the events of 1798, the United Irishmen rebellion, which provide a common ground for all three strands of nationalism, are ignored by loyalist iconography, for, although Protestants figured widely in the rebellion, they fought for a united and independent Ireland. The AOH, INF and Sinn Féin all root their contemporary ideology in this movement, and claim its martyrs as their own, although by emphasising different heroes.

The Hibernians commemorate this period by three heroic failures. Father Michael Murphy joined the rising in Wexford, and was killed leading the rebel forces in the battle of Arklow on 9 June 1798 (Kee 1989a). The Battle of Antrim of June 1798, when Henry Joy McCracken's army was overcome by the government forces, marked the beginning of the end of the rising in Ulster (Pakenham 1992). And finally, 'Bold Robert Emmett, The Darling of Erin', whose attempted rising of 1803 'ended in a scuffle in a Dublin street' (Beckett 1981:285), achieved immortality in Ireland with his final speech in court, in which he asked that no man should write his epitaph until Ireland was free (Kee 1989a). The Hibernian banners recall a series of tragic failures in which each event or individual is immortalised as another heroic sacrifice for the ideal of Ireland.

However, as we shall see, other points of emphasis can be used: the Foresters focus on the radical Presbyterian involvement in 1798, while for republicans it marks the beginning of the modern sequence of armed uprisings. Each of these readings can be justified within the differing strands of nationalism, and they serve to illustrate the continued significance of this pivotal event in Irish history.

Collectively, the Hibernian banners identify the Catholic faith, and by extension the Church itself, as an active agent in the desire for Irish freedom, while still offering some support for the argument for armed rebellion or some form of active resistance to perceived injustice. The Church as an institution has always opposed the successive attempts at armed nationalist risings in Ireland, although it has been more willing to acknowledge the heroism of sacrifice in a noble cause. But the distance of time allows many rebels and their actions to be reinterpreted and validated by later generations.

The role of individual members of the Church as active participants in resistance to the law, exemplified in extreme manner through Father Murphy, is also drawn out and emphasised on the many banners depicting the 'Rock Mass' that refer back to the Penal Laws imposed after the Williamite victories. Under these Catholics (and Presbyterians) were barred from public office and from bearing arms, and had restricted rights in trade, employment and land purchases. While the Catholic religion was not formally banned, the archbishops and bishops were banished from Ireland, and the secular clergy had restrictions placed on their movements. Religious services ('rock' or 'penal' mass) were held in the countryside away from civil and military authorities. The Penal Code had largely been abandoned or repealed by the end of the eighteenth century, although full rights to public political life only followed O'Connell's election to Parliament in 1829 (Beckett 1981; Jackson 1947). The Church is therefore depicted as being on the side of the people and against injustice, while attempting to focus an acceptable form that opposition and resistance should take.

The Roman Catholic Church in Ireland has never been able to hold the line on this issue consistently. While it has attempted to maintain its ethical stance, opposing violence, it has remained conscious of the feelings of the Catholic people, of the justness of the cause that drives people to desperate measures. This has meant that it has condemned the violence of the Easter Rising and of the IRA, but taken the perpetrators back into the body of the Church. The Church continues to walk a fine line: it opposes violence, yet often implicitly sanctions it retrospectively.

The dominant theme running through the images is therefore the importance of religion in forging and maintaining Irish national identity. Catholicism is depicted as the primal force in the creation of that identity; in the scenes of Patrick and Erin there are no signs of human agency on the natural landscape except for the churches. The Church is the agent that brings together the people, their culture (harp) and the natural world (wolfhound, shamrock) to forge them into a specific Irish Catholic Nation. Further, it is the Church and its supporters who are portrayed as the prime examples of resistance to English and Protestant domination. Physical resistance is perpetrated either in the name of the Catholic faith or directly by its sons acting within the faith of their fathers. Erin symbolises the passive spirit of the people, who need the leadership of the Church to mobilise them towards their destiny. The historical events commemorated by the AOH are remembered as successes for Catholic Ireland against England. But they were only ever short-term victories that necessitated further resistance:

victory at Benburb was followed by the arrival of Oliver Cromwell, who ruthlessly crushed resistance; Sarsfield was forced to capitulate to the Williamite forces and went into exile in the service of the King of France; the Wexford Rebellion, the most successful part of the United Irishmen's rising, was smashed after the defeat at Arklow, and the battle of Antrim paved the way for the suppression of the Ulster Rising.

The emphasis therefore is on both the legitimacy of rebellion and the importance of undertaking resistance to those forces that pose a threat to Catholic Ireland. But the banners also stress the mediating role of the Church and the importance of Church authority in defining the validity of the form. This helps explain the somewhat incongruous inclusion of the leaders of the 1916 Easter Rising on a banner, since the portraits of Pearse, Connolly, Clarke and McDonagh are contextualised by their adjacency to Emmett and O'Connell. The United Irishmen and the Repeal Association both represent the earlier tradition of struggle for emancipation in Ireland and also define the failed forms, mass peasant rising and popular civil protest, that give legitimacy to the urban, vanguardist military rising of 1916. Easter 1916 can be justified and understood not simply by the circumstances in Ireland at the time, but also by what had passed before. Finally, what links the socialist trade union leader (Connolly), the full-time revolutionary (Clarke), the poet and headmaster (Pearse) and the university lecturer (McDonagh) is their Catholicism and, following their surrender and execution (which generated the support and sympathy for the Rising that the reading of the Proclamation of the Republic had failed to do), their martyrdom and self-sacrifice for the cause of Ireland. It is their willingness to risk all for the cause that links Connolly and Pearse with Robert Emmett and in turn with Oliver Plunkett and keeps them as nationalist heroes, when the historical leaders of the AOH cause – Devlin, Dillon and Redmond – are largely forgotten.

Erin Risen – The Foresters Banners

The Maid of Erin is less important than images of Catholicism on the Hibernian banners; but she is the most popular image on the banners of the INF (Table 9.1). She is associated with the same symbols, harp, wolfhound and round tower, as on the AOH banners; but there are numerous subtle changes of emphasis. In most pictures Erin is standing rather than sitting, in three she is playing the harp rather than merely using it as a support, as the AOH Erin does, and in another four cases she is holding a green flag aloft. All of these images convey a sense of a more assertive character. The figure faces the viewer; frequently she is holding a sprig of shamrock, and in only one case is she pointing to the round tower as she does on the AOH banners. The round towers are more prominent, and in most cases a Celtic cross features in the foreground, while the rising sun is less prominent. There are no signs of angels or modern churches.

The impression that is being conveyed is that Erin is less a figure passively awaiting assistance than one confident in asserting her self-proclaimed identity. This invokes a sense of Irishness based on a history of self-justified actions, rather than one legitimated by reference to outside forces such as the Catholic Church. The green flag is held high. The harp is played, and is therefore less a symbol of a long lost past, than an expression of a still living and distinct culture. This living culture is further expressed by the use of the Irish language (*Eire go Bragh* – 'Ireland for Ever'), 'Celtic'-style lettering, and interlacing designs around the central image. These differences with the AOH banners are not absolute, but rather are expressed in terms of priorities and preferences. The INF banners in general also exhibit a wider range of forms in respect of frames, borders and border designs than those of all the other organisations; although remaining within a distinctive banner-making practice, the boundaries are being pushed out to embrace a broader range of styles and historical traditions.

Religious images do appear on the INF banners, however. Apart from the pictures of local ruined churches and churchmen, the most interesting images are of Saint Brigid and Saint Moninna. With St Patrick and St Columba, Brigid is the most important of the Irish saints, all three having shrines at the most famous Irish pilgrimage centre at Lough Derg (Taylor 1995; Toibin 1994). Brigid was the principal goddess of pagan pre-Christian Ireland, and was symbolised by a serpent and by the sun. Her feast day of Imbolc (1 February) marked the first day of spring and the first stirrings of new life. Although the historical St Brigid is credited with the founding of a monastic settlement at Kildare, very little is actually known of her life, and it is possible that she is no more than the adoption of pagan traditions into the body of early Irish Christian mythology (Condren 1989:Chapter 4). In her turn Brigid, as saint and virgin, has been made subordinate to Mary by the Irish church, replacing the active female ideal with its opposite.

St Moninna represents another version of the active and independent women in the growth of the early church: she too is accredited with the founding of numerous religious houses in England, Scotland and Ireland, but ultimately suffered from the power struggles in the male-dominated hierarchy (Condren 1989:101–2). That these two female saints should be represented on INF banners fits with the more assertive femaleness of the Erin figure. The AOH, on the other hand, prefers to stress the role of male figures like Patrick and Columba, and relegates any reference to Brigid to minor placings. The INF ideology supports a more active expression of Irish identity, one less constrained by the Roman Catholic Church and one more responsive to local trad-itions. If the AOH banners acknowledged the quandary of the Church in opposing but yet understanding political violence, then the INF banners are less equivocal: Irish nationhood will only be achieved through an active assertion of Irish identity.

Most of the remaining images depict a wide range of historical figures, each of whom is portrayed on a single banner. Each can be held as an example of the assertion of Irish identity. The individuals represent a diverse range of historical events that extend from the struggles of the Gaelic chiefs to the 1916 Rising. Red Hugh O'Donnell, who was an ally of Hugh O'Neill in the rebellion of the 1590s, and Patrick Sarsfield exemplify the earlier tradition of military rebellion; but the majority of those com-memorated date from the 1790s onwards, and many of them represent the modern tradition of armed rebellion. Henry Joy McCracken and William Orr were both members of the United Irishmen. Orr was executed in April 1796 for administering the UI oath to two soldiers: as a result he became the organisation's first martyr. McCracken was himself executed in 1798 after leading the unsuccessful Antrim rising (Elliot 1982). Father Theobold Mathew was a successful temperance campaigner across Ireland in the 1830s and 1840s (Malcolm 1986), while John Mitchel was a radical propagandist in the same period, who was exiled in May 1848 immediately before the Smith O'Brien rising (Kee 1989a).

Other figures include Sir Charles Russell who defended the nationalist leader Charles Stewart Parnell against charges that he was implicated in the Phoenix Park murders, and Thomas Sexton elected as MP for West Belfast in 1880 as part of the Home Rule landslide. He was Parnell's lieutenant for many years before they fell out (Lyons 1977). Finally, Roger Casement, who organised a supply of guns from Germany, and Padraic Pearce, who led the Provisional Government of the Irish Republic in the failed 1916 Easter Rising, are both commemorated. Both men were subsequently executed by the British Government.

All these men are depicted in simple portraits with just their names underneath. The banners, then, commemorate some of the most important characters and events in nineteenth-century Irish history. While they avoid Daniel O'Connell's activities, and make brief acknowledgement to the heroes of earlier times, the banners concentrate on those personalities and resistances to British rule in Ireland that were couched in terms of nationality rather than being expressed as religious differences. A significant point that can be made about the personalities who are featured on these banners is that Orr, McCracken, Mitchel, Parnell and Casement were all Protestants (Roger Casement converted to Catholicism while he was in prison following the Rising, and received his first and last Communion on the day of his execution (Kee 1989c)).

The Catholic Church is not invoked here to legitimise action (although Church leaders and buildings are depicted), but instead the broader ideal of national unity, encompassing the Presbyterian, Church of Ireland and Roman Catholic faiths, is the aim. The contemporary polarisation, in which political ideals are ascribed by religious faith, and the Protestant 'inevitable and natural' self-identification as British rather than Irish were not self-evident through the eighteenth century, but only emerged in the course of the nineteenth century, at a time of rapidly changing political and economic circumstances. The fusion of the politico-religious identities Catholic–Nationalist and Protestant–Unionist has never been completed; and, in particular, the tradition of radical Protestants who have maintained an Irish identity is well documented (Campbell 1991; Elliott 1985).

The widely used symbols of the Irish nation – the harp, the wolfhound, the round tower and the Celtic Cross – all allude to a sense of national identity that has continued, in spite of the British, from the far-distant past; but these symbols were in fact only brought together as such in the nineteenth century, within the context of the wide-ranging populist emancipation movement and the often apolitical cultural revival movement (Sheehy 1980). As was noted above, Hibernia/Erin and the harp were non-sectarian national symbols immediately prior to the United Irishmen rising in 1798, and it was not until the nineteenth century that they were redefined as icons of a Catholic and Gaelic identity. The United Irishmen movement was the first to adopt the ideals of nationality, made prominent by the French Revolution, as its aims; but the history of Irish rebellion throughout the following century was one that involved a constant struggle to raise this proud ideal above the more practical aspirations such as land rights, which were the real issues capable of motivating the mass of the impoverished peasantry. Nevertheless, it is the propagandists of the ideals of nationhood who are celebrated and commemorated: from Orr and McCracken onwards to the activities of the Foresters themselves, the INF banners uphold the ideals of 'Unity, Nationality and Benevolence' as the way forward for Ireland.

The AOH and the INF have a small membership compared with that of comparable loyalist organisations, and politically they are of little importance. Nevertheless, they remain an important facet of the parading tradition, and their displays represent a significant part of nationalist ideology. In the period between the end of the Second World War and the beginning of the Troubles, the AOH and the INF were prominent in maintaining a public presence for the nationalist tradition; but since 1968 constitutional nationalist supporters have largely abandoned the streets. Sinn Féin and the IRA have become the dominant public force within the nationalist movement. Republican parades and paintings have been the most visible displays of nationalism within the media; but their militant ideology represents only a fraction of nationalist supporters.

In recent years Sinn Féin has attracted some 35 per cent of the nationalist vote, while the constitutional nationalist Social Democratic and Labour Party (SDLP) attracts the other 65 per cent. The SDLP do not participate in parades, and their support is therefore largely invisible except at election time. While the AOH and the INF are not connected to the SDLP, the conservative, Catholic, constitutionalist ideologies that are displayed on their banners probably represent the ideals of a broader nationalist movement beyond the membership of these organisations. While advocating a religious and/or constitutionalist approach to contemporary politics, Irish nationalism can still celebrate the heroes of the long-dead past, and can continue to express a desire for a United Ireland while claiming to reject the tactics of the IRA. The visual displays of the AOH and INF commemorate many features of the broader traditions of nationalism that have been largely overwhelmed and obscured by the resurgence of the republican movement in the past twenty-five years.

However, the continued celebration of the heroes of 1798 and 1916, and by extension of their tactics, ultimately makes it difficult to reject out of hand the contemporary violence of the IRA. The distinction between acknowledging the legitimate violence of the 'heroes of 1798' or the Easter Rising and that of the present-day IRA becomes a fine one, just as the distinction between the historical and contemporary Protestant tradition of forming paramilitary groups for defence is a fine one. If the past is readily understood by reference to hindsight, then the present can also be understood by reference to the past. The lessons of the past continue to be propagated through the medium of highly decorated banners carried at public parades. The ideology of the AOH and INF remains grounded in the same historical roots as the republican movement. The images give support to the historical traditions of rebellion, of persecution and of the valorisation of secular saints who have offered their lives to the cause of Ireland. Ironically, Protestant/Unionists and Catholic/Nationalists celebrate and commemorate many of the same events, or at least the same narrow period. The 1640s, 1688–91, 1916 remain important historical dates for both communities. Even if the mirror is viewed from two different and mutually exclusive perspectives, the effect, to legitimise and reaffirm the importance of the gun in Irish political life, is the same on both sides. The banner displays by supporters of both Orange and Green obscure much of the more obvious support for the gun within the commemoration of a heroic and glorious past. Freed from the constraints of a formal tradition, and the need to be accountable to a wider constituency, the displays of support for the various paramilitary groups have no such coyness; they explicitly valorise the power and success of the gun. These images rarely appear on public parade, however; but in the past decade they have become highly visible on the walls of the working-class areas of Belfast and Derry. It is to the mural painting tradition that I now turn.

Trevor King Memorial; Disraeli Street, Belfast.

Part IV

Painting the Streets

Graffiti, Gobnascale, Derry, August 1992.

The practice of painting murals on gable walls in working-class areas dates from just before the First World War. Until 1981 it was almost totally a unionist preserve; but the republican hunger strikes of that year inspired a dramatic outpouring of slogans and images on the walls of the nationalist areas (Rolston 1991, 1992). This marked a new beginning in terms of the quantity of paintings being produced and the range of subjects that were depicted. Republican mural painting drew on designs and styles grounded in both Catholic and Celtic imagery, which were used to elaborate and visualise slogans graffitoed on the walls. This in turn led to a resurgence of loyalist paintings, which utilised both long-established subjects and also explored new themes and practices generated during the Troubles. Contemporary loyalist murals have moved away from the traditional subject-matter to constitute a distinct discourse that differs from, and sometimes conflicts with, mainstream unionist positions. The two bodies of mural works have developed in parallel over the past decade or so, and depict many similar themes and images; but the two communities are not engaged in a debate with each other via the murals – rather it is the shared socio-political environment that has helped to generate the similarities. The murals remain a part of two largely separate internal discourses.

Most murals are to be found in the working-class estates of Belfast and Derry, the areas that have been most affected by the violence and most polarised by sectarian divisions; but wall paintings can be found in many other towns and villages across the north. The impetus for much of the painting is the commemorative parades of the summer marching season, when these areas are extensively decorated with flags and bunting. Loyalist areas are decorated with red, white and blue bunting, and Union Jacks and Scottish and Ulster flags flown from permanently fixed flag-holders on houses and shops, while kerbstones, bollards, postboxes, lampposts and traffic lights are often painted red, white and blue and, more rarely these days, Orange arches are erected. In nationalist areas the displays of colour are more muted, and are often confined to flying the Irish tricolour, although lampposts and kerbstones are painted green, white and orange and bunting is hung out in some areas. The flags and bunting appear only for the marching season, and encode a restricted range of largely uncontested meanings; but the murals are on display more permanently, and may be visible for many years. They permit more elaborate ideas to be expressed: ideas that increasingly challenge or refocus the traditional values of the community, which are displayed on the banners, and re-present them as revalued by the experiences of the Troubles.

The colour-coded lampposts and kerbstones often mark the entry into a distinct territory; but most murals tend to be hidden away in back streets. They are rarely painted as provocative statements, and rarely make any obvious reference to the other community or any sense of conflict. In part this restraint has been to avoid the dangers of painting political statements in areas where one might be exposed to either the security forces or one's political enemies, but it also exerts a degree of control over the image and its meaning. It targets the image at the people who will more readily understand the nuances and allusions. Just as the marching orders control access to their images through restricted temporal display, so access to the murals is of a restricted spatial nature. The messages on the murals are not intended to convert the unbelievers.

Gable walls at the end of terraces provide the largest, most prominent sites on which to paint murals, although extensive redevelopment throughout the city has meant that murals are nowadays painted on a wide variety of walls. Sometimes images are painted on a board, which allows elaborate details to be included and enables the paintings to be replaced more readily, or to be protected from bad weather. The gable ends offer a large space to create an image; but this does not mean that all available space will be utilised. Some murals are painted two storeys high; but as this involves more work and more equipment – at least a ladder and sometimes scaffolding – many are therefore painted only to a height accessible to a pavement-level painter or use only a proportion of the wall area. In theory the consent of the owner of the building must be obtained before painting begins; but with much of the working-class housing rented from the Housing Executive, this is not possible: the Executive do not allow wall paintings on their properties. However, it is also known that they will not remove murals as they would graffiti, primarily because of the association between murals and paramilitary groups, and so their houses are often used. A controversy was generated at Easter 1993 after a letter to the *Belfast Telegraph* complained about a UDA mural on the Newtownards Road that had been painted without permission by 'three or four youths' over a period of days some months earlier. Although residents advocated that the painting should be removed, the police were unwilling to do anything and the Housing Executive would not send workers in because of the involvement of the paramilitaries (*BT* 6.4.1993, 13.4.1993; *News Letter* 14.4.1993). Three years later the murals were still on the walls; they have been repainted at least twice, and additional walls have since been incorporated into the display. Furthermore, the images are regularly and widely reproduced both in print and on television.

The earliest murals were the work of skilled paint craftsmen, house or shipyard painters, for whom it was an extension of their existing skills (Loftus 1990). But nowadays murals are more often the works of untrained, often unemployed men and youths (there are only a few murals that have been done by women) who are prepared to 'have a go'. Lyttle (n.d.), for example, records that a number of murals in the Mersey Street area of east Belfast were painted by two schoolboys. Usually the painting is done by people living in the area rather than by outsiders, although there are exceptions. Murals may even be collective efforts, with a more skilled designer setting out the main outline in chalks while friends help by filling in the colours. One Sandy Row painter claimed that the King Billy mural he was painting was his first attempt, although he had 'tidied up' another painting the previous week. He claimed no previous artistic experience, and based his design on a small photograph that he carried. The impetus for the mural was the Twelfth of July parade, and he worked steadily for several days to finish it on time. However, he returned to add some more detail and improve the framing columns in the week leading up to the march to mark the Tercentenary of the Boyne in September 1990. This painting was finished in time for the parade; but murals that are not ready by their appointed deadline may well be abandoned and left partly finished. Two years later the outline of a UDA emblem had been sketched out next to the King Billy, but no paint had been added: it was only completed after the loyalist ceasefire was declared, over four years after it had been started.

More recent (1995) encounters with mural painters suggests

some changes in the practice. The man who painted the Cúchulainn series in east Belfast was asked to paint them because of his
known artistic skills. He has subsequently established himself as
a sign-writer. A commemorative mural in the Shankill was also
'commissioned' from a man who painted landscapes and portraits
professionally. In this case an extensive array of gloss paints and
scaffolding were provided for the work. In 1995 the West Belfast
Festival commissioned a series of murals to commemorate the
150th anniversary of the Famine: these were designed and
overseen by a varied group of artists who worked with local
schoolchildren during the summer holidays. A small group of
painters now work almost full-time producing murals and other
political images for the republican movement.

Once the work is finished, the painter loses control of the mural.
It becomes the property or responsibility of the householder, the
organisation who had commissioned it, or the community. They
can be added to and changed as required. In this sense, a mural
need never be regarded as complete or finished. There is no
sanctity surrounding the painter's relationship to the work or the
form of the image. Some murals are clearly valued: they are
repainted if damaged or worn, and maintained over several years.
But both loyalist and republican murals are frequently painted
over and their sites reused. Sometimes, if the painting has been
damaged or if it related to a specific political campaign, it will
painted out and the wall left bare; on other occasions the image
will be replaced with a more up-to-date image. Several walls could
in theory be 'excavated' to reveal a succession of layers accumu-
lating as the different images have been painted over the years.
But there is little sentiment about mural paintings: a few have been
maintained almost as monuments, but most are expected to have
a short life. Whereas the images on banners have been restricted
to a limited number of traditional images and avoid commenting
on contemporary events, murals are much more closely reflective
of political events and processes. They represent the most dynamic
element in the commemorative political cycle.

Ulster Freedom Fighters; Snugville Street, Belfast, July 1994.

UVF – Still Undefeated; Woodstock Link, east Belfast, October 1994.

Chapter 10

At the Going Down of the Sun. . .

In the post-war period and during the early years of the Troubles, loyalist mural painting was in decline; but the appearance of republican murals in, and after, 1981 stimulated loyalist painters. From about 1984 a new wave of paintings began to appear, which were dominated by paramilitary figures and symbols. Unionist opposition to the Anglo-Irish Agreement of 1985 was a further stimulation to visual displays that placed stress on Ulster's British identity. In the past decade the emblems, flags and heraldic devices of the paramilitary groups have become more elaborate, and gunmen have appeared on walls with greater frequency. Within this shift of symbolism the relationship with Great Britain has become more uncertain and ambiguous; increasingly, Ulster has come to be defined in its own terms, independent of external authority, although there is still little visual support for an Independent Ulster. This period marks a transition from murals that espoused a unionist, i.e. a British-orientated, ideology to a loyalist position, in which Ulster appears as the principal focus of identity.

Although paramilitary images have come to dominate the murals of loyalist Belfast, the practice remains embedded within the commemorative calendar. The anniversaries of the Somme and the Boyne, and more recently Armistice Day in November, remain the events that encourage painters, even if traditional meanings and assumptions are no longer duplicated on the walls. The paramilitary groups have also begun to use murals to extend the commemorative process by painting memorials to their own dead. In this chapter I discuss the semiotics of the paramilitary iconography, and consider how these groups use both new and established symbols to situate themselves within the wider unionist tradition and legitimise themselves in the political arena. As part of this process the murals must be viewed as images in space as well as in time: analysis must be aware of how the location and juxtaposition of images can affect their meaning, a process that Barthes (1977) terms 'relay'. This encourages the viewer to interpret images not as self-contained statements, but rather within the wider context of adjacent and interacting images.

This is particularly important in the way in which established images of King Billy are now juxtaposed to paramilitary gunmen. The Orange banners largely ignore the Troubles and paramilitary groups; but mural paintings are used to force a confrontation between traditional meanings and contemporary values. This focus of analysis can be extended to explore variations in the subject-matter of murals in different areas of the city. Although murals are confined to working-class areas, they do not appear in all such areas: a close geographical analysis suggests that distinctive patterns of allegiances are displayed on the walls. While on one level murals are used to develop a working-class critique of the traditional middle-class dominance of the unionist legacy, these differences also express competitive territorial antagonisms within the loyalist working class. Both levels confirm the murals as part of an internal unionist discourse, rather than aimed at the republican enemy.

Paramilitary Iconography

Although King Billy is no longer the dominant image on the walls of Belfast, there are still at least ten paintings of him across the city. This represents only a small proportion of mural paintings; but they are so distributed that each working-class loyalist area has at least one wall devoted to him. The most recent King Billy painting appeared on Sandy Row in July 1990, while the long-established site at Rockland Street (dating from the 1920s) was repainted in both 1990 and 1991. King Billy therefore remains an important touchstone of continuity and certainty within loyalist visual displays. A few other murals depict the traditional images that are found on Orange banners: the Closing of the Gates at Derry, the Londonderry coat of arms, the Crown and Bible and commemorations of the battle of the Somme; but the most widespread images nowadays are representations and emblems of the paramilitary groups. The two main paramilitary groups are the Ulster Volunteer Force (UVF) and the Ulster Defence

Association (UDA) (for the history and development of these groups see Boulton 1973; Bruce 1992, 1994; and Nelson 1984).

The contemporary UVF appeared in 1966, and was banned the same year when its leaders were convicted of sectarian murder. It has since been a shadowy organisation without a public face, except in symbolic form. To define its identity and to legitimise its activities within the loyalist working class, the UVF adopted the name and emblems of the, widely admired, organisation from the Home Rule period. In so doing it claimed the inheritance of the Protestant tradition of forming into paramilitary groups when their position was perceived to be under threat, thus emphasising the similarity between past and present political situations. Although the UVF attempted to extend this link back to the eighteenth-century Volunteers in the early issues of their journal *Combat* (see Vol. 1 No. 2, April 1974), this has not been continued. Instead, the UVF emphasises the continuity with its predecessor and, by placing itself at the vanguard of loyalist activity, demands the support that the UVF received in the past. Their central symbol is an upright, gold-coloured oval with the Red Hand of Ulster in the centre and the words 'For God and Ulster' around the rim. UVF flags, purple with the Union flag in the upper left quadrant, are also common on murals. The use of the date 1912, and reference to the battle of the Somme, further stress the continuity between the two bodies. The symbol of the youth wing of the UVF, the Young Citizen Volunteers, a green shamrock with an initial on each leaf, which also dates from 1912, is also widely used on murals. A number of UVF and YCV murals were painted in 1987 at the 75th anniversary of the original body.

The UDA was formed in 1971 from a number of local vigilante groups that had sprung up to provide 'defence' for Protestant areas, as rioting and violence increased across the city. Initially it was a mass movement, and was able to demonstrate its strength by parading publicly and manning barricades in no-go zones of loyalist Belfast. In 1974 the UDA was involved in organising the Ulster Workers' Council strike, which was a catalyst in the dismantling of the new power-sharing assembly at Stormont (Anderson 1994). Unlike the UVF, the UDA was unable to claim an obvious history, and had to create an elaborate iconography to locate itself within the loyalist tradition. Their emblem was developed from the Ulster coat of arms, a red cross on a white shield, with the Red Hand in a six-point star in the centre. The initials appear over the shield in a scroll, and their motto 'Quis Separabit' ('Who Shall Separate Us') similarly underneath. Each quadrant contains the symbol of one of the four groups within the organisation, the UDA, the Ulster Freedom Fighters (UFF), the Loyalist Prisoners Association (LPA) and the Ulster Defence Force (UDF): all involve variations of the Red Hand. The UDA emblem has a Red Hand on a blue field under a crown; the UFF (the name used by the UDA when carrying out acts of violence, and banned since 1973) use a simple clenched red fist; the LPA emblem shows the red hand entwined in barbed wire, but, with the crown over it, emphasises continued loyalty despite imprisonment. Finally, the UDF depicts a winged Red Hand with the motto 'Sans Peur'. Usually the UDA shield is flanked by the Union Jack and the Ulster flag, although sometimes the Scottish flag replaces one of these. This coat of arms is based on the device adopted by Ulster Unionists as their version of the historical Ulster symbol during the Home Rule crisis. The composite UDA emblem appeared in the UDA journal in July 1986 (the simple UDA emblem had appeared in April 1985). Initially the UDA used the motto 'Cedant Arma Togae' ('Law Before Violence'), but their ancestry was enhanced by adopting the motto 'Quis Separabit'. This was first used on the insignia of the Knights of the Most Illustrious Order of St Patrick, founded in 1783 by George III (Hayes-McCoy 1979:40); it was later taken up by the Ulster Unionist Convention in Belfast in 1892 (Kee 1982:136), and became the motto of the Royal Irish Rifles, who fought at the Somme. Although they have followed a less direct path, the UDA adopted a similar strategy to the UVF, and have linked their activities with those of an earlier generation of loyalists. But where the UVF favoured open identification with the paramilitary tradition, the UDA immersed themselves among constitutional emblems and symbols.

Shankill Murals

By juxtaposing paramilitary and traditional emblems the UDA and UVF use the walls of Belfast to locate themselves within the loyalist community. These conjunctions veil their own overt militarism, but also adapt the dominant meanings and values of unionist symbols and historical icons by emphasising the militaristic possibilities of the 'legal' traditions. The process by which the meaning of traditional or Orange symbols is reinterpreted can be seen by the group of murals in Percy Place, a small cul-de-sac at the bottom of the Shankill Road. These were painted by a local man, Alan Skillen, in July 1984, with materials that were bought with money donated by local people (*BT* 3.7.84); they were repainted in 1993. On one side of the road are two large paintings, one of King Billy on horseback, with next to it an outline map of Northern Ireland on which the Union Jack and the words 'Shankill, No Surrender' are superimposed. Facing these are five painted gables: the first has a crowned shield in Scottish colours flanked by a Union Jack and the Ulster flag and the slogan 'No Surrender 1690'; the next depicts a crowned Red Hand with the Scottish and Ulster flags and the words 'Ulster, Scotland, United We Stand'; the central painting is a shield, based on the UDA emblem, but which here includes both UDA and UVF emblems in the four quadrants – behind the shield are two Union Jacks, and the slogan reads 'Shankill Supports All the Loyalist Prisoners'; the fourth mural is a Red Hand on a blue shield with the words '1690, God Save the Queen'; while on the fifth wall a Bible and Crown has the words 'One Faith, One Crown' written across the pages. Collectively, these seven murals depict established unionist themes, and, apart from the reference to the loyalist prisoners, would not seem out of place on an Orange parade; but the reference to paramilitarism is muted and presented as an act of solidarity with the prisoners, rather than support for militarism.

However, beneath these large murals are four smaller paintings extending across the lower garden walls: these constitute a sub-text that changes the whole tone of the display. The first also depicts a Union Jacked outline of Ulster, but in the centre a hooded gunman raises a clenched fist and proclaims 'We Will Never Accept a United Ireland, Ulster Still Says No'; the second is a blue UDA shield with other paramilitary emblems around it; the third portrays a hooded gunman in front of an Ulster and a UVF flag and two UVF shields, and the slogan states 'This is Loyalist West Belfast, Shankill No Surrender'; on the final painting the UDA shield sits in front of the Scottish and Ulster flags. In contrast to the large paintings, this group of images focuses solely on paramilitary concerns; but their proximity to the larger unionist murals means that the meaning of the latter is both elaborated and re-orientated.

If the paramilitary groups are attempting to define themselves as the contemporary expression of traditional values, then these traditional values must be reconsidered as well. The paramilitary allusion to the potential and actual violence behind the Protestant Ascendancy forces recognition of the darker side of Ulster history. Thus the Red Hand proclaiming 'God Save the Queen' is directly above a Red Hand in the centre of a UDA shield; the gunman on the red, white and blue Ulster is opposite a similar map with the Ulster star in the centre. The Union Jack features prominently on the larger paintings, but has virtually disappeared from the symbolic repertoire of the paramilitary groups (although the Crown is still loyally invoked by the UDA), and the Scottish flags become an extension of Protestant solidarity rather than con-stitutional unity.

Rolston states that collectively these murals depicted 'an intense representation of loyalist armed struggle that had not been witnessed previously' (1991:40); and this group remains one of the most elaborate of such displays. The paintings link the aims and ideals of the UDA/UVF with those of mainstream Unionism in defending Ulster's links with Britain. But, as we have already seen with regard to Orange iconography, the ambivalence as to what those links are at heart remains a problem: Ulster is still British but, apart from the Crown, Scotland is the only clearly identified embodiment of that union. These murals suggest the emergent working-class critique of Orangeism that foreshadowed the rise of the two loyalist political parties, the Progressive Unionist Party and the Ulster Democratic Party, since the ceasefire of October 1994. Although the paintings reframe the traditional meanings of unionist symbols, they make no attempt to question the sectarian nature of Ulster's political system, and their reinterpretation can only be taken so far. The loyalists may challenge the middle-class values of the political order of Unionism, but their paintings do not challenge Protestant unity.

Murals and Local Identity

On the Shankill the murals of the main paramilitary groups can be found side by side; but in south Belfast murals are used to express the distinctive local identities within the Protestant community, rather than create an appearance of paramilitary unity. The people of Sandy Row, Donegall Pass, Roden Street and the Village are united by their membership of the Orange Order, and they are symbolically linked by the mini-Twelfth parades; but there remains a degree of hostility and competitiveness between the people of these areas (Holloway 1994a,b). The sense of antagonism and difference between locales within the loyalist community is here made visible in the patterns of allegiance that are displayed on the walls. Although paramilitary murals predominate in south Belfast, Orange subjects are more numerous than elsewhere: each of the four areas has a prominent painting of King William, and five of the ten King Billy paintings in the city are in this small area. At Rockland Street, in the Village, King Billy has occupied the same site since the late 1920s. Another painting on the Donegall Pass, and the adjacent memorial to the late Robert Bradford MP, are replicas of murals that were located in nearby Lindsay Street until redevelopment destroyed them. In both cases the paintings themselves provide a touchstone of continuity within areas that have undergone major physical and demographic change. They provide a visible expression of the seemingly unchanged ideals of unionism through times of uncertainty.

However, the King Billy on Sandy Row has been adapted to the context of the Troubles: here the king is accompanied by two gunmen, one in seventeenth-century costume and the other in contemporary fatigues. An adjacent scroll bears the words 'We the loyalist people of Sandy Row remember with pride the 300th anniversary of the Battle of the Boyne, No Surrender, signed UFF'. Here William is less the champion of civil and religious liberties and more a warrior king. Elsewhere, apart from a small UVF painting, UDA murals dominate Sandy Row, and, in response to the IRA ceasefire of September 1994, the UDA presence was reaffirmed. Two new UDA and UFF murals were painted, and a UDA shield was added beside King Billy.

In contrast, in nearby Donegall Pass there are no references to the UDA: the most prominent murals, besides King Billy, commemorate the 36th Ulster Division and the battle of the Somme. One depicts three soldiers with heads bowed mourning their fallen comrades, while nearby the emblem of the South Belfast Young Conquerors Flute Band is incorporated among the symbols of the UVF, the YCV, the Royal Irish Rifles and the 36th Ulster Division. The most recent addition, in late 1995, was an elaborate memorial mural to the UVF dead, depicting a piper playing a lament for fallen comrades. Through such displays of support for the paramilitary groups the sense of distinction and local identity is displayed in this area, and a clear difference is marked from neighbouring loyalist areas.

A similar contrast between adjacent and otherwise seamless areas is apparent between the Village and Roden Street. At the head of Roden Street a large memorial to John McMichael, a former leader of the UDA, incorporates references to the local flute band, the Roden Street Defenders and the UFF. In nearby streets there are a number of UDA emblems and a hooded UFF gunman, as well as the King Billy. There are no references to other paramilitary groups. But only a few streets away, in the Village, the murals proclaim support for the UVF and the small Red Hand Commando paramilitary group, of which little has been written. In contrast to the Shankill, the paramilitary groups in south Belfast appear to have distinct, separate territories, with no common space for combined displays.

But this territorial division may have as much to do with music as guns. As Bell (1990) noted in his study of young loyalists in Derry, it is the young men, often members or supporters of the blood and thunder bands, who play the most prominent role in decorating the areas and building the bonfires for the Twelfth celebrations. The bands often form a centre of social life; band halls function as social clubs and illegal bars, and many bands attract a sizeable following of friends and neighbours when they parade. It is the bands who have introduced paramilitary emblems to Orange parades, and this has been extended on to many walls, as bandsmen have co-opted mural painting for their own interests: a number of paintings celebrating flute bands have appeared among paramilitary images.

These paintings vary between those which create a trade mark image for the band and those which link a band with a paramilitary group. The Roden Street Defenders band link themselves sym- bolically and linguistically with the UDA, while the neighbouring Pride of the Village Flute Band incorporated their name into the Red Hand Commando mural adjacent to the King Billy on Rockland Street. The division of allegiance between the UDA in Roden Street and the UVF/RHC in the Village coincides with the support for the two different bands. By no means all bands are closely connected with paramilitary groups; but newspaper reports, following a particularly vicious murder in 1994, suggested that a number of members of the Pride of the Village were members of the Red Hand Commando. The band is no longer in existence, although it lives on through its mural.

The relationship between bands and the paramilitary groups is complex and shadowy, but both use murals to leave a more permanent mark on the city. Band murals are widespread, and give a permanent presence to groups who are otherwise only visible on parading days. They often impress themselves on the viewer with the unlikely juxtaposition of cartoon figure emblems and paramilitary symbols. The South Belfast Young Conquerors mural on Donegall Pass contains a cartoon viking figure alongside many references to the 36th Ulster Division. The Gertrude Star Flute Band on Templemore Avenue, in east Belfast, use a bulldog, Donald Duck and UDA emblems as the basis for their designs. In both cases the band have constructed their iconography within parameters established by the two main paramilitary groups, as well as including their own distinctive characters.

Clearly many murals are painted both for and by supporters of the paramilitary groups; but, at the same time, the bands frequently adopt paramilitary regalia, and often transfer their support on to the walls around where they live. It may be impossible to distinguish between areas where 'genuine' support for the paramilitaries is strong and areas where the young are claiming allegiance as a mark of distinction. But it would also be wrong to suggest that there is no 'real' paramilitary involvement in the murals. The UDA mural to John McMichael, on Roden Street, has, on occasion, been defaced by UVF graffiti (presumably by lads from the Village); but these have always been quickly removed. In April 1993 the UDA magazine *New Ulster Defender* carried photographs of three paint-bombed UDA murals in the Roden Street area, the report ended with an ominous remark 'It is hoped that those responsible for defacing the murals will be caught and the punishment will fit the crime.' Although there is no evidence that any punishment resulted from this defacing of the mural, it is an indication that the paramilitary groups regard at least some of the paintings as more than mere transient graffiti.

Lest We Forget

The practice of honouring the dead on murals is an extension of
the wider process of legitimising paramilitary activities that began
with the adoption of the 1912 UVF emblems, and of the battle of
the Somme as the epitome of the courage, heroism and military
prowess of the Ulstermen. It is the Somme that provides the
imagery and rhetoric for many of the memorial murals. One of
the earliest of these was a UVF mural in Ballysillan, north Belfast,
dating from 1986, which commemorated the dead and the
imprisoned members of the organisation. The design was based
on the UVF banners carried on parades, but with the list of
campaigns fought in the First World War replaced by the names
of UVF volunteers. The first UDA memorial mural appeared the
following year on Dee Street, in east Belfast, and forms a 'Roll of
Honour' to seventeen members of the East Belfast UDA who have
been killed in the Troubles. Painted in the apex of a gable wall,
the names of the dead appear on scrolls wrapped around classical
columns. In the centre the UDA shield is suspended from a cross.
A similar, but larger design, commemorating the south Belfast
UDA, with John McMichael's name prominently displayed, was
painted on a gable on Sandy Row in October 1994. Another
common image is derived from the Somme mural on Donegall
Pass: this painting features three silhouetted figures mourning
their fallen comrades; their heads are bowed and their hands rest
on their weapons. This is the pose the guard of honour adopts at
the state Armistice Day commemorations. This representation of
sorrow has subsequently been used on a number of murals to the
paramilitary dead. Two figures flank the memorial to UDA leader
John McMichael at Roden Street, while a single figure mourns UVF
gunman Brian Robinson in Woodvale; on Hopewell Avenue two
figures mark the memorial to Red Hand Commando member
Stevie McCrea. In a further comparison between the sacrifice on
the Somme and the sacrifice for modern Ulster, the Hopewell
Avenue mural quotes and adapts lines from Laurence Binyon's
poem 'For the Fallen', which is the standard eulogy at First World
War commemorations:

> For he shall not grow old
> As we that are left grow old
> Age shall not weary him
> Nor the years condemn
> At the going down of the sun
> And in the morning
> We will remember him.

This process, by which the paramilitary groups compare themselves and their dead with those who fell at the Somme, has been made more explicit elsewhere:

> At this time of year when Ulster Loyalists everywhere commemorate and celebrate the sacrifices and victories throughout our proud history in general, but in particular at the siege of Londonderry and the great battles of the Boyne and the Somme. Let us not forget those, who during our present conflict, have made the supreme sacrifice, and those who have sacrificed their liberty, in our struggle. (Communiqué 1 July 1991, from UDA Inner Council, *Ulster*, July/August 1991).

As well as appearing on murals, McMichael, Robinson and McCrea are also commemorated by bands and on banners carried at Orange parades. While the Orangemen commemorate the sacrifice of Protestant martyrs for their faith and for the 'Glory of God', and remember the men of the 36th Ulster Division who died for King and Country, the paramilitary fight is fought for Ulster alone. Another memorial, painted in 1991 in Percy Place to 'Councillor and Assemblyman George Seawright' (who was expelled from the DUP after suggesting that all Catholics should be incinerated, and later killed by the Irish People's Liberation Organisation (Bruce 1992)) is symbolically linked to the Somme by a bunch of red poppies, but contextualised with the lines 'In remembrance of all those who have given their lives and their freedom in the struggle to keep Ulster Protestant'. Militarism alone is seen as insufficient to establish the broader morality of the cause, but once the sacrifices of today are seen to match the sacrifices of 1916 then the cause is ennobled and the paramilitary campaign can legitimately map itself on to the heroic history of Ulster; and just as the UVF claim of the Somme dead that 'Not just today, seventy-five years on, but for ever more shall their name liveth . . . Ne Obliviscaris' (*Combat* July 1991), and while the contemporary paramilitary groups remember the fighting heroes of the past, they also intend that the volunteers of the contemporary campaign will be remembered 'at the going down of the sun, and in the morning'.

Changing Allegiances

The resurgence of mural painting within the loyalist working-class areas peaked about 1988. The signing of the Anglo-Irish Agreement at Hillsborough in 1985 had heightened political tension in the north, with widespread unionist opposition expressed on the streets by the 'Ulster says No' campaign. These protests, and the 75th anniversary of the UVF in 1987, gave an opportunity and the impetus to the paramilitary groups to extend their public presence and the chance to legitimise their place within the loyalist tradition. The paintings in Percy Place and a similar extensive group in the Mersey Street area of east Belfast (Jarman 1992) exemplified the way in which the loyalists initially situated themselves ideologically within the unionist tradition. Their ideals built on and extended the established icons and symbols of the Ulster Protestants. The paramilitaries only claimed or extended the meaning of symbols that were already widely recognised and understood.

But, in recent years, images have begun to appear that ignore or reject many of the traditional symbols, and instead incorporate new designs that express something of a shift in publicly expressed beliefs. Since 1992 a group of paintings has been built up over four gables and the connecting garden walls on the Newtownards Road, in east Belfast. These explore and develop the theme of the changing nature of Ulster's identity. The first painting appeared as the Ulster Defence Regiment was being amalgamated with the Royal Irish Rangers to create the Royal Irish Regiment. Many loyalists saw the replacement of Ulster by Irish in the name as a significant reflection of the influence of Dublin on Ulster affairs. A UDR man and a 'B' Special policeman are identified with the slogan 'Ulster's Past Defenders'; behind them are the Ulster flag and the Union Jack, and beneath them the question 'Who will Defend Ulster Now?' The 'B' Specials were an almost totally Protestant police reserve formed at the same time as the Northern Ireland state in 1920, and disbanded in 1970 because of their violence and sectarianism (Farrell 1983; Weitzer 1995). The Ulster Defence Regiment, a locally raised unit of the British Army, was regarded as a Protestant regiment, and there had been a number of accusations of collusion and co-membership between the UDR and the UDA/UVF (Bruce 1992). On the gable wall to the right of this mural a UDA gunman, identified as one of 'Ulsters Present-Day Defenders', stands beside the mythical hero Cúchulainn, described as an 'Ancient defender of Ulster from Irish attacks over 2000 years ago'. They stand over a Union Jack and beside a shield decorated with the Ulster cross. Connecting these two images are the words 'Our message to the Irish is simple, Hands off Ulster, Irish Out. The Ulster Conflict is about Nationality.'

These paintings make explicit claims for the UDA as a continuation of the 'B' Specials and the UDR tradition; but more significantly they also mark the debut of Cúchulainn on the walls of loyalist Belfast. Whereas the UVF have presented themselves as the inheritors of the tradition of the Protestant volunteer militias, this is the first time that the UDA have spelled out their claimed ancestry rather than simply alluded to a history through heraldic emblems and Williamite images. The tradition of the loyalist defenders of Ulster is extended to the dawn of Ulster's history. Cúchulainn, central figure of the Celtic epic *Táin Bó Cuailnge*, has until recently been regarded solely as a nationalist hero and is widely used in republican visual memorials (see below); but within the past twenty years he has begun to be invoked as an Ulsterman as part of a revision of Irish prehistory that includes asserting that the Protestants are more Irish than the Irish (Adamson 1974, 1982, 1991; Adamson, Hume and McDowell 1995; Hall 1986; Ulster Young Unionist Council 1986).

Over Easter 1993 another painting was added and changes were made to the Cúchulainn mural. The new mural, to the Ulster Young Militants, included the red, blue and yellow Independent Ulster flag next to a Scottish flag and a UYM shield with a clenched Red Hand; it also included the established Orange refrain, 'Our civil and religious liberties we will maintain.' Large letters designated the area 'Ulster's Freedom Corner.' The Cúchulainn mural was repainted and the UDA emblem made more prominent (this also now uses the Independent Ulster colours) and, more significantly, the shield design was changed from the red and white Ulster cross to the new Independent Ulster design. Although the idea of an

Independent Ulster has been floated periodically within the UDA (Graham and McGarry 1990; UDA 1979; UPRG 1987) and by the small Ulster Independence Committee, it had not been taken up in the popular political arena until Independent Ulster flags began appearing at parades and in street decorations in July 1992. They now appear widely in areas where the UDA is prominent. Finally, in 1994, a fourth wall was claimed by the muralists: this was dominated by a hooded UFF gunman and a large clenched red fist, and beside the figure was an acknowledgement of the loyalist prisoners: 'Their only crime is loyalty – We forget them not.'

This painting completed a sequence that set out the ideological position of the various groupings within the UDA: although it anchors itself on the touchstones of loyalty to the Crown and Britain, it also clearly defines a position of self-reliance based on the security of the gun. Rolston (1991) has argued that since the onset of the Troubles the Protestant community have gone through a period of confusion and uncertainty regarding their identity and status within the United Kingdom, that old symbols and values have lost their meaning and new ones have not been forthcoming to replace them. It has been left to the young males to reaffirm and redefine a sense of community, and this, in turn, has led to a increasing reliance on militaristic values rather than the religious traditions of their parents. Traditional images have not disappeared or been abandoned, and they are still paraded at every opportunity; but they are now being challenged and redefined more systematically from within.

As the Unionist certainties have been undermined, so the Orange hegemony has faded: the supporters of the UDA and UVF have literally created a space within the Protestant community to challenge accepted notions of loyalty. Politicians have increasingly been seen as ineffectual in providing the economic security and standards they once delivered, and the role of the security forces, especially when they have confronted loyalists, has also seemed open to question. The Ulster Protestant working class have always had an ambivalent attitude to the British state, loyalty being balanced by fear of betrayal, and it is this relationship that the idea of an Independent Ulster confronts head on. Although the idea is regularly talked down by all parties, it regularly resurfaces. Previous attempts to construct a political framework for loyalism have been defeated from within, the fear of compromise stronger than the desire for change; but the calling of a loyalist ceasefire in October 1994 and the emergence of the loyalist political parties into the public arena seems to indicate a desire to develop and express new ideas.

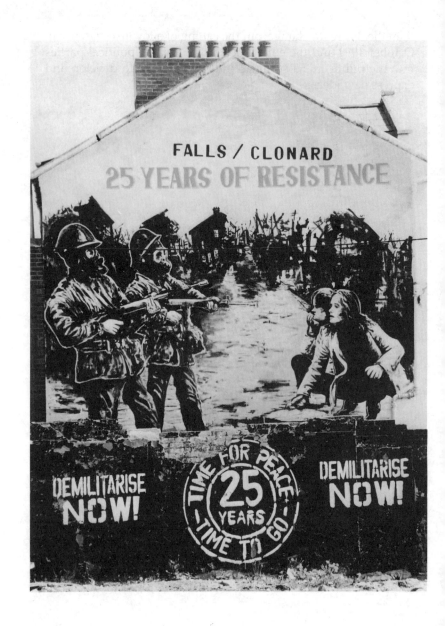

25 Years of Resistance; Falls Road, August 1994.

Unbowed – Unbroken; Lenadoon, October 1995.

Chapter 11

Hungering for Peace

Under the Stormont government the 1954 Flags and Emblems Act was used to ban nationalist visual displays wherever they were likely to cause an offence; in practice this was often interpreted to mean anywhere in Northern Ireland. This meant that public commemorations of Irish nationalist history or republican heroes were largely muted, and any attempts to mount prominent displays were inevitably opposed by loyalists. When a tricolour was displayed at the Republican Party offices in Divis Street in the Lower Falls in the run-up to the 1964 general election, Ian Paisley threatened to lead a protest to remove it. This threat forced the police to act first (the RUC station was next door to the offices), and they smashed their way into the offices and removed the offending flag. It was replaced the next day. When the offending flag was removed a second time, rioting broke out, and at least 30 people were taken to hospital with serious injuries (Boyd 1987).

In 1970, two men were sentenced to six months' imprisonment for painting a tricolour and the slogan 'Ireland Unfree shall never be at Peace' in Annadale Street in Belfast (*Irish News* 23.7.1970). Ten years later, a sixteen-year-old youth was shot dead by the RUC as he painted republican slogans. The constable claimed that he thought the paint brush was a gun, and was found not guilty of murder (Rolston 1991:102). These examples illustrate the measures that were taken to prevent displays of support for republicans, and indicate how the police were instrumental in maintaining the public face of the 'Protestant State' (see Bryson and McCartney (1994) for an extended discussion on the use of flags and emblems in Northern Ireland). Excluded from contributing to the broader political or cultural identity of Northern Ireland, the identity of the nationalist community was maintained and developed through the Catholic Church, Gaelic sports, music and dancing. The cultural practices of the two dominant communities scarcely overlapped, operating in different spaces, at different times and at times in different languages, and the public domain remained unionist and loyal to a British identity.

However, the explosion of painting that appeared in the nationalist estates of Belfast, Derry and elsewhere during the hunger strikes of 1981 did not emerge from a vacuum. The expansion of the IRA armed struggle throughout the 1970s led to a growing prison population. Some of these prisoners had been convicted, but many had simply been interned since the practice was introduced in August 1971. The internment centres in turn became (among other things) educational centres, as the prisoners taught themselves political theory, Irish history and the Irish language. Among other activities, many inmates turned to crafts and artistic works, producing paintings, woodcarvings and leather work to be sent out to friends and relatives, featuring such images as Celtic crosses, harps, the phoenix and portrayals of republican political heroes such as Pearse and Connolly (Adams 1990; Rolston 1991). They also decorated their own quarters in the compounds of Long Kesh (as they do today in the H Blocks): 'there were murals . . . the Proclamation of the Irish Republic with the heads of the signatories drawn around it, and on the opposite side was a big portrait, the red face, black beret, and star of Che Guevara. So you had Guevara and 1916' (internee Jake Jackson quoted in O'Malley (1990:45)).

Religious, Gaelic and historical symbols and images were forged together with internationalist icons to create a new republican iconography that would later be reproduced on the nationalist streets of Belfast, Derry and elsewhere. The first republican murals appeared in support of the hunger strikers in the H Blocks of Long Kesh prison. From 1976, as part of a wider process designed to depoliticise the situation in Northern Ireland, Special Category (political) Status was revoked for new prisoners. Many of the republican prisoners in Long Kesh and in the women's prison at Armagh who were subsequently denied special status refused to wear prison clothing and went 'on the blanket', with only prison issue blankets as covering. After four years the Blanket Protest had failed to achieve its aims, and pressure was increased with a hunger strike. This ended after 53 days, without any deaths, when a compromise agreement seemed to have been reached; but, when it appeared that this agreement was not being implemented, a second hunger strike began on 1 March 1981. This was led by Bobby Sands, the Officer Commanding the IRA prisoners (Beresford 1987; Clarke 1987; O'Malley 1990).

In the summer of 1979, while the prisoners were still on the blanket protest, Bobby Sands had sent a 'comm' (a smuggled communication between prisoners and the movement on the outside) suggesting that 'a massive Paint and Poster campaign' and a painting spree 'that would cover the countryside' should be started to increase awareness and support for the prisoners (O'Malley 1990:54). The appearance of these standardised slogans and simple images prepared the ground for the murals. But this style of painting only took off after Sands died after 66 days on strike, having been elected Westminster MP for Fermanagh and South Tyrone in the meantime. In the months after his death, over 150 murals were painted in Northern Ireland (Rolston 1991). The early murals were dominated by the hunger strikes, especially paintings of Bobby Sands portraying him as a smiling young man. Other images depicted prison brutality, or linked the long-haired emaciated appearance of the prisoners with Catholic images of the suffering Christ. Alongside these representations of the prisoners, images of IRA volunteers with assorted weapons also appeared. After the hunger strikes ended, murals supporting the continuing political and military campaign appeared, as the initially spontaneous outburst of painting was co-opted within the resurgent republican movement and became part of the Sinn Féin publicity machine.

Mural paintings were one facet of a broader movement that sought to 'draw support' for republicanism and also elaborate on the cultural traditions that provide the ideological framework for resistance to British rule in Ireland. Alongside the small number of militarily active members of the IRA, the republican movement includes a wide range of political and cultural activists who may give more or less support for the tactics of the armed struggle, while endorsing the aim of a United Ireland. Mural painting is part of this broad 'culture of resistance', which has flourished, particularly in west Belfast, since the 1980s (Scott 1990; Sluka 1992, 1995). While their initial focus was in the prison struggles, mural paintings have been used to address a range of political issues, and more recently many have focused on subjects that appear to have little to do with the generally accepted demands of the IRA. However, I will attempt to draw the strands of this corpus together.

At any one time there are around 100 murals in Belfast and 20 or so in Derry. Some of these date back to the mid-eighties, but the majority have been painted in more recent years. Having established a 'tradition' of mural painting, the range of the subject-matter of republican murals has been expanded beyond its original narrow focus. They are now used to commemorate their history, to celebrate their culture in its widest sense, and as part of their political campaign. The expansion of murals and other public imagery following the IRA ceasefire in 1994 merely confirms how the medium has become central to the political process in the past fifteen years.

Sinn Féin and the IRA have a near-monopoly of mural paintings in nationalist areas. None of the smaller republican groups have a visual presence on the streets, other than graffiti, and neither does the larger political grouping within the nationalist movement, the Social Democratic and Labour Party. The types of territorial variation in support for the paramilitaries found in loyalist areas are not a factor in the development of republican murals. The major exception to this republican monopoly are a number of murals sponsored by the Catholic Church. The Church has always had a visual impact in nationalist areas, with statues of the Madonna outside churches and streetside grottoes in some areas; but the use of murals was a new departure that followed in the wake of the republican movement. Depictions of the Madonna and Child can be found in most nationalist areas, in the same way as King Billy can be found in loyalist areas. Often found near to an IRA mural, these paintings represent the two ideological poles of the nationalist community.

Although republican murals began as a part of a political campaign, they have been adapted to the commemorative process in nationalist areas just as they have by loyalists. However, republicans more readily focus on the events of the recent past, as part of the continuity of resistance and suffering against imperialism. The 1981 Hunger Strikers are still recalled, particularly through depictions of the portrait of Bobby Sands or more indirectly by the representation of a lark, which was Sands's prison pen name. Sands is portrayed prominently in Twinbrook where he lived, and again on the wall of the Republican Press Centre on the Falls Road. Both murals bear his insistent claim: 'Everyone, Republican or otherwise has his/her own part to play.' The Falls

Road mural (repainted after the ceasefire) is seen by everyone coming up the main thoroughfare of west Belfast.

Until the winter of 1992, this portrait faced a mural of Nelson Mandela that had been painted to mark his seventieth birthday in 1988. This was one of a number of solidarity murals used to link the IRA campaign with other national liberation struggles (these include the Basques, Catalans, PLO, native Americans and most recently Australian Aborigines). In this case an analogy was made between the position of the two men and the state of their countries. Mandela, the imprisoned radical whose cause was taken up by Western governments, and who was soon to become the President of South Africa, was confronted by Bobby Sands MP, who was regarded as a criminal and allowed to die by Margaret Thatcher's government (or 'murdered by fellow members of Parliament' as one painting in Andersonstown states).

Joe McDonnell was another hunger striker commemorated on a mural, which was painted to mark the tenth anniversary of his death. This painting was unveiled at a formal opening ceremony, only to be damaged by a paint bomb three days later (*An Phoblacht* 25.7.1991). Having been repainted at least once and then further damaged it was replaced by a mural proclaiming Irish–Basque solidarity in August 1992. This wall has in turn been painted twice more since then.

In fact, most of the H Block paintings have been replaced as the sites have been used for new images, but a small number of them remain. Some, like the one on the New Lodge Road, use an early design of a bearded blanket man staring out above the prison skyline with the slogan 'You stood by them then! Remember them now!' This generalised and depersonalised representation of gaunt, unkempt blanket men appears in stark contrast to other recent paintings, which return to portraits of the ten who died, and who remain immortalised in their pre-prison appearance as smiling, youthful, healthy and well-groomed young men.

Republicanism as Tradition

The Hunger Strike memorial in Derry's Shantallow estate, and the Sands memorial in Twinbrook, symbolically situate the Hunger Strikes within the wider republican tradition, by including a prominent representation of a phoenix rising from the fires of death. The phoenix was adopted into Irish politics as the emblem of the Irish Republican Brotherhood (the Fenians), who appeared in the 1860s and were centrally involved in the 1916 Easter Rising (Newsinger 1994). The phoenix symbolises the process of rebirth from the ashes of defeat and thereby the indestructibility of the republican cause. It affirms the inevitability and certainty of continued risings until a United Ireland is obtained. Its historical resonance therefore is to link the IRA with their nineteenth-century counterparts. But it also resonates with the early years of the Troubles, as it was the rioting and burning of Catholic houses in the lower Falls area that brought about the rebirth of the IRA itself from an almost moribund position in 1969 (Conroy 1988). Just as republicans proclaim that the Irish people cannot be defeated, so the IRA rose from the ashes of previous defeated armed rebellions. The phoenix is one of a number of symbols that the republican movement uses to situate itself and its activities historically, and many of these are brought together on murals to the Easter Rising, the seminal historical event for modern republicanism.

One of the most vibrant of these is on the Whiterock Road, where the seven signatories to the proclamation of Irish Independence, along with the Countess Markievicz (the first woman elected as a Westminster MP, but also an acknowledgement of the role of women within the republican movement: see Benton 1995; Ward 1983, 1995), appear over the date 1916, which is painted in huge flaming numbers. The Dublin GPO, headquarters of the rebels, burns in the corner, while on the apex of the gable the phoenix rises from the flames, beside the Starry Plough, symbol of the Irish Citizen Army, and an orange sunburst, a symbol used by the Repeal Association in the 1840s, the Fenians in the 1870s and the Irish Volunteers in 1914, and now the symbol of the *Fianna Éireann*, the republican youth movement. The painting therefore includes a dense and elaborate array of historical and political reference points; such connections are made on a number of paintings.

Other murals to the Rising also include important symbols such as the Easter lily and the flags of the four provinces of Ireland. With its white petals, orange stamen and green leaves, this lily replicates the Irish tricolour: these days paper lilies are widely worn at Easter time as a symbol of remembrance of the Rising; but they also reaffirm a link with the Church. Although this lily was adopted as a symbol by Cumann na mBan, the republican women's movement, in the 1920s, the white lily also has a long association as a Christian symbol of the Virgin, and as such is used to decorate churches at Easter time (Goody 1993b; Loftus 1994). The coats of arms of the four historical provinces of Ireland, Connacht, Leinster, Munster and Ulster, appear together on numerous republican murals and are carried at all republican parades. The Ulster emblem is, of course, the older red and yellow nationalist shield of pre-partition Ulster, rather than the red and white version used by loyalists. Carried or displayed together, they reaffirm the essential unity of the island.

These main symbols, the tricolour, phoenix, sunburst, starry plough, easter lily and coats of arms, signify the position of the IRA as inheritors of a long-standing tradition reaching back into the eighteenth century, encompassing many diverse historical strands of political thinking within the contemporary republican umbrella. These republican symbols relate not just to their own political tradition, but also connect their aims and aspirations to those of the broader and more conservative nationalist community, in a similar way to that in which the loyalist paramilitaries situate themselves within unionism.

While republicans claim a long ancestry of rebellion, the Provisional IRA claim legitimacy for their present armed struggle by arguing that they are the direct inheritors of the Irish Republic proclaimed in 1916 by the Provisional Government.

> The moral position of the Irish Republican Army, its right to engage in warfare, is based on: (a) the right to resist foreign aggression; (b) the right to revolt against tyranny and oppression; and (c) the direct lineal succession with the Provisional Government of 1916, the first Dáil of 1919 and the second Dáil of 1921. (From the *Green Book*, quoted in Coogan 1987:685.)

The subsequent Governments of the Republic are derived from the 1922 Dáil, which, republicans claim, betrayed the ideals of the 1916 declaration by approving the Treaty of Surrender with Britain, and have therefore forfeited both their legitimacy and the support of the IRA (Coogan 1987). Easter 1916 provides the historical legitimacy, the ideology, the heroes and the models of activity for the contemporary republican movement. The ideology, a combination of nationalism and socialism, is derived from, and embodied in, the persons of Pearse and Connolly. The first, a poet and schoolteacher steeped in Catholicism and the Celtic revival, invoked the rejuvenating power of a blood sacrifice: 'the old heart of the earth needed to be warmed with the red wine of the battlefields' (Lee 1991). The second was a socialist, trade union organiser, Marxist political theorist and founder of the Irish Citizen Army. But, like Pearse, Connolly recognised that 'as of mankind before Calvary, it may be truly said without the shedding of Blood there is no Redemption' (quoted in Kee 1989:273). Pearse and Connolly, iconic heroes of 1916, have been adopted as models of the revolutionary in action. They are retained as the ancestors of the contemporary republican icon, Bobby Sands, who, like Connolly, went to his death knowing that although he might be certain to fail, he would inspire others to take up the challenge.

The resort to armed rebellion at Easter 1916 is seen as justified by the eventual success in achieving at least a partial self-rule in the face of a wavering British support for Home Rule. It is as the inheritors of the republican tradition that the IRA claim themselves justified in continuing the armed struggle. Although a number of paintings do emphasise the armed struggle, paramilitary figures are not a dominant image on republican murals. On the Falls Road a gunman in a balaclava representing 'Freedom's Sons' and 'D Company, 2nd Battalion, Belfast Brigade' stares out from amongst the shields of the four provinces (which are linked by razor wire), the tricolour and the *Fianna* sunburst, and on the South Link in Andersonstown a mural entitled 'Ireland's Soldiers of Freedom' depicts IRA Volunteers, encompassed by republican symbols, in action poses. Like the paramilitary figures on loyalist murals, IRA Volunteers pose in a landscape of emblems and symbols, in which harps, rifles, tricolours, the phoenix and larks, the symbols of tradition, are used to legitimise their activities. As a counterpart to these celebrations of the gun, the sacrifices of these often anonymous volunteers remain an important link in the symbolic chain. The importance of the dead, as an example to others, is recalled on the Beechmount Avenue mural, in a quotation from Padraic Pearse:

> The fools the fools the fools!
> they have left us our Fenian dead,
> and while Ireland holds these graves,
> Ireland unfree shall never be at peace.

These words serve as a counterpart to the loyalist sentiments expressed by Laurence Binyon's words, and emphasise how the memory of dead comrades provides people on both sides with a determination to achieve some form of justification for the loss. However, few of the republican dead are commemorated as significant events in their own right. Apart from the Hunger Strikers only the eight IRA men killed in an ambush at Loughgall, Co. Armagh, and the three volunteers killed in Gibraltar by the SAS, both in 1987, have been commemorated on recent murals. These both celebrate the triumph that will eventually be achieved through the willingness of people to risk their lives for the cause of Ireland. But their deaths are remembered, and the events commemorated, less as examples of willing sacrifice than as martyred victims.

This is an attitude that also extends to the commemorations of civilians who have been killed in the Troubles by the security forces. Most nationalist areas have plaques or stone memorials erected to people who have been killed over the past twenty-six years: in Derry the fourteen victims of Bloody Sunday are remembered by individual but nameless paintings on Westland Street in the Bogside, close to where the killings took place. The site itself is marked by a small obelisk, while nearby two other paintings commemorate the deaths of Sean Downes and eleven-year-old Stephen McConomy from plastic bullet wounds.

The counterpoint to these murals that remember the victims of violence are paintings that focus on and condemn the violence of the security forces. In Beechmount Avenue, on a site that has housed a number of images over the past decade, the face of a loyalist paramilitary is uncovered to reveal a 'Terminator'-like robot. Behind the portrait is the Union Jack. On the New Lodge Road a skeletal death figure is draped in a Union Jack, and beside it the word 'Murderer' has the letters UDR picked out in red, white and blue.

As O'Malley (1990) has discussed in relation to the period of the hunger strikes, republicans, as much as any of the other parties involved in the Troubles, make a distinction between 'good' and 'bad' violence. Each side justifies and sometimes celebrates its own good violence, while virulently criticising that of the other side. The British Government represents IRA violence as criminal and terrorist, while the IRA explain their actions in the language of national liberation and anti-colonial struggles. Republican murals go further than those of the loyalists in noting the sacrifices made by their members and the cold-bloodedness of the enemy. Whereas for loyalists the enemy is the IRA, which has often been equated with the wider Catholic population, the IRA can sidestep the issue of sectarian violence by representing the enemy as the agents of an oppressive state. But the rhetoric of the republican murals is broadly similar to that of loyalist paintings: both valorise the armed struggle by paramilitary groups, and legitimise their tactics and actions by co-opting the history and symbols of both the recent and a more distant past. Both imply that truth and justice will be proved through sacrifice, and both emphasise an apparent readiness to continue without compromise.

The Celtic Tradition

The majority of republican murals are grounded in the documented histories of this century, but an increasing number turn to Ireland's Celtic past as further legitimisation of the republican position. One of the earliest of these was a mural in Derry's Chamberlain Street featuring a Celtic warrior, which appeared in the early 1980s. The warrior is accompanied by the (unacknowledged) opening words of Padraic Pearse's poem *Mise Éire* ('I am Ireland'), in which Ireland, personified as a woman, recounts both her glory (Cúchulainn) and her shame (betrayal by her family) (Dudley Edwards 1977). In recent years such images have become more prominent. A mural on North Queen Street, demolished in 1990, featured the dying Cúchulainn, his horse, the bulls from the *Táin* saga, dolmens and other Celtic animal and bird symbols, in a riot of background colours. In Springhill Avenue, King Nuada of the Tuatha Dé Danann was portrayed among dolmen and ogham stones, in a painting based on the work of Jim FitzPatrick, who specialises in mythical Celtic characters, portrayed in a 'heavy metal' style (FitzPatrick 1978). In Armagh, an extensive mural, painted over a gable and two walls of a small extension, depicts the dying Cúchulainn in a romanticised lake-filled landscape, with a wolfhound at his feet and a dolmen nearby. Finally, a Celtic cross (also used on the memorials to the Loughgall and Gibraltar volunteers) provides the centrepiece of a mural on New Lodge Road to 'The heroes of 1916', which features both an IRA volunteer in 1916 uniform and Cúchulainn.

Cúchulainn has long been an established figure in republican iconography. A statue of him, sculpted by Oliver Shepherd and cast in bronze, was installed as a memorial to the Easter Rising in the General Post Office in Dublin in 1935 (Turpin 1994). The statue depicts the death of Cúchulainn, which, although warned of its approach, he faced with martial honour. Having received the fatal wound, he has tied himself to a stake so that he will die on his feet; the crow landing on his shoulder signifies that he has expired his last breath. Most subsequent politicised representations of Cúchulainn are copies of this Dublin original, including the sculpted stone centrepiece of the republican plot in the City Cemetery in Derry and all the mural paintings. Cúchulainn and Nuada represent the deep history of the Irish martial tradition inherited by the IRA.

Although only the New Lodge Road mural directly compares the historical with the mythical within a single painting, the locations of many of the Celtic murals make these connections explicit. Facing the New Lodge Road mural is a painting commemorating the 1981 hunger strikers, and next to it another to Volunteer Joe Doherty, who escaped from Long Kesh prison and lived in the USA until he was extradited in 1992. The Springhill painting of Nuada is between the Loughgall memorial and an anti-censorship mural. In conjunction with the Celtic Cross the mythic heroes represent a claim to an ancient history that has been largely ignored in the republican movement in recent years. The attempts to expand their traditions to include more than the rebellious military past, a move into the cultural world of Irish myth and beliefs, has been balanced by the increased role of the Irish language within the republican movement. Although Pearse was deeply involved with the Gaelic League and its interests in regenerating the Irish language and culture, the contemporary concerns of the republican movement have focused more on the practical social and political matters that will lead to self-determination. But Irish words, slogans and designs feature prominently on a number of murals; many street names in the nationalist areas have been changed into Irish or at least become bilingual; and on Ardoyne Avenue a series of murals celebrate Gaelic sports and Irish music and dancing.

Much of the impetus for these developments began in the prisons. The cultural expressions of an Irish republican identity that were generated there included learning and using the Irish language both as part of a previously neglected heritage, and as a practical tool that permitted communication between prisoners that the warders could not understand. An extension of this has been a resurgence of interest in Irish mythology. The current (1996) body of mural paintings within the republican blocks of the Maze prison are dominated by images of mythical warriors, long-haired women and other Celtic-style symbols and designs. While the use of Cúchulainn and Celtic mythology within republican murals might seem to be a 'natural' and obvious step for a political culture legitimating itself through an anti-imperialist struggle of long duration and emphasising the importance of a distinctive indigenous culture, the more recent interest in Cúchulainn by loyalists and his subsequent appearance on their murals has been more of a surprise. However, it follows a similar logic of politically structured identity. To understand this contest over Cúchulainn, it is necessary to know something of the myth of the *Táin Bó Cuailnge* or 'Cattle Raid of Cooley' itself.

The *Táin* tells the story of the attempt of Medb, Queen of Connacht, to borrow the brown bull of Cuailnge for a year, so that her herds will match those of her husband Ailill. Having been refused the loan, Medb and Ailill gather their armies together to ride to Ulster and seize the animal. As a result of an ancient curse, the warriors of Ulster become afflicted with 'labour' pains at the time of their greatest difficulty, which leaves them unable to defend their kingdom. The only warrior in Ulster not afflicted is Cúchulainn, who is spared because of his supernatural ancestry. Cúchulainn meets the invading armies and slows them down by challenging their finest warriors in single combat. He defeats all his opponents. Nevertheless, the bull is captured, and Medb and Ailill begin their return to Connacht. Only after Cúchulainn has killed Ferdia, his foster brother, in single combat and been severely wounded himself, are the men of Ulster freed from their afflictions; then, with the partially revived Cúchulainn, they defeat the Connacht forces at a last great battle. Cúchulainn spares Medb's life, and peace is made between the opposing forces (Kinsella 1970). The *Táin* ends at this point, but another story tells how Medb plots revenge and, with the aid of magic, is able to draw Cúchulainn out alone to face her armies, where he suffers mortal wounds, but ties himself to a tall stone to die on his feet (Gregory 1902).

Set sometime in the first centuries after Christ, the *Táin* is thought to have been written down in the eighth century AD although the oldest surviving manuscript, the *Lebor na hUidre* ('Book of the Dun Cow') dates from the twelfth century. The tale was recounted orally and recited literally into the seventeenth century (Carney 1987; O'Cuiv 1976), and received widespread recognition when it was translated and published as part of the Gaelic revival in the late nineteenth century. The *Táin* represents the finest and most complete piece of writing among the body of Celtic literature that has survived. It can be read as an example of the Irish cultural heritage, which describes in detail the lives and customs of life in Ireland before the English arrived; but it also offers an example of the skill, courage, bravery and persistence of the Irish fighting men.

The spirit of Cúchulainn was invoked by Padraic Pearse in the GPO in 1916, his willingness to meet his fate and his death with bravery have led him to be widely adopted as a republican icon. Loyalists read the *Táin* rather differently. Instead of the tale of ritualised combat between Gaelic warriors, it is seen to recount how Ulster was attacked by the combined armies of the other three kingdoms of Ireland. Cúchulainn is usually interpreted as a semi-magical figure with otherworldly ancestry; but Adamson argues that he should be seen as a member of the pre-Celtic people, the Cruthin. Cúchulainn, he says, is described as short and dark, compared with the normally tall and fair Celts, and comes from the region of Murtheimne, a 'well defined Cruthin territory' (1991:18). The Cruthin were eventually forced into exile into south-west Scotland, thereby providing the ancestry of the Scottish settlers who came to Ireland from the seventeenth century onwards. Therefore, rather than a colonisation process, the plantation by Scots was the return of the exiles (Adamson 1974).

Adamson claims that the *Táin* records the Cruthinic defence of Ulster from the invading forces of a United Ireland, and the nationalist reading of Irish history, in which all Irishness is Celtic, is therefore wrong. Rather the Ulster Protestants are more Irish than the Celts, and Ulster has always been a distinct and separate cultural region. Instead of being an Iron Age IRA volunteer, Cúchulainn has been claimed by loyalists as the first UDA man. Besides Cúchulainn, some Ulster loyalists argue that the early Christian monastic expansion is also substantially the work of members of the Cruthin population, and that the Celtic Cross is actually 'a symbol of our forgotten past' (*New Ulster Defender* Vol. 1 No. 5); however, the Celtic Cross and St Patrick have yet to appear on loyalist murals.

Loyalist and republican mural paintings began from very different starting positions, one celebrating a seventeenth-century military victory and the other a twentieth-century political campaign, but have drawn close together through the central role of the paramilitary groups in using wall paintings as a medium for expressing their political identity and trying to legitimise their opposing actions and tactics. They finally collided on the contested common ground of a 1500-year-old mythological warrior. While both sides use Cúchulainn to situate their identity in the deep historical or mythological past, this is not a coming together of opposing ideals, or an acknowledgement of shared roots; rather it is indicative of the gulf between them. It also illustrates how symbols need to be read within a specific context to understand how they are being used: they have no essential meaning outside that context. While the republican use of Cúchulainn is established, even traditional, and appears 'logical' or obvious, the loyalist claim is no less authentic, and their reading of the *Táin* has a certain legitimacy. But a general acceptability for this interpretation will only come from within the wider loyalist community, which to date has not been forthcoming.

Ceasefire Murals

The loyalist Cúchulainn appear to have been a one-off, an attempt to move beyond the established boundaries of their iconography; but the murals that have been painted since the ceasefires have shown no indication of following that path. The paramilitary ceasefires of August and October 1994 generated a sustained output of paintings, in which both sides used the walls to elaborate their position and their expectations (Jarman 1996a; Rolston 1995; Woods 1995). The murals on both sides show significant differences from earlier paintings, but overall, loyalist and republican paintings have begun to exhibit a greater divergence than previously. Many of the recent paintings are much more elaborate and of a higher quality than earlier murals, and they are being used to express complex arguments through attractive and readily absorbed images. Although these paintings are principally orientated to a local audience, they are also more consciously constructed with an eye on the global media and a wider international consumption. They serve to reassure local supporters, but also convey the messages of both sides to a larger audience. This new body of work illustrates something of the dynamic element of mural painting, which is eminently suited to changing political demands and circumstances.

At the time the republican ceasefire was declared the most widely seen image was a mural in the Ardoyne depicting a file of British soldiers marching down a road, which an adjacent signpost indicated led to England. Above this image a banner, decorated with green, white and orange balloons, wished the troops *Slán Abhaile* ('Safe home'), while below it declared '25 Years – Time to Go.' Similar images under the slogan of *Slán Abhaile* appeared throughout Belfast and across the north. There are no images of hooded paramilitaries on these paintings; the only gunmen are the British army. The paintings reiterate the broadly stated claim that the army were the problem rather than part of the solution. These paintings, and slogans like '25 Years, Time for Peace – Time to Go', which were stencilled throughout nationalist areas, convey a sense that the IRA were laying down their arms from a position of strength.

Twenty-five years of resistance should be enough to convince everyone that the troops must first *Fag ár Sraideanna* ('Leave our Streets') and then leave Ireland altogether. The claimed victory is therefore moral rather than military. Some of the older murals that celebrated the armed struggle and republican history have subsequently been painted over and replaced with new demands. On the Falls Road 'Equality, Freedom and Fraternity' and 'Dialogue, Trust and Respect' were set out as the 'Foundation Stones for Lasting Peace', while nearby, the British demand for a republican commitment to a permanent ceasefire was turned back on the government with counter-demands to end the Unionist veto, disband the RUC, open all roads and release all POWs – 'PERMANENTLY'. These, the murals state, are among the other essential ingredients for 'A Just and Lasting Peace'.

Instead of focusing on the military struggle the new murals emphasised the broad base of the republican campaign. In Andersonstown, it is the 'People of the Shaws Road' who demand an immediate withdrawal of the troops. On the Falls Road '25 years of Resistance' is celebrated by two women defying masked soldiers by banging bin-lids. In St James the 'The Spirit of Freedom' is expressed by two silver-haired women haranguing a paratrooper. Not only were there no IRA gunmen, but there is scarcely a mention of either the IRA or Sinn Féin; instead it is daily resistance of the people that is celebrated.

The old militaristic language of national liberation s. been replaced by a broader celebration of a total c resistance. The principal agents in this are female: on o ﹏ this is a belated acknowledgement of the role that wome.. have played in the Troubles, but on another it signifies a retreat into the old identification of Ireland as a woman, as Mother Ireland. This resistance draws not only on some ineffable spirit, but also on an essential sense of cultural difference, a difference that has in turn been emphasised and extended by a widespread use of the Irish language and Celtic-style designs as both content and/or frame for many paintings.

These two themes have been most extensively used by a series of paintings commemorating the 150th anniversary of the Famine, commissioned for the 1995 West Belfast Festival, which are dominated by images of starving struggling women and children, and by a large number of Celtic epic paintings that began to appear in August 1996. The republican mural painters appear to have turned aside from their traditional symbols and heroes to imply that the IRA ceasefire marked a real break with the past and that future resistance will be grounded in the kind of street actions that Sinn Féin have begun to lead and encourage. However, Irish nationalism has always been a diverse movement in which militarism is but a strand, sometimes dominant, sometimes dormant; and a cultural expression of national identity has always been a prominent part of the broader struggle.

In contrast recent loyalist murals remain firmly based on a celebration of the military capacity of the UFF and UVF, and there has been little indication of either political demands or cultural differences. The only paintings that make broader political demands have been two murals that have asserted a general demand for peace, linked with a desire for the need to free the loyalist prisoners. Beyond these, gunmen dominate the corpus, and only seem to emphasise the continued readiness of loyalist paramilitaries to 'resist any Eire involvement in our country'. The most clearly set out statement from the UFF appeared beside a masked gunman on the Newtownards Road mural complex (it has subsequently appeared at Roden Street and Sandy Row). It states 'For as long as one hundred of us remain alive we shall never in any way consent to submit to the rule of the Irish. For it's not for glory we fight but for freedom alone which no man loses but with his life.'

The UVF make no such grandiose statements on their recent murals, they merely reaffirm their presence, a painting in east Belfast stating 'Ulster Volunteer Force, 1912–1994, Still Undefeated', while a year into the ceasefire two hooded gunmen stared out from a painting in north Belfast and declared that the UVF were 'Prepared for Peace – Ready for War'. These murals appear to offer no hints of compromise, no suggestion of political analysis and no moves away from the rhetoric of the gun. The paintings offer a stark contrast with the expressions of 'abject remorse' voiced by the Combined Loyalist Military Command in their ceasefire statement.

However, at a time of political uncertainty when the parties linked to the paramilitary groups have begun to break with traditional unionist rhetoric, it was perhaps necessary to offer a reassurance that loyalist interests would be defended and that there would be no sell-out. And when one looks closely at the gunmen on the walls it is clear that they are not all threatening violence. The majority of them have been painted as part of memorial murals, where (as in the 1920s), surrounded by the symbolic repertoire of war and death, poppies, wreaths, lowered flags and bowed heads, they publicly honour their dead comrades. These memorials appear to signify the end to conflict, or a form of conflict, in the same way as the republican murals signified a change of tactic. The paintings suggest that while the paramilitaries remain to defend the interests of the loyalist community, they acknowledge that a significant break has been made with the recent past.

There are also other changes in the symbolic structure of these murals that are worth considering. Throughout the Troubles loyalist paramilitary imagery largely relied on representations of gunmen and/or a limited range of flags and symbols; the most prominent of these have been the Union Jack and the Ulster flag. However, only a small number of post-ceasefire murals painted have included either of these two central symbols of Unionism, and instead there has been a greater reliance on the flags and emblems of the organisations themselves. At a time when mainstream unionists have caused an outcry at any attempts to dilute the symbolic displays of the Union, this seems a significant change. The moves towards political dialogue, generated by the

Progressive Unionist Party and the Ulster Democratic Party, have not been matched by the loyalist mural painters, who make no overt political statements; but neither is there any suggestion of a desire to retreat into the comfortable traditional icons and symbols of Unionism. This might suggest a more significant break with the past and a greater willingness to consider new ideas, although this optimism must be balanced by the hardlined retrenchment into the comfort of the gun, which in turn suggests another reality, that of an uncompromising retreat into an 'Ulster Alone' siege mentality.

Since 1981 mural painting has become the one of the principal media through which republican and loyalist groups have revealed themselves in the public sphere. Such paintings have been used to situate and legitimise the two movements historically and symbolically within the wider nationalist and unionist com-munities. They have been used to display explicitly the case for paramilitary action in support of political ideals, a form of activity that is more implicit within the constitutional political domain. Mural paintings often appear to be somewhat removed from the wider practice of commemoration, which is enacted through the parades, but I have argued that murals are an integral part of this extensive process. Besides the formal commemorative content of many of the paintings, murals have also often been used as the site of a more overt commemoration: a parade, an oration, a wreath-laying, or a final military salute. They are used most extensively in this way by loyalists, for whom the culture of parading is most deeply embedded.

Many of the recent memorial murals, particularly those on the Shankill Road, are symbolically linked each year by band parades that are held on the anniversaries of prominent paramilitary figures. These anniversaries have increasingly provided an alternative focus for mural painting that has extended the season beyond the Orange commemorative calendar. A distinct loyalist marching season, somewhat similar to the established republican practice of holding small locally orientated parades to honour their dead, is beginning to emerge. There is no suggestion that the ceasefires indicate a desire to forget the past and forge a common future: if anything they affirm an insistence on the irreconcilable difference between the two dominant identities in the north of Ireland, identities that are mapped out and displayed through the recurrent parades of culture and the culture of parading.

Protest I: No Sectarian Parades; Derry, August 1995.

Protest II: Anger; University Street, Belfast, June 1995.

Chapter 12

In Conclusion

This study began by asking how the people of Northern Ireland maintained and expressed their understanding of the past, how a collective or social memory of historical events and past conflicts was created and used to influence and direct activity in the present. Following the work of Paul Connerton, which stressed the importance of the collective involvement in ritual as a way of consolidating or embodying a social memory, I have focused attention on the local custom of holding commemorative parades to mark important anniversaries. But I also tried to move beyond Connerton's rather narrow focus on the performative aspects of ritual and to look as well at what else is being conveyed on these occasions through the production and display of paintings on banners and walls. This has involved a consideration of both the form of these events and the production of meaning through the elaborate visual displays.

I

I began by sketching out something of the history of these practices. Unionists in general, and Orangemen in particular, lay great store by the concept of tradition with regard to parading practices. Tradition for them implies a sense of permanence, an unchanging deep-rooted custom, a continuity between what is done today and what was done by their forefathers. This sense of tradition is used to legitimise their current expectations of a right to march where and when they will. The history of parading that I have set out gives some support to this idea of tradition, in so far as it is possible to draw out a more or less continuous practice of holding parades to honour certain anniversaries from the late seventeenth century until the present.

Through this span of time the form of the parade seems to have changed little: many of the essential elements of contemporary parades were already part of the ritual process in the late eighteenth and early nineteenth centuries. But in their detail and their meaning, the parades have changed considerably. The contemporary emphasis on tradition tends to ignore these numerous changes and prefers to see parading as a cultural practice that is somehow beyond time, a custom outside the world of politics and social change. However, if parading is undoubtedly a traditional practice, it is also intimately linked with the world of politics. Contemporary parading practices have been shaped by the broader political world, and have been an important element in creating that world. Throughout the nineteenth century, anniversary commemorations were of major importance in helping to mould the sectarian divide in the north of Ireland and, once established, the parades have been instrumental in perpetuating the divisions. They pass the memory of difference through the generations.

I also showed how the visual displays were an important element in this process. The early use of flags and the building of floral arches began a process of mapping the sectarian divide on to geography in a more permanent manner than the relatively transitory parades could ever achieve. These fixed displays became more prominent and elaborate in the period of the Home Rule crisis, a time that also saw the emergence of extensive professional banner displays. The earlier parades had used the displays to make relatively simple statements of allegiance; but from the end of the nineteenth century they have been used in a more intensive manner to define the Protestant and Catholic communities in terms of opposing national identities. The images on the banners in particular have been used to flesh out and give substance to these oppositions by locating them in an essentialist and primordial difference. These visual displays were not the only medium used to reformulate these identities; but, in so far as they were an expression of the grass-roots attitude, they give an insight into the way the polarisation of society into conflicting national identities developed at the bottom as well as the top.

II

The three other parts of the study then explored these diverse but connected aspects of the tradition to consider how they are currently used by the contemporary unionist and nationalist communities in Northern Ireland. In each case I tried to show how both communities used parades, banners and murals as part of the process of commemoration, and how the three media related to one another within each community. While this involved dealing with a quantity of empirical data, I feel it was important because those few studies that have been made of parades, banners and murals have tended to treat them in isolation rather than to consider how they are connected and how they are used to focus, elaborate, challenge or change understandings of collective identity. Although the three media of display all relate to com-memorating the past, they are not simply three methods of saying the same thing: in each community differing factions of the community utilise different forms of representation to convey their particular understanding of what it means to be a unionist or a nationalist.

Among the unionists the main commemorations are inclusive events that allow diverse groups to come together and subsume their major differences for a public affirmation of strength and unity. The Twelfth of July, and the weeks leading up to it, is a time for Protestants to affirm their control over the whole of Northern Ireland. Parade after parade gradually spins a web of connections across the entire six counties and beyond. On the Twelfth itself, a large proportion of the Protestant population take to the streets, men and boys marching, women and girls watching, for the symbolic re-enactment of the battle of the Boyne. The majority of discussions of the unionist parading tradition have focused on the parade itself: the form, the scale and the responses they generate. When any reference is made to the particularity of the material culture of the displays it is to comment on the anachronistic use of symbols of Britishness: the bowler hats, white gloves and Union Jacks. But to understand the importance of the event it is also necessary to consider what is being said and by whom. Although the performance is central to this process, the major parades are also an annual opportunity to witness the collective display of political and martial heroes, religious leaders, martyrs and saints, and to be shown the religious and moral ideals that provide the foundation of faith and identity. The visual displays are used to elaborate on the meaning of the anniversary by situating it within a broader ideological frame. But while the sight of marching men and the sound of banging drums are heard extensively, the images are seen only by the faithful. The triumphalist and provocative rhetoric of marching feet too easily masks the complexity of the visual messages.

In the introduction I suggested that visual images had long been recognised as an important factor in the mnemonic process, that they were useful as a means of encoding a broad range of information that they did not constrict overmuch in interpretation. Images as symbols retain power because of their ambiguity, because of their ability to convey different things to different people. This is part of the importance of the use of images in the Irish commemorative process, and explains why King Billy can retain a sense of importance to a range of political opinion among the unionists and why Pearse and Connolly can be celebrated by groups as diverse as the Hibernians and Sinn Féin. As symbols it is hard to be precise about their meaning.

But, by juxtaposition, by bringing a range of images together, what Barthes refers to as the processes of relay and anchoring may be brought into play. Juxtaposition invites recognition of the connection between seemingly disparate images; but it can also be used to focus or anchor the meaning. In use there is always a tension between the potential multivocality of the symbol and the attempt to impute specific meanings at specific places. In part this tension is resolved by making meaning appropriate to the time or place: at the ritual events, where the banner images appear as almost sacred icons revealed only to the faithful, or on the gables of the working-class estates, where similar images may allude to another form of ethereal or secretive presence. But this closure is always only partial. If in social usage images do not contain endless meanings, they nevertheless retain multiple meanings, and therefore their power.

Parades are awash with colour as the lodges and bands display their regalia and emblems. The visual rhetoric of the younger elements on parade has become more prominent over the period of the Troubles, but the main displays on the banners remain under the control of the conservative membership of the Orange Order. The widely quoted speeches give the view of the Orange leadership; but the visual displays give a more democratised view from the ranks. These pictures seem unconcerned with contemporary issues, being mainly restricted to historical or religious themes, and as such are used to depict the basic tenets of the Protestant faithful in Ireland. The fact that the images have hardly changed this century only seems to confirm this sense of permanence.

However, when one moves away from an analysis of the banners as singular images, and begins to look at them as a body and in the context of the process of the parade, it becomes clear that they are being used to display a more elaborate text. The celebration and commemoration of past events and heroes aims to guide action in the present, and so the recurrent celebration of martial heroes and military victories helps to legitimise and sustain faith in a violent solution to Ulster's problems. The displays at the parades remain relatively coded behind a rhetoric of civil and religious liberty or biblical authority. Those who have taken the message of history to heart, the paramilitaries of the UDA and UVF, are not very prominent at these parades, although they maintain a surrogate presence within the visual displays of some of the bands. As illegal organisations their displays have largely been restricted to the walls of the working-class estates of Belfast, where the murals commemorate the fallen paramilitary heroes and their ideals of national identity. However, they use the murals to situate their activities within the broad range of beliefs of the mainstream Protestant ideology. King William remains the anchor on which the paramilitaries justify their actions; but the murals move his importance away from the guardianship of civil and religious liberties to refocus on his role as a man who was prepared to fight for his faith.

The nationalist community utilises a similar triad of commemorative practices. In some ways these appear as little more than a pale reflection of the larger-scale unionist traditions; but just as the Orangemen seem to overcompensate for their feelings of being under siege by parading more intensively, so nationalists have often been restrained by the dominant unionist community from mounting their own displays. Nevertheless, parading is still the core practice for commemorative displays. Although all the nationalist groups aspire to the same end, a United Ireland, differences over the best way to achieve that aim have meant that each group marks its commemoration independently. The difference in form between the parades of the constitutional nationalists, the Hibernians and Foresters, and the parades of the republican movement reflects their different histories. The nationalist parades draw on the same roots as the Orange tradition, although they have increasingly diverged in much of the style, with the adoption of American-style bands and marching. The republican parades in turn reflect their emergence from the more sombre custom of funeral processions and the more recent tradition of political demonstrations.

These differences are also evident in the visual displays: nationalist banners celebrate the military heroes and battles alongside the religious leaders and saints. By emphasising the form and without reference to the visual displays it would be difficult to distinguish the Orange and Green parades or the parades of the Hibernians from the Foresters. Even the categories of images on the banners are similar, the church and the battlefield forming the two poles around which the collective difference is expressed. Only by considering the details does the ideological gulf between nationalist and unionist become clear. But by looking at the collective displays of the nationalist banners, one can also be more aware of the differences within the community at the same time as one is aware of the common themes that link the conservative and Catholic with the nationalist and then on to the republican elements. Just as the Orange displays reveal the underlying tension between a faith in a biblical sense of destiny and the need for self-reliance, between prayer and the gun, so the nationalist banners also help to justify the recourse to violence, by celebrating the recurrence of rebellion against the British.

Visual displays at republican parades are less prominent: the threat or the reality of violence at these demonstrations in recent years has militated against spending large sums of money on relatively fragile artefacts, and the banners have been largely *ad hoc* affairs. Over the past two or three years more elaborate banners have begun to appear on parades; and although these are not on the same scale as those of the other nationalist groups, it is these that have clearly provided the inspiration. Instead, republicans rely on mural painting for their most impressive visual displays. Like their loyalist counterparts, murals provided the opportunity for illegal groups to make prominent public statements about their aims and ideals and the legitimacy of their tactics. Since republicans began to paint murals in the early 1980s, they have expanded the scope of the genre dramatically and they have inspired loyalist paramilitaries to develop their visual rhetoric similarly. At the beginning of the Troubles mural painting was thought to be a dying tradition; in the past fifteen years it has been transformed into the most vibrant of practices. Although parades and commemorative anniversaries remain the stimulus for painting or repainting many of the murals, the form has become more widely used as a way of 'drawing support', and has also become the most common mass media signifier of the Troubles (Jarman 1996b).

Throughout this study I have tried to illustrate not only the distinctiveness of the two broad traditions, nationalist and unionist, and the importance in this of their three component parts, the parades, banners and murals, but also the important con-nections and shared traditions between the two communities and their commemorative practices. The extensive and repetitive practice of parading and the intensive visual displays associated with parades have become the most prominent of the ways and means that the people of the north of Ireland use to construct their collective memories, but also to display their differences. These anniversaries are displays of strength and resolve: they reaffirm territorial identities, confirm boundaries and demonstrate col-lective rights of way. Most of the time these are symbolic displays; but, at times of crisis, the ritual process may be transformed into an open confrontation. Despite this occasional descent into real rather than symbolic violence, the parades themselves are seen by those taking part as being directed inwards rather than as attempts to antagonise. They are 'part of our culture' rather than 'triumphalist coat-trailing'. They are a time to express solidarity and to declare and display faith by replaying and remembering the battles or sacrifices of old.

III

While there is something of a timeless permanence implied in the naming of these communities of difference, or at least a sense of a distinction nourished by hundreds of years of religious divergence, I have tried to show how this has been created within a much shorter period of time. It is only within the past two hundred years that the communal polarisations that dominate the contemporary

political and social life of the north have become the overriding
determinants of identity, and only in the past century have these
polarisations become rooted in a conflicting sense of nationality.
Protestant and Catholic have been historically the dominant bases
for identity; but other anchors for non-sectarian collective action
have surfaced from time to time. The Volunteers, the Freemasons
and trade unions have been most prominent among the social
movements that have attempted to counter the sectarian drift.
Although these remain underused or ignored at present, they
remain as a possible basis for a future reclaimed history of Ireland,
and, as a recent study has indicated, a substantial proportion of
the population of the north are consistently opposed to a narrow
sectarian polarity (Boyle and Hadden 1994).

For the time being, however, there remain two dominant
collective memories in the north of Ireland, which are expressed
by the social identities of Protestant or Catholic. Although the
parades are opportunities for displays of unity and expressions
of collective strength, this also conceals a multitude of more tightly
focused identities that are based on shared experience in particular
residential areas, places of work, variations in political or religious
belief, gender, class and age. Focusing purely on the form of the
commemorative process tends to obscure the differing or multiple
meanings given to these events by the participants: the visual
displays are used to extend meaning, while the reliance on images
rather than words leaves the meaning open and by extension
ensures the complexity and vitality of the event. A detailed
consideration of the content of the displays also shows how
marginal or minority groups are able to participate in these public
displays of unity while retaining some degree of autonomy. I have
tried to draw out some of these divisions and alternative perspectives as they are played out in public, and, while these differences
do achieve some form of collective and public expression, that
expression largely remains within the dominant framework
structured by the culture of parading.

Within the nationalist community political strategy has been
a consistent fracture zone, and while the overall demand for a
United Ireland remains consistent and strong among all groups,
differences over the appropriate tactics have led to the fragmentation of the nationalist body politic. Nevertheless, agreement
remains over the key elements of the collective past, the constant

stream of warriors and saints who have struggled and sacrificed themselves for faith and fatherland, and who must be commemorated in the most appropriate way.

The unionist community has shown a similar disagreement over the best way to ensure that its political desires to remain part of the United Kingdom are fulfilled; but while the activities of the loyalist paramilitary groups have been condemned, they have claimed a space within the public displays of strength. And, although relatively small, these public displays continue to grow. While the Protestant community has readily broken into small confessional congregations, in political terms it has remained solidly bounded by the threat of betrayal and the feeling of being under siege.

What has emerged from this study is that the nationalist and unionist communities have increasingly come to use a common form, or series, of practices with which to display their apparently contradictory identities. Although the custom of parading with decorated banners is rooted in the eighteenth-century past, and was part of a much wider custom that extended across Britain and Ireland, it has in the late twentieth century come to represent one of the constituent features of northern Irish political and social life. The attempt to offer a broad sweep over the comparative commemorative and visual practices has perhaps led to an understatement of the sheer scale of social parading; but given the extent of the material, this was probably inevitable. But the scale, visibility and sheer ubiquity of parading is also to an extent contingent on the broader political process. The Troubles themselves have been prominent in expanding the practice of parading, in part to reinforce position, to confirm collective rights and strength, but also by generating events and heroes that need to be incorporated into the commemorative calendar.

The emphasis on the traditional parades to mark dates such as 1688, 1690, 1798 and 1916 obscures the fact that this traditional practice is being expanded all the time. Loyalist bands now parade to honour the paramilitary dead, and in support of political demands as well as socially in competitions. Republicans similarly honour their dead and, with increasing weight given to constitutional and non-violent strategies, have returned to the streets *en masse* to push their demands.

The two ceasefires in the autumn of 1994 fuelled this process rather than cause it to abate. The anniversaries of the ceasefires have in turn become events to commemorate. The years 1995 and 1996 witnessed the most violent and confrontational marching seasons since the beginning of the Troubles: the right to parade and the right not to have to suffer a parade have become key issues of strength for both communities (Jarman and Bryan 1996). Increasingly, both sides recognise (although often only grudgingly) each other's rights: witness Sinn Féin's increasing access to the centre of Belfast, which only a few years ago was a no-go zone for any but unionist parades; but each side also seeks to put boundaries on those rights. The right to parade exists, but not anywhere, any time; and no one can agree on who should have the right to say yea or nay.

Simon Harrison has recently argued that among some peoples of Melanesia violence is not so much a product of antagonistic relations between fixed groups of individuals as a constituent part of the creation of those groups: 'violence is one of a range of symbolic practices by means of which groups act to constitute themselves within the system of relationships encompassing them' (1993:14). In Ireland, the custom of parading has been central to the constitution of the antagonist collective communities identified as Protestant and Catholic. As a symbolic practice, predicated on the rhetoric of war, parades have been and remain formative events in the sectarian polarisation of the north. The parade has not simply been an expression of an existing communal identity, so much as part of the practice of constituting difference on which competing identities could be constructed. Over the past two hundred years the competing displays of strength have served to reinforce a sense of collective opposition that has now become solidified as 'tradition'. 'Tradition' forms the basis for an insistence of our right to parade freely and the denial of that same right to the other, traditional oppositions that are re-confirmed over and over again each marching season, because it is at this time that the collective Other is most visible. Time and again people say 'I've got nothing against this individual Catholic or Protestant' or 'Some of my best friends are Catholics', but the individual is always the exception, the one that is known from personal contact at work, or sometimes as a neighbour; in contrast, one knows the collective Other only from a distance as an indistinct mass of marching men. The parade is the cultural medium for constructing that collective Other that at other times is largely invisible.

But while the practice of parading serves to define the collective

Other, and provides the means by which Protestant/Unionists recognise Catholic/Nationalists and vice versa, the parade is also perhaps distinctive of an emergent specific northern Irish culture, one which is not really British, despite the protestations to the contrary, and not as singularly Irish as would be desired. It is probably unwise to speculate on the emergence of a distinctive cultural pattern; but nearly four hundred years of colonisation and sharing the same 'narrow ground', and seventy-five years of political separation have left their mark on the north of Ireland. For the past two hundred years (and for the foreseeable future) it has been, and will remain, the commemorative, celebratory or social parade that has become the distinctive means of displaying faith in the contested (occupied) six counties of Northern Ireland/ Ulster.

Enniskillen War Memorial, Easter, 1992.

Bibliography

Newspapers and Journals

Andersonstown News
An Phoblacht/Republican News
Belfast News Letter (later *Newsletter*)
Belfast Telegraph
Belfast Weekly News
Combat
Derry Journal
Fortnight
Irish Democrat
Irishman
Irish News
Irish Reporter
Londonderry Sentinel
New Ulster
New Ulster Defender
Northern Whig
Orange Standard
Sunday Life
Sunday World
Ulster

Books and Articles

Adams, G. (1990). *Cage Eleven*. Dingle, Brandon Books.
Adams, J. R. R. (1987). *The Printed Word and the Common Man: Popular Culture in Ulster 1700–1900*. Belfast, Institute of Irish Studies.
Adamson, I. (1974). *The Cruthin: The Ancient Kindred*. Bangor, Donard Publishing.
Adamson, I. (1982). *The Identity of Ulster: The land, the language, the people*. Belfast, Pretani Press.

Adamson, I. (1991). *The Ulster People: Ancient, Medieval and Modern.* Bangor, Pretani Press.

Adamson, I., Hume, D. and McDowell, D. (1995). *Cuchulain the Lost Legend, Ulster the Lost Culture.* Belfast, Ulster Young Unionist Council.

Agulhon, M. (1981). *Marianne into Battle: Republican Imagery and Symbolism in France 1789–1880.* Cambridge, Cambridge University Press.

Anderson, B. (1983). *Imagined Communities: Reflections on the Origin and Spread of Nationalism.* London, Verso.

Anderson, D. (1994). *14 May Days. The Inside Story of the Loyalist Strike of 1974.* Dublin, Gill and Macmillan.

Baddeley, O. and Fraser, V. (1989). *Drawing the Line: Art and Cultural Identity in Contemporary Latin America.* London, Verso.

Banks, M. (1996). *Ethnicity: Anthropological Constructions.* London, Routledge.

Bardon, J. (1992). *A History of Ulster.* Belfast, Blackstaff Press.

Barnard, T. C. (1991). The Uses of 23 October 1641 and Irish Protestant Celebrations. *English Historical Review*, October 1991.

Barrington, J. (1803). *Personal Sketches of his Own Times*, Vol. 1. London, Coburn and Butley.

Barthes, R. (1973). *Mythologies.* London, Paladin.

Barthes, R. (1977). *Image–Music–Text.* London, Fontana.

Bartlett, T. (1992). *The Fall and Rise of the Protestant Nation: The Catholic Question 1690–1830.* Dublin, Gill and Macmillan.

Beames, M. (1983). *Peasants and Power: The Whiteboys Movement and their Control in Pre-famine Ireland.* Brighton, Harvester Press.

Beattie, G. (1993). *We are the People: A Journey through the Heart of Protestant Ulster.* London, Mandarin Paperbacks.

Beatty, W. J. (1933). *Freemasonry in Benburb.* Dungannon.

Beckett, J. C. (1981). *The Making of Modern Ireland, 1603–1923.* London, Faber and Faber.

Beckett, J. C., Boyle, E., Hewitt, J. *et al.* (1983). *Belfast: The Making of a City, 1800–1914.* Belfast, Appletree Press.

Bell, D. (1990). *Acts of Union: Youth Culture and Sectarianism in Northern Ireland.* London, Macmillan.

Benton, S. (1995). Women Disarmed: The Militarization of Politics in Ireland 1913–23. *Feminist Review*, No. 50.

Beresford, D. (1987). *Ten Men Dead: The Story of the 1981 Irish Hunger Strike.* London, Grafton Books.

Berger, J. (1977). *Ways of Seeing.* Harmondsworth, Pelican.

Berger, J. and Mohr, J. (1975). *A Seventh Man.* Harmondsworth, Penguin.

Bergeron, D. (1971). *English Civic Pagentry, 1558–1642.* London, Edward Arnold.

Bew, P., Gibbon, P. and Patterson, H. (1995). *Northern Ireland 1921–1994: Political Force and Social Classes.* London, Serif.

Bloch, M. (1986). *From Blessing to Violence: History and Ideology in the Circumcision Ritual of the Merina of Madgascar*. Cambridge, Cambridge University Press.

Boal, F. W. (1982). Segregating and Mixing: Space and Residence in Belfast. In Boal, F. W. and Douglas, J. (eds), *Integration and Division*. London, Academic Press.

Boal, F. W. (1995). *Shaping a City. Belfast in the Late Twentieth Century*. Belfast, Institute of Irish Studies.

Boissevain, J. (1965). *Saints and Fireworks: Religion and Politics in Rural Malta*. London, Athlone Press.

Boissevain, J. (1984). Ritual Escalation in Malta. In Wolf, E. (ed.), *Religion, Power and Protest in Local Communities*. Berlin – New York – Amsterdam, Mouton.

Boissevain, J. (1992a). Play and Identity. Ritual Change in a Maltese Village. In Boissevain, J. (ed.).

Boissevain, J. (ed.) (1992b). *Revitalising European Rituals*. London, Routledge.

Boulton, D. (1973). *The UVF, 1966–73: An anatomy of loyalist rebellion*. Dublin, Torc Books.

Bourdieu, P. (1977). *Outline of a Theory of Practice*. Cambridge, Cambridge University Press.

Bowyer Bell, J. (1989). *The Secret Army. The IRA 1916-1979*. Dublin, Poolbeg Press.

Boyce, D. G. (1990). *Nineteenth Century Ireland: The Search for Stability*. Dublin, Gill and Macmillan.

Boyce, D. G. (1991). *Nationalism in Ireland*. London, Routledge.

Boyd, A. (1987). *Holy War in Belfast*. Belfast, Pretani Press.

Boyle, J. (1988). *The Irish Labour Movement in the Nineteenth Century*. Washington, Catholic University of America Press.

Boyle, K. and Hadden, T. (1994). *Northern Ireland: The Choice*. Harmondsworth, Penguin.

Bruce, S. (1992). *The Red Hand: Protestant Paramilitaries in Northern Ireland*. Oxford, Oxford University Press.

Bruce, S. (1994). *The Edge of the Union: The Ulster Loyalist Political Vision*. Oxford, Oxford University Press.

Bryan, D. (1996). Ritual, 'Tradition' and Control: The Politics of Orange Parades in Northern Ireland. Unpublished Ph.D. Thesis, University of Ulster, Coleraine.

Bryan, D., Fraser, T. G. and Dunn, S. (1995). *Political Rituals: Loyalist Parades in Portadown*. Coleraine, Centre for the Study of Conflict, UUC.

Bryson, L. and McCartney, C. (1994). *Clashing Symbols: A report on the use of flags, anthems and other national symbols in Northern Ireland*. Belfast, Institute of Irish Studies.

Buckland, P. (1980). *James Craig, Lord Craigavon*. Dublin, Gill and Macmillan.

Buckley, A. D. (1982). *The Gentle People: A study of a peaceful community in Ulster*. Holywood, Ulster Folk and Transport Museum.

Buckley, A. D. (1985–6). The Chosen Few. Biblical Texts in the Regalia of an Ulster Secret Society. *Folk Life*, Vol. 24.

Buckley, A. D. (1987). 'On the Club': Friendly Societies in Ireland. *Irish Economic and Social History*, XIV.

Buckley, A. D. (n.d.) The Urban Brotherhoods of Ireland. Unpublished Paper.

Buckley, A. D. and Anderson, K. (1988). *Brotherhoods in Ireland*. Cultra, Ulster Folk and Transport Museum.

Buckley, A. D. and Kenney, M. (1995). *Negotiating Identity: Rhetoric, Metaphor and Social Drama in Northern Ireland*. Washington, Smithsonian Institute Press.

Burke, P. (1978). *Popular Culture in Early Modern Europe*. London, Temple Smith.

Burton, F. (1978). *The Politics of Legitimacy*. London, Routledge and Kegan Paul.

Campbell, F. (1991). *The Dissenting Voice: Protestant Democracy in Ulster from Plantation to Partition*. Belfast, Blackstaff Press.

Carney, J. (1987). Literature in Irish 1169–1534. In Cosgrove, A. (ed.), *A New History of Ireland*, Vol. II, *Medieval Ireland 1169–1534*. Oxford, Oxford University Press.

Carruthers, M. (1990). *The Book of Memory: A Study of Memory in Medieval Culture*. Cambridge, Cambridge University Press.

Cecil, R. (1993). The Marching Season in Northern Ireland: An Expression of a Politico-Religious Identity. In MacDonald, S. (ed.), *Inside European Identities: Ethnography in Western Europe*. Oxford, Berg.

Chaplin, E. (1994). *Sociology and Visual Representation*. London, Routledge.

Clarke, L. (1987). *Broadening the Battlefield: The H-Blocks and the Rise of Sinn Féin*. Dublin, Gill and Macmillan.

Cohen, A. (1993). *Masquerade Politics*. Oxford, Berg.

Condren, M. (1989). *The Serpent and the Goddess: Women, Religion and Power in Celtic Ireland*. San Francisco, Harper and Row.

Connerton, P. (1989). *How Societies Remember*. Cambridge, Cambridge University Press.

Connolly, S. J. (1982). *Priests and People in Pre-famine Ireland, 1780–1845*. Dublin, Gill and Macmillan.

Connolly, S. J. (1992). *Religion, Law and Power: The Making of Protestant Ireland, 1660–1760*. Oxford, Clarendon Press.

Conroy, J. (1988). *War as a Way of Life: a Belfast Diary*. London, Heinemann.

Coogan, T. P. (1987). *The IRA*. London, Fontana.

Coser, L. (1992). Introduction to M. Halbwachs, *On Collective Memory*. Chicago, University of Chicago Press.

Crawford, P. I. and Turton, D. (eds), (1992). *Film as Ethnography*. Manchester, Manchester University Press.

Crawford, W. H. (1972). *Domestic Industry in Ireland: The Experience of the Linen Industry*. Dublin, Gill and Macmillan.

Crawford, W. H. and Trainor, D. (eds) (1969). *Aspects of Irish Social History*. Belfast, HMSO.

Cressy, D. (1989). *Bonfires and Bells: National Memory and the Protestant Calendar in Stuart England*. London, Weidenfeld and Nicolson.

Crossle, F. (1909). *A History of Nelson Masonic Lodge, No 16, Newry*. Newry.

Crossle, P. (1973). *Irish Masonic Records*. Dublin, Grand Lodge of Ireland.

Da Matta, R. (1977). Constraint and License, a preliminary study of two Brazilian national rituals. In Moore, S. and Myerhoff, B. (eds), *Secular Rituals*. Assen, Van Gorcum.

Darnton, R. (1984). *The Great Cat Massacre and Other Episodes in French Cultural History*. London, Allen Lane.

Davis, S. (1986). *Parades and Power: Street Theatre in Nineteenth Century Philadelphia*. Philadelphia, Temple University Press.

de Baroid, C. (1990). *Ballymurphy and the Irish War*. London, Pluto Press.

de Certeau, M. (1984). *The Practice of Everyday Life*. Berkeley, University of California Press.

de Vere White, T. (1973). The Freemasons. In Williams, T. D. (ed.), *Secret Societies in Ireland*. Dublin, Gill and Macmillan.

Dewar, M. W., Brown, J. and Long, S. E. (1969). *Orangeism: A new historical perspective*. Belfast, Grand Orange Lodge of Ireland.

Doak, C. (1978). Rioting and Civil Strife in the City of Londonderry during the Nineteenth and Early Twentieth Centuries. Unpublished MA Thesis, Queen's University, Belfast.

Donnelly, J. (1981). Hearts of Oak, Hearts of Steel. *Studia Hibernica*, No. 21.

Dudley Edwards, R. (1977). *Patrick Pearse: The Triumph of Failure*. London, Victor Gollancz.

Edwards, E. (1992). *Anthropology and Photography*, 1860-1920. New Haven and London, Yale University Press.

Elias, N. (1982). *The Civilising Process*, Vol. 2: *State Formation and Civilisation*. Oxford, Basil Blackwell.

Elliott, M. (1982). *Partners in Revolution: The United Irishmen and France*. New Haven and London, Yale University Press.

Elliot, M. (1985). *Watchmen in Sion: The Protestant Idea of Liberty*. Derry, Field Day.

Eriksen, T. H. (1993). *Ethnicity and Nationalism: Anthropological Perspectives*. London, Pluto Press.

Evans, K. (1992). The Argument of Images: Historical representation in Solidarity underground postage, 1981–87. *American Ethnologist*, 19 (4).

Farrell, M. (1980). *Northern Ireland: The Orange State*. London, Pluto Press.

Farrell, M. (1983). *Arming the Protestants: The Formation of the Ulster Special Constabulary 1920–27*. Dingle, Brandon Books.

Feld, S. (1982). *Sound and Sentiment: Birds, Weeping, Poetics and Song in Kaluli Expression*. Philadelphia, University of Pennsylvania Press.

Feldman, A. (1991). *Formations of Violence: The Narrative of the Body and Political Terror in Northern Ireland*. Chicago, University of Chicago Press.

Fentress, J. and Wickham, C. (1992). *Social Memory*. Oxford, Blackwell.

FitzPatrick, J. (1978). *The Book of Conquests*. Limpsfield, Paper Tiger.

Foucault, M. (1977). *Discipline and Punish: The Birth of the Prison*. Harmondsworth, Allen Lane.

Foucault, M. (1981). *The History of Sexuality: An Introduction*. Harmondsworth, Penguin Books.

Foy, M. T. (1976). The AOH: An Irish politico-religious pressure group, 1884–1975. Unpublished MA Thesis, Queen's University, Belfast.

Frazer, J. G. (1923). *The Golden Bough: A Study in Magic and Religion*, Vol. 1. London, Macmillan.

Garvin, T. (1981). *The Evolution of Irish Nationalist Politics*. Dublin, Gill and Macmillan.

Garvin, T. (1987). Defenders, Ribbonmen and Others: Underground Political Networks in Pre-Famine Ireland. In Philpin, C. H. E. (ed.), *Nationalism and Popular Protest in Ireland*. Cambridge, Cambridge University Press.

Gellner, E. (1994). *Encounters With Nationalism*. Oxford, Blackwell.

Gerald of Wales (1982). *The History and Topography of Ireland*. Harmondsworth, Penguin.

Gibbon, P. (1975). *The Origins of Ulster Unionism*. Manchester, Manchester University Press.

Gillespie, R. (1992). The Irish Protestants and James II, 1688–90. *Irish Historical Studies*, Vol. XXVIII, No. 110.

Goldring, M. (1991). *Belfast: From Loyalty to Rebellion*. London, Lawrence and Wishart.

Gombrich, E. (1980). *Art and Illusion: A Study in the Psychology of Pictoral Representation*. Oxford, Phaidon.

Goody, J. (1993a). Knots in May: Continuities, Contradictions and Change in European Rituals. *Journal of Mediterranean Studies*, Vol. 3, No. 1.

Goody, J. (1993b). *The Culture of Flowers*. Cambridge, Cambridge University Press.

Gorman, J. (1986). *Banner Bright: An Illustrated History of Trade Union Banners*. Buckhurst Hill, Scorpion.

Gosden, P. H. (1961). *The Friendly Societies in England, 1815–75*. Manchester, Manchester University Press.

Graham, C. and McGarry, J. (1990). Co-determination. In McGarry, J. and O'Leary, B. (eds), *The Future of Northern Ireland*. Oxford, Clarendon Press.

Grange, R. T. (1980). *The Story of Cogry Lodge. A History of Cogry Union Masonic Lodge No. 148*. Cogry.

Gray, J. (1983). Popular Entertainment. In Beckett, J. C. *et al.*

Gregory, Lady A. (1973). *Cuchulain of Muirthemne: The Story of the Men of the Red Branch of Ulster*. Gerrards Cross, Colin Smythe.

Gregory, A. (1994). *The Silence of Memory: Armistice Day 1919–1946*. Oxford, Berg.

Habermas, J. (1992). *The Structural Transformation of the Public Sphere: An Inquiry into a Category of Bourgeois Society*. Cambridge, Polity Press.

Halbwachs, M. (1980). *The Collective Memory*. New York, Harper and Row.

Halbwachs, M. (1992). *On Collective Memory*. Chicago, University of Chicago Press.

Hall, M. (1986). *Ulster: The Hidden History*. Belfast, Pretani Press.

Handelman, D. (1990). *Models and Mirrors*. Cambridge, Cambridge University Press.

Harper, D. (1987). *Working Knowledge: Skill and Community in a Small Shop*. Berkeley and Los Angeles, University of California Press.

Harris, R. (1972). *Prejudice and Tolerance in Ulster: A study of neighbours and strangers in a border community*. Manchester, Manchester University Press.

Harrison, S. (1993). *The Mask of War: Violence, Ritual and the Self in Melanesia*. Manchester, Manchester University Press.

Harwood, F. (1976). Myth, Memory and the Oral Tradition: Cicero in the Trobriands. *American Anthropologist*, Vol. 78.

Hayes-McCoy, G. A. (1979). *A History of Irish Flags from Earliest Times*. Dublin, Academy Press.

Hepburn, A. C. (1996). *A Past Apart: Studies in the History of Catholic Belfast 1850–1950*. Belfast, Ulster Historical Foundation.

Hewitt, J. (1951). Ulster Poets, 1800–70. Unpublished MA Thesis, Queen's University Belfast.

Hill, J. (1984). National festivals, the state and "protestant ascendancy" in Ireland, 1790–1829. *Irish Historical Studies*, XXIV, No. 93.

Hobsbawm, E. (1983). Introduction: Inventing Traditions. In Hobsbawm, E and Ranger, T. (eds).

Hobsbawm, E. and Ranger, T. (1983). *The Invention of Tradition*. Cambridge, Cambridge University Press.

Holloway, D. (1994a). Pass Masters. *Fortnight*, No. 332.

Holloway, D. (1994b). Territorial Aspects of Cultural Identity: the Protestant Community of Donegall Pass, Belfast. *Causeway*, Vol. 1, No. 5.

Jackson, T. A. (1947). *Ireland Her Own: An outline history of the Irish struggle*. London, Cobbett Press.

Jarman, N. (1992). Troubled Images. The Iconography of Loyalism. *Critique of Anthropology*, Vol. 12, No. 2.

Jarman, N. (1993). Intersecting Belfast. In Bender, B. (ed.), *Landscape, Politics and Perspectives*. Oxford, Berg.

Jarman, N. (1996a). The Ambiguities of Peace: Republican and Loyalist Ceasefire Murals. *Causeway*, Vol. 3, No. 1.

Jarman, N. (1996b). Violent Men, Violent Land: Dramatizing the Troubles and the Landscape of Ulster. *Journal of Material Culture*, Vol. 1, No. 1.

Jarman, N. (1997). Material of Culture, Fabric of Identity. In Miller, D. (ed.), *Why Some Things Matter*. London, UCL Press.

Jarman, N. and Bryan, D. (1996). *Parade and Protest: A Discussion of Parading Disputes in Northern Ireland*. Coleraine, Centre for the Study of Conflict, UUC.

Jenkins, R. (1982). *Hightown Rules: Growing up in a Belfast housing estate*. Leicester, National Youth Bureau.

Jenkins, R. (1983). *Lads, Citizens and Ordinary Kids: Working class youth lifestyles in Belfast*. London, Routledge and Kegan Paul.

Jenkins, R., Donnan, H. and MacFarlane, G. (1986). *The Sectarian Divide in Northern Ireland Today*. London, RAI Occasional Paper No. 41.

Jewsiewicki, B. (1986). Collective Memory and its Images: Popular urban painting in Zaire – A source of the 'present past'. *History and Anthropology*, Vol. 2.

Johnston, J. (1977). *A Masonic Monograph, Clogher Masonic Lodge No. 451*. Enniskillen.

Joy, H. and Bruce, W. (1792–3). *Belfast Politics or A collection of debates, resolutions and other proceedings of that town in the years 1792 and 1793*. Belfast.

Kapferer, B. (1988). *Legends of People, Myths of State*. Washington, Smithsonian Institute Press.

Kee, R. (1982). *Ireland: a History*. London, Abacus.

Kee, R. (1989a). *The Most Distressful Country: The Green Flag*, Vol. I. Harmondsworth, Penguin.

Kee, R. (1989b). *The Bold Fenian Men: The Green Flag*, Vol. II. Harmondsworth, Penguin.

Kee, R. (1989c). *Ourselves Alone: The Green Flag*, Vol. III. Harmondsworth, Penguin.

Kelly, J. (1994). 'The Glorious and Immortal Memory': Commemoration and Protestant Identity in Ireland 1660–1800. *Proceedings of the Royal Irish Academy*, Vol. 94C.

Kemp, W. (1991). Visual Narrative, Memory and the Medieval 'esprit du system'. In Küchler, S. and Melion, W. (eds), *Images of Memory: On Remembering and Representation*. Washington, Smithsonian Institute Press.

Kertzer, D. (1988). *Ritual, Politics and Power*. New Haven, Yale University Press.

Kinsella, T. (1970). *The Tain*. Oxford, Oxford University Press.

Küchler, S. (1987). Malangan: Art and Memory in a Melanesian Society. *Man (n.s.)*, 22.

Küchler, S. (1989). Malangan: Objects, Sacrifice and the Production of Memory. *American Ethnologist*, 15.

Lane, C. (1981). *Rites of Rulers*. Cambridge, Cambridge University Press.

Larsen, S. S. (1982). The Glorious Twelfth: A Ritual Expression of Collective Identity. In Cohen, A. (ed.), *Belonging: Identity and Social Organisation in British Rural Cultures*. Manchester, Manchester University Press.

Lee, J. J. (1991). In Search of Patrick Pearse. In Ní Dhonnchadha, M. and Dorgan, T. (eds), *Revising the Rising*. Derry, Field Day.

Leighton, S. (1938). *A History of Freemasonry in the Province of Antrim*. Belfast.

Leonard, J. (1988). 'Lest We Forget': Irish War Memorials. In Fitzpatrick, D. (ed.), *Ireland and the First World War*. Dublin, Lilliput Press and Trinity History Workshop.

Leyton, E. (1974). Opposition and Integration in Ulster. *Man (n.s.)*, 9.

Loftus, B. (1978). *Marching Workers*. Belfast and Dublin, Arts Councils of Ireland.

Loftus, B. (1990). *Mirrors: William III and Mother Ireland*. Dundrum, Picture Press.

Loftus, B. (1994). *Mirrors: Orange and Green*. Dundrum, Picture Press.

Lowenthal, D. (1986). *The Past is a Foreign Country*. Cambridge, Cambridge University Press.

Lyons, F. S. L. (1973). *Ireland Since the Famine*. London, Fontana/Collins.

Lyons, F. S. L. (1977). *Charles Stewart Parnell*. London, Collins.

Lyttle, C. (n.d.). The Development of Political Wall Murals in Northern Ireland. Unpublished dissertation.

McAuley, J. (1994). *The Politics of Identity*. Aldershot, Avebury Press.

McCann, E. (1980). *War and an Irish Town*. London, Pluto Press.

McCann, E. (1992). *Bloody Sunday in Derry: What Really Happened*. Dingle, Brandon Books.

McClelland, A. (1980). Orange Arches of the Past. In Belfast County Lodge, *The Twelfth*. Belfast, Orange Order.

McClelland, A. (1990). *William Johnston of Ballykilbeg*. Lurgan, Ulster Society.

MacDonagh, O. (1983a). *States of Mind: Two Centuries of Anglo-Irish Conflict 1780–1980*. London, George Allen and Unwin.

MacDonagh, S. (1983b). *Green and Gold: The Wrenboys of Dingle*. Dingle, Brandon Books.

McFarlane, G. (1986a). Violence in Rural Northern Ireland: Social Science Models, Folk Interpretations and Local Variation. In Riches, D. (ed.), *The Anthropology of Violence*. Oxford, Basil Blackwell.

McFarlane, G. (1986b). 'Its not as simple as that': the expression of the Catholic and Protestant boundary in Northern Irish rural communities. In Cohen, A. P. (ed.), *Symbolising Boundaries: Identity and Diversity in British Cultures*. Manchester, Manchester University Press.

McFarlane, G. (1989). Dimensions of Protestantism: The Working of Protestant Identity in a Northern Irish Village. In Curtin, C. and Wilson, T. (eds), *Ireland From Below: Social Change and Local Communities*. Galway, Galway University Press.

McGuffin, J. (1973). *Internment*. Tralee, Anvil Books.

McGuffin, J. (1974). *The Guinea Pigs*. Harmondsworth, Penguin.

Mach, Z. (1992). *Continuity and Change in Political Ritual: May Day in Poland*. In Boissevain, J. (ed.).

MacNeill, M. (1962). *The Festival of Lughnasa: A Study of the Survival of the Celtic Festival of the Beginning of Harvest*. Oxford, Oxford University Press.

Macrory, P. (1988). *The Siege of Derry*. Oxford, Oxford University Press.

Malcolm, E. (1986). *Ireland Sober, Ireland Free: Drink and Temperance in 19th Century Ireland*. Dublin, Gill and Macmillan.

Malcolmson, R. (1973). *Popular Recreations in English Society 1700–1850*. Cambridge, Cambridge University Press.

Marin, L. (1987). Notes on a Semiotic Approach to Parade, Cortege and Procession. In Falassi, A (ed.), *Time Out of Time: Essays on the Festival*. Albuquerque, University of New Mexico Press.

Miller, D. (1989). *Still Under Siege*. Lurgan, Ulster Society.

Miller, D. W. (1978). *Queen's Rebels: Ulster Loyalism in Historical Perspective*. Dublin, Gill and Macmillan.

Miller, D. W. (1983). The Armagh Troubles, 1784–95. In Clark, S. and Donnelly, J. S. (eds), *Irish Peasants: Violence and Political Unrest, 1780–1914*. Manchester, Manchester University Press.

Miller, D. W. (1990). *Peep O'Day Boys and Defenders: Selected Documents on the County Armagh Disturbances, 1784–96*. Belfast, PRONI.

Montgomery, G. and Whitten, J. R. (1995). *The Order on Parade*. Belfast, GOLI.

Morgan, A. (1991). *Labour and Partition: The Belfast Working Class 1905–1923*. London, Pluto Press.

Morphy, H. and Morphy, F. (1984). The Myths of Ngalakan History: Ideology and Images of the Past in Northern Australia. *Man (n.s.)*, 19.

Mosse, G. (1975). *The Nationalisation of the Masses*. New York, Fertig.

Muir, E. (1981). *Civic Ritual in Renaissance Venice*. New Jersey, Princetown University Press.

Nelson, S. (1984). *Ulster's Uncertain Defenders: Loyalists and the Northern Ireland Conflict*. Belfast, Appletree Press.

Newsinger, J. (1994). *Fenianism in Mid-Victorian Britain*. London, Pluto Press.

Ní Dhonnchadha, M. and Dorgan, T. (1991). *Revising the Rising*. Derry, Field Day.

Nora, P. (1989). 'Between Memory and History: Les Lieux de Memoire.' *Representations*, 26.

O'Cuiv, B. (1976). The Irish Language in the Early Modern Period. In Moody, T. W., Martin, F. X. and Byrne, F. J. (eds), *A New History of Ireland* Vol. III, *Early Modern Ireland 1534–1691*. Oxford, Oxford University Press.

O'Cuiv, B. (1978). The Wearing of the Green. *Studia Hibernica*, No. 17/18.

O'Dowd, L. (1993). Craigavon: Locality, Economy and the State in a Failed 'New City'. In Curtin, C., Donnan, H. and Wilson, T. (eds), *Irish Urban Cultures*. Belfast, Institute of Irish Studies.

O'Keefe, T. J. (1992). "Who Fears to Speak of '98": The Rhetoric and Rituals of the United Irishmen Centennial, 1898. *Eire-Ireland*, XXVII:3.

O'Malley, P. (1990). *Biting at the Grave: The Irish Hunger Strikes and the Politics of Despair*. Belfast, Blackstaff Press.

Ortner, S. (1973). On Key Symbols. *American Anthropologist*, 75.

Ozouf, M. (1988). *Festivals and the French Revolution*. Cambridge MA, Harvard University Press.

Pakenham, T. (1992). *The Year of Liberty: The History of the Great Irish Rebellion of 1798*. London, Orion.

Panofsky, E. (1970). *Meaning in the Visual Arts*. Harmondsworth, Peregrine.

Papadakis, Y. (1993). The Politics of Memory and Forgetting in Cyprus. *Journal of Mediterranean Studies*, Vol. 3, No. 1.

Parkinson, R. E. (1957). *History of the Grand Lodge of Free and Accepted Masons of Ireland*, Vol. II. Dublin, Lodge of Research.

Pat Finucane Centre (1995). *One Day in August*. Derry, Pat Finucane Centre.

Pat Finucane Centre (1996). *In the Line of Fire*. Derry, Pat Finucane Centre.

Peirce, C. (1940). *Philosophy of Peirce, Selected Writings*, ed. J. Buchler. London, Routledge and Kegan Paul.

Phoenix, E. (1994). *Northern Nationalism: Nationalist Politics, Partition and the Catholic Minority in Northern Ireland 1890–1940*. Belfast, Ulster Historical Foundation.

Purdie, B. (1990). *Politics in the Streets: The origins of the civil rights movement in Northern Ireland*. Belfast, Backstaff Press.

Quinn, F. (1994). *Interface Images: Photographs of the Belfast 'Peacelines'*. Belfast, Belfast Exposed Photography Group.

Rafferty, O. (1994). *Catholicism in Ulster, 1603–1983: An Interpretative History*. Dublin, Gill and Macmillan.

Redfield, P. (1994). Remembering the Revolution, Forgetting the Empire: Notes after the French Bicentennial. In Taylor, L. (ed.), *Visualising Theory. Selected Essays from VAR, 1990–1994*. New York, Routledge.

Reid, T. (1823). *Travels in Ireland*. London, Longman.

Richardson, J. (1993). The Curious Case of Coins. Remembering the Appearance of Familiar Objects. *Psychologist*, Vol. 6, No. 8.

Ricoeur, P. (1981). *Hermeneutics and the Human Sciences*. Cambridge, Cambridge University Press.

Roach, J. (1993). Carnival and the Law in New Orleans. *Drama Review*, 37, No. 3.

Rogers, P. (1934). *The Irish Volunteers and Catholic Emancipation, 1778–93*. London.

Rolston, B. (1991). *Politics and Painting: Murals and Conflict in Northern Ireland*. Cranbury, NJ, Associated University Presses.

Rolston, B. (1992). *Drawing Support: Murals in the North of Ireland*. Belfast, Beyond the Pale Publications.

Rolston, B. (1995). *Drawing Support 2: Murals of War and Peace*. Belfast, Beyond the Pale Publications.

Rosaldo, R. (1980). *Ilongot Headhunting 1883–1974: A Study in Society and History*. Stanford, Stanford University Press.

Rose, R. (1971). *Governing Without Consensus*. London, Faber and Faber.

Rubin, M. (1991). *Corpus Christi*. Cambridge, Cambridge University Press.

Saxl, F. and Wittkower, R. (1948). *British Art and the Mediterranean*. Oxford, Oxford University Press.

Schudson, M. (1989). How Culture Works: Perspectives from Media Studies on the Efficacity of Symbols. *Theory and Society*, Vol. 18.

Scott, J. C. (1990). *Domination and the Arts of Resistance*. New Haven CT, Yale University Press.

Select Committee. (1835). *Report from the Select Committee, appointed to Inquire into the Nature, Character, Extent and Tendency of Orange Associations or Societies in Ireland*. London, House of Commons.

Sennett, R. (1993). *The Fall of Public Man*. London, Faber and Faber.

Sheehy, J. (1980). *The Rediscovery of Ireland's Past*. London, Thames and Hudson.

Silverblatt, I. (1988). Political Memories and Colonizing Symbols: Santiago and the Mountain Gods of Colonial Peru. In Hill, J. D. (ed.), *Rethinking History and Myth: Indigenous South American Perspectives on the Past*. Urbana and Chicago, University of Illinois Press.

Simms, J. G. (1974). Remembering 1690. *Studies*, Autumn 1974.

Simpson, W. G. (1924). *The History and Antiquities of Freemasonry in Saintfield, County Down*. Saintfield.

Simpson, W. G. (1926). *Masonry of the Olden Time in the Comber District*. Lisburn.

Sluka, J. (1989). *Hearts and Minds, Water and Fish: Support for the IRA and INLA in a Northern Irish Ghetto*. Greenwich, CT, AI Press.

Sluka, J. (1992). The Politics of Painting: Political Murals in Northern Ireland. In Nordstrom, C. and Martin, J.-A. (eds), *The Paths to Domination, Resistance and Terror*. Berkeley, University of California Press.

Sluka, J. (1995). Domination, Resistance and Political Culture in Northern Ireland's Catholic-Nationalist Ghettos. *Critique of Anthropology*, Vol. 15, No. 1.

Smith, A. D. (1986). *The Ethnic Origins of Nations*. Oxford, Basil Blackwell.

Smyth, D. H. (1974). The Volunteer Movement in Ulster: Background and Development 1745–85. Unpublished Ph.D. Thesis, Queen's University, Belfast.

Smyth, P. D. H. (1979). The Volunteers and Parliament, 1779–84. In Bartlett, T. and Hayton, D. W. (eds), *Penal Era and Golden Age: Essays in Irish History 1690–1800*. Belfast, Ulster Historical Foundation.

Smyth, J. (1992). *The Men of No Property: Irish Radicals and Popular Politics in the late Eighteenth Century*. Dublin, Gill and MacMillan.

Smyth, J. (1993). Freemasonry and the United Irishmen. In Dickson, D., Keogh, D. and Whelan, K. (eds), *The United Irishmen: Republicanism, Radicalism and Rebellion*. Dublin, Lilliput Press.

Stevenson, D. (1990). *The Origins of Freemasonry: Scotland's Century 1590–1710*. Cambridge, Cambridge University Press.

Stewart, A. T. Q. (1989). *The Narrow Ground*. London, Faber.

Stewart, A. T. Q. (1993). *A Deeper Silence: The Hidden Roots of the United Irish Movement*. London, Faber and Faber.

Storch, R. (1982). 'Please to Remember the Fifth of November': Conflict, Solidarity and Public Order in Southern England, 1815–1900. In Storch, R. (ed.), *Popular Culture and Custom in Nineteenth Century England*. London, Croom Helm.

Taylor, L. (ed.), (1994). *Visualising Theory: Selected Essays from V.A.R. 1990–1994*. New York, Routledge.

Taylor, L. (1995). *Occasions of Faith. An Anthropology of Irish Catholics*. Dublin, Lilliput Press.

Tilley, C. (1994). *A Phenomenology of Landscape: Places, Paths and Monuments*. Oxford, Berg.

Tóibín, C. (1994). *Bad Blood: A Walk along the Irish Border*. London, Vintage.

Turner, V. (1969). *The Ritual Process*. Chicago, Aldine.

Turner, V. (1974). *Dramas, Fields and Metaphors: Symbolic Action in Human Society*. Ithaca, Cornell University Press.

Turpin, J. (1994). Cúchulainn lives on. *Circa*, Autumn 1994.

UDA (Ulster Defence Association) (1979). *Beyond the Religious Divide: Papers for discussion*. Belfast, UDA.

UPRG (Ulster Political Research Group) (1987). *Common Sense: Northern Ireland – An Agreed Process*. Belfast, UPRG.

UYUC (Ulster Young Unionist Council) (1986). *Cuchulain, the Lost Legend, Ulster, the Lost Culture?* Belfast, UYUC.

Vincent, J. (1989). Local Knowledge and Political Violence in County Fermanagh. In Curtin, C. and Wilson, T. (eds), *Ireland From Below: Social Change and Local Communities*. Galway, Galway University Press.

Vogt, E. and Abel, S. (1977). On Political Rituals in Contemporary Mexico. In Moore, S. and Myerhoff, S. (eds), *Secular Rituals*. Assen, Van Gorcum.

Walker, B. (1992). 1641, 1689, 1690 and all that: The Unionist Sense of History. *Irish Review*, No. 12.

Walker, B. (1996). *Dancing to History's Tune: History, myth and politics in Ireland*. Belfast, Institute of Irish Studies.

Ward, M. (1983). *Unmanageable Revolutionaries: Women and Irish Nationalism*. London, Pluto Press.

Ward, M. (1995). Finding a place: women and the Irish peace process. *Race and Class*, Vol. 37, No. 1.

Warner, M. (1985). *Monuments and Maidens: the Allegory of the Female Form*. London, Weidenfield and Nicolson.

Webb, J. J. (1929). *The Guilds of Dublin*. Dublin.

Weber, M. (1985). *The Protestant Ethic and the Spirit of Capitalism*. London, Unwin Paperbacks.

Weitzer, R. (1995). *Policing Under Fire: Ethnic Conflict and Police–Community Relations in Northern Ireland*. Albany, State University of New York.

Werbner, P. (1991). Stamping the Earth with the Name of Allah; Zikr and the Sacralising of Space among British Muslims. Paper presented at SSRC NY Conference, Harvard University.

Whelan, K. (1996). *The Tree of Liberty: Radicalism, Catholicism and the Construction of Irish Identity 1760–1830*. Cork, Cork University Press.

Wiener, R. (1978). *The Rape and Plunder of the Shankill*. Belfast, Farset Press.

Woods, O. (1995). *Seeing is Believing? Murals in Derry*. Derry, Guildhall Press.

Wright, F. (1987). *Northern Ireland: A Comparative Analysis*. Dublin, Gill and Macmillan.

Wright, F. (1996). *Two Lands on One Soil. Ulster Politics before Home Rule*. Dublin, Gill and Macmillan.

Yates, F. (1966). *The Art of Memory*. London, Routledge and Kegan Paul.

Index